COLUMBIA UNIVERSITY STUDIES IN ENGLISH
AND COMPARATIVE LITERATURE

THE SOUTHERN PLANTATION

THE
SOUTHERN PLANTATION

*A Study in the Development and the
Accuracy of a Tradition*

BY

FRANCIS PENDLETON GAINES, Ph.D.

GLOUCESTER, MASS.

PETER SMITH

1962

To

JOHN CALVIN METCALF

PREFACE

THE purpose of this study is to suggest in general outline the popular conception of the old plantation, to trace the development of that conception, and to make an analysis of it in comparison with the plantation as it actually existed.

That there is a plantation tradition in American literature and thought is a thesis that needs no defense. If authority were called for, we could cite Thomas Nelson Page, who, as he says in his introduction to the writings of Dr. Bagby, recognized in much ante-bellum work a consistent " ideal coloring." It was, of course, the generation of Page himself which did most to fix this coloring as the light of plantation romance. The tradition varies; in the hands of certain sincere workers, it is a thing of dignity; in the presentation of many theatrical spectacles, it is a thing of tinsel. In most of its occurrences, however, it is after a well defined, a uniform pattern.

It should be borne in mind that the present approach to the subject is through the popular conception. This fact explains the inclusion of material which is not *belles lettres* and the exclusion of some which, though valuable, had but limited appeal. No one supposes, for instance, that "Daddy " Rice had such insight into plantation life as manifested by Irwin Russell or Howard Weeden; yet Russell's poems and Miss Weeden's etchings have been far less influential than " Jim Crow," who jumped his way into international fame, who fathered a great line of minstrel men, who penetrated unexpected corners, even going, in gingerbread effigy, into the House of Seven Gables.

vii

The careful student of the real plantation may feel that the treatment of the important and difficult matters in the last three chapters is almost bold in its summarization. The field is so large that it is no easy task to confine the investigation to just the suggestions of the tradition. Such action was necessary, however, unless violence were done the unity proposed. Economic problems, for example, important as they are in the realm of fact, are barely indicated in the tradition and must be considered in the present study on a correspondingly reduced scale.

It is but fair to acknowledge the work done by competent scholars who have been sifting the materials of plantation chronicle. Every subsequent investigator must feel himself in the debt of Ballagh, Bassett, Bruce, Dodd, Fleming, Hart, Phillips, and others. The present writer has, however, gone back to original sources as far as possible.

Not because it is a convention of the preface but because of abiding gratitude, I record here my personal obligations. My life-long friend and former colleague, J. L. King, has been helpful in a measure that I can not easily repay. Professor A. H. Thorndike, in a few preliminary conferences, clarified my own thinking and has assisted me all along the way. Professor W. P. Trent, whose mastery of the whole field in which I have worked is a matter of common knowledge, has made available for me the fruits of his long study and his wisdom. Dr. Carl Van Doren guided me; his scholarship and critical acumen have been invaluable; his courtesy has made the task a joy. Simple justice demands that I add in conclusion that my wife has made possible whatever achievement is here represented.

CONTENTS

THE SOUTHERN PLANTATION

CHAPTER I

THE POPULAR CONCEPTION OF THE PLANTATION

A few years ago the leading periodicals of the country carried a handsomely illustrated advertisement of a phonograph company. The scene represented an old negro who sat on a little eminence and gazed wistfully across a valley. On the opposite hill the world of actuality merged into a cloud-like vision, the semblance of the ex-slave's dream: the old plantation; a great mansion; exquisitely gowned ladies and courtly gentlemen moving with easy grace upon the broad veranda behind stalwart columns; surrounding the yard an almost illimitable stretch of white cotton; darkies singingly at work in the fields; negro quarters, off on one side, around which little pickaninnies tumbled in glad frolic. It is not a far-fetched analogy to consider the gray-haired darkey, with longing in his eyes, symbolic of the American public. On the plain of reality, as it were, we gaze across a vale of desire to the heights of illusion, to the delectable hill — and see thereon the Southern plantation.

Of all native resources which have yielded contribution to the popular imagery, the plantation is most spacious and most gracious. Other local color types have been as sharply differentiated, as persistently exploited, but no other has proved so rich in romantic values. Unique in its structure, varied in its characters from the stately to

1

the grotesque, suggestive of many sentimental moods, the ante-bellum Southern estate has appealed strongly. Various sections, institutions, epochs, have been the theme of a relatively full tradition, but the plantation legends have a luxuriance lacking in the others. These may exhibit swiftness of action, vividness of personage, even the clash of large motives; but the plantation has the atmosphere of enchantment; they may be, in certain respects, distinct from the every-day world, but the plantation is most nearly the ideal. Perennially, thus, romantically inclined Americans yield themselves to the mood of reminiscent dreaming after the fashion of Billy's vision: "dee voices soun'in' low like bees, an' the moon sort o' meltin' over de yard, an' I sort o' got to studyin', an' hit 'pear like de plantation 'live once mo', an' de ain' no mo' scufflin', and de ole times done come back ag'in, an' I heah meh kerridge-horses stompin' in de stalls, an' de place all cleared up ag'in, an' fence all round de pahsture, an' I smell wet clover-blossoms right good, an' Marse Phil and Meh Lady done come back —."

The penetration of the plantation concept, as romances have interpreted it, into the popular consciousness and the lodgment gained there invite interesting speculation. The vigor of this particular tradition is probably due to the temperament of people who have cherished the fancy. Without going too far afield by way of philosophical analysis, we may suggest at least three reasons for the sweep of the plantation legend.

This tradition, in the first place, appeals strongly to the innate American love of feudalism. It is curiously true that however violent may be our profession of political equality, however we may vaunt our democracy, our imaginative interests are keenly appreciative of social gradations and our romantic hunger is satisfied by some

allegory of aristocracy. This fact is true to some extent
in our actual life; witness the reception we give foreign
princes, or the conduct of many of our countrymen in
foreign courts. Particularly does this feeling seem to en-
joy free scope in our sentimental fancies as expressed, for
example, in literary preferences. Now the plantation,
alone among native institutions, satisfies this craving for
a system of caste. The ante-bellum Southern estate is
rich in both the pageantry and the psychology of feudalism. It offers the spectacle of the irresponsible lordly
class and the scale of life that appertains to it. It offers,
too, the spectacle of the lower class, obsequious in attitude toward this ruling group, cheerful in acceptance of
a humble lot, unambitious, ignorant, superstitious, fan-
tastically funny. On the one hand, we see rich modes
of life and a hereditary authority, exercised with the
graciousness of condescending mercy; on the other, a comic
inferiority and a devoted concurrence in the scheme of
government. Here, then, are the American equivalents
for Camelot, for Ivanhoe.

The plantation, again, furnishes through the person of
the genuine darkey, essentially the most conspicuous figure
of the tradition, the closest native approximation to a type
almost as old as history, proverbially dear to the masses,
as opposed to the literati: the folk figure of a simple,
somewhat rustic, character, instinctively humorous, irra-
tionally credulous, gifted in song and dance, interesting
in spontaneous frolic, endowed with artless philosophy.
We have other figures associated with these separate ideas
but the plantation black, more than any other type, com-
bines these qualities which have exercised immemorial
charm. It is worthy of note in this connection that, as
if in rough conformity with this role of folk personage,
the darkey is the assumed source of a large body of un-

written humor, or at least is credited with a larger collection of floating anecdotes, real and spurious, than any other of our makers of vulgar comedy.

The plantation calls forth a response, in the third place, because, specially since its epoch is closed and the system has passed, it stands as a kind of American embodiment of the golden age. It is the custom of the imagination to dwell on the past as the era of happier things, to feel that " There hath passed away a glory from the earth," a feeling that finds expression from Greek mythology to such gentle reminiscences as Thackeray's recollections in *The Newcomes* of the preceding generation. The extreme youth of our country, together with its consistent development during these few decades, has denied to us the privilege of associating with our national tradition many legendary records of a misty, heroic long ago. Makers of our historical romance have, however, manifested marked facility in creating the illusion of antiquity; their success, moreover, has been most pronounced when they treated an order of life that no longer exists. The plantation has come to be seen, then, in a long and rosy perspective. Though it ceased to function less than sixty years ago, it seems so remote that it suggests a different and a more resplendent age. The plantation romance remains our chief social idyl of the past; of an Arcadian scheme of existence, less material, less hurried, less prosaically equalitarian, less futile, richer in picturesqueness, festivity, in realized pleasure that recked not of hope or fear or unrejoicing labor.

Theories that may account for the relative power of plantation concept in the popular imagination are less important for our purpose than a consideration of what that conception is. By way of arriving at a fairly accurate idea of the prevailing notion, we may glance at some

out-croppings in modern life which serve at once to reveal and to perpetuate the popular conviction.

The stage affords favorable opportunity to study the
occurrence of the conception. Theatrical interpretation
of the plantation romance, or some of its derivations, has
persisted with greater vitality than the tradition in fiction.
It was possible, for example, during the season of 1922–
1923 to witness in New York alone half a dozen plays or
pageants which featured plantation customs; and there
was an uninterrupted presentation of spectacles in which
this material received minor elaboration. Popular relish
for " the old-time stuff " is still keen. Reviewing a negro
musical comedy, a critic commented sadly that it was
" a pity such evident talent could not be utilized for the
production of something racially distinctive." But the
executive of the company was wise in his own generation.
He knew that the theatre-going public does not, in any
considerable proportion, want racial distinctiveness; it
wants the standard portrayal of plantation characteristics
as developed by the tradition.

There is a measurable dramatic representation of plantation life in relative fulness. The pattern is constant.
The setting reveals the conventional mansion, a large white
house with commodious grounds, the latter lovely with
prodigal growth of flowers and shrubbery considered
Southern. The background is usually the cotton field;
if a moon-light scene can be introduced, so much the
better. The characters fall into stock types: the old
planter, or, if the time is post-bellum, the former general;
his daughter or ward, heroine of the drama, owner of an
elaborate wardrobe, marked particularly by hoop-skirts
and delicate bodices; the butler, who may also be the
body-guard, clothed in grotesque finery; the old mammy,
who may also be the cook, with her inevitable bandanna.

Various suggestions of the old regime are brought out. The famed hot biscuits and fried chicken are usually provided for the gustatory delight of the whites, while the bare mention of 'possum, 'taters, or watermelon, occasions eloquent lip-smacking on the part of the blacks. Dignified dances, particularly the Virginia reel, are emblematic of the recreational life of the big house, as the jigging and clogging reveal the merry-making of the quarters. Always present and never too subtle is the inter-racial psychology: blustering kindness on the part of the master, tender consideration on the part of the heroine, matched by a hollow sham of frightened obedience and a real affection and self-immolation on the part of the slaves.

The dramatic tradition persists most hardily, however, in the negro show. Pure minstrelsy no longer holds its place in popular affection, though the type is not extinct; but the vogue of burnt cork in the vaudeville circuits and the popularity of the all-negro musical comedy, a species that has flourished in the last few years, give no indication of waning. The significant thing here is that each entertainment runs true to form. Without attempting original departures, these spectacles present over and over again the stereotyped devices long fixed in popular conception. The common " sets " are the cabin by the cotton patch, the levee by the river side — really a wharf piled high with cotton bales which are pushed aside when the dancing begins — and sometimes a graveyard for the effects of superstition. Comedy is the principal objective; and the comedians are conventional, black-faced, grossly exaggerated scarlet lips, shining teeth, adaptable eyes, nappy hair, and a costume of either inharmonious assortment of poorly-fitting garments or of iridescent pomp. Equally conventional are the tricks of conduct by which the resultant comedy is achieved: eccentricities of vocabulary, whether by reason of poor grammar or ambitious struggling after impressive phraseology; inherent dishonesty, for which myriad opportunities are provided; deep-rooted superstition, with special reference to ghosts, hoodoos, or the rabbit-foot; elaborate bombast of courtship; even religion fantastic in intense emotionalism. A secondary emphasis, not entirely divorced from the humorous, is put upon singing and dancing. The banjo is usually conspicuous. The repertoire of song runs the gamut from a little lullaby or a romantic ballad to the ridiculous " blues "; not all the effects are comic, for even one of these " blues " may swing the imagination back to sorrow songs that must have swelled from many a slave ship. Dancing, whether in the abandon of the jig or the pompous strutting of the cake-walk, is one of the common transplantings of supposed plantation customs.

Casual occurrences of the plantation motive in other dramatic types are to be observed. It is not an unusual thing, for example, to see a negro in a fairly serious piece, his service generally being for sentimental relief. This practice is certainly as old in our drama as Mrs. Mowatt's *Fashion* and it has been adopted by many producers of moving pictures; cinema dramas varying from William Allen White's *A Certain Rich Man* to Harold Lloyd's *Dr. Jack*. So universally has this dramatic mode been accepted that when Eugene Walter introduced a colored maid in *The Easiest Way* he deemed it necessary to add a note warning the audience that she was not the typical Southern mammy. Other dramatic manifestations are found in the vaudeville houses; negro acts may not be so popular as they were a generation ago, but they still make up no small program of the variety houses. In New York there has recently been in operation a cabaret which featured exclusively striking motives of the tradi-

tional plantation darkies. Borrowings of the material by
the eye and ear spectacles of our day are not unknown.
One can hardly attend the lighter musical performance,
from the "revue" to the burlesque, without witnessing
some adaptation.

At the present time a rather conspicuous appearance of
the background and motives of plantation life is to be
found in moving pictures. D. W. Griffith's *The Birth of
a Nation* occurs to the mind at once. For a more recent
illustration we may select the same producer's *The White
Rose*. The time of this story is emphatically modern,
certainly if we judge by the most recent forms of jazz
dancing and the latest scraps of slang. Yet the atmosphere of the old plantation is consistently suggested. We
see the large Louisiana mansion, the slave quarters, the
costume balls, the splendor of a rural Southern civilization, the devotion of Mammy, and all the standard resources of negro character, fidelity, humor, musical talent,
indolence, all handled so as to create the illusion of the
ante-bellum regime.

Intimately associated with the stage, in fact largely de-
rived from it, are the songs which with more or less pertinency continually interpret some phase of the plantation or
its typical figures. It is amazing to reflect on the vitality
of some of these sentimental ditties. A recent symposium,
according to a report made to the convention of music
supervisors in Cleveland, April 11, 1923, revealed the fact
that out of eighteen favorite songs of the nation, five are
plantation ballads, and a sixth is a more recent "coon
song." From time to time public concerts of the negro
spirituals awaken renewed enthusiasm. The stream of
new melodies is almost inexhaustible. One needs only to
inspect the windows of a music store or to consult the
catalogue of a phonograph company to be impressed with

the persistence of the theme. The matter of the plantation songs will be considered in a subsequent chapter; in the present connection the important fact is the manner in which these lays, most of them gross exaggerations, continue to feed to the popular imagination the same old concepts. However alien to the real Southern estate, these ephemeral hymns contain what is accepted as plantation material: a levee, a cotton field, a Southern meal, a mammy, a Dixie girl, even the names of the Southern states or the suggestive quality of certain Southern rivers which, presumably, fringe the estates. The immediate setting may be most incongruous; the columnist who predicted, apropos of the recent Shakespearean revival, that shortly a famous black-face comedian would appear as Hamlet with a specialty " Carry me back to my Elsinore mammy " understood how detached the plantation may be from its musical interpreters. Absurd as some of these songs are in the light of logical analysis, their emotional appeal, which is not dependent upon rational content, is undeniable and they are of significance in perpetuating the tradition. Thackeray's reaction to a plantation melody has been often cited, but it will bear repeating as typical of a fairly general response: " I heard a humourous balladist not long ago, a minstrel with wool on his head and an ultra-Ethiopian complexion, who performed a negro ballad that I confess moistened these spectacles in a most unexpected manner. I have gazed at thousands of tragedy queens dying on the stage and expiring in appropriate blank verse, and I have never wanted to wipe them. They have looked up, be it said, at many scores of clergymen without being dimmed, and behold; a vagabond with a corked face and a banjo sings a little song, strikes a wild note, which sets the heart thrilling with happy pity."

Significant revelations of the elements that compose the

plantation ensemble, as it exists in popular fancy, are found in many phases of modern life. One of the most interesting is plantation cooking. The prestige of delicious food peculiar to the ante-bellum South is hinted at by almost every menu of contemporary restaurants with appetizing suggestions of old Virginia ham, Maryland chicken, Southern waffles, hot biscuits, yams, various Creole concoctions, and the like. The authentic quality of this element in public imagination is attested by the number of cook books that intimate some connection with the kitchen glories of the past; volumes entitled, in some modification, Dixie recipes or aunt somebody's cook-book are conspicuous in the bibliography of household economy. It makes little difference whether such titles are descriptive or merely tempting; the implication is unmistakable. Many daily papers carry the column devoted to the preparation of food under the caption of a mammy's name. On Broadway at the time of this writing a large electric sign invites to a "Dixie dinner." Business houses have capitalized this plantation appeal; thus we have a nationally known brand of pancake flour sponsored by an old mammy and recommended as based upon a Southern formula; and the graphic scenes that accompany many advertisements are reminiscent of plantation food.

A minor filament of the plantation pattern is negro humor. Reference has been made to the prominence of this factor on the stage and to the large body of unwritten material. We must remember also the accumulation of this fund of humor in joke columns, in humorous departments of magazines, in the professedly funny books. The utilization of negro comedy by journalistic mediums was already an established practice when, before the war, " Q. K. Philander Doe-Sticks," as M. M. Thompson signed himself, was bringing out in Northern papers such sketches

as *The Colored Camp Meeting;* and the custom has grown
steadily. Our own day has seen the negro in the serial
cartoon, not always exclusively featured as in J. P. Alley's
Hambone, but often in some other panel as a subordinate
resource.

One cannot go far in this ultra-modern world without
seeing tokens of the survival in the public consciousness
of the traditional conception. Here, for example, a great
department store shows in a window an array of black
and white materials. The display is set against a typical plantation background outlined entirely in these two
colors: in the distance the fields of white cotton, thronged
with happy workers; two powerful negro women, issuing
from the nearest patch, swing along in a bodily rhythm
harmonious with the tune they are singing, though their
heads are held immobile in order not to endanger the full
baskets carried in characteristic African fashion; in the
side foreground are the cabins, somewhat tumble-down
but eloquent of good cheer; before these the pickaninnies
gambol and one adult negro thrums a banjo while several
of his friends are dancing to the intoxicating strains; inside the cabin appears the smiling face of a plantation
mammy, busy in the preparation of her meal. In another shop window, there is a striking exhibition of a
fascinating new style for women, an audaciously colored
scarf, even an over-blouse, which, a fashion authority as-
sures us, represents " the Paris version of mammy's old
Southern bandanna "; and sure enough it is a bandanna
in a flame of gorgeous colors. Elsewhere the windows
feature a mechanical toy, dignified with alliterative title
of Jazz-a-bo Jim; a negro in conventionally fantastic attire stands on a miniature cabin and automatically dances.
During the season of 1922–1923 a popular dance was
known as the plantation trot, the central idea, according

to a terpsichorean scholar, "being to plant the feet firmly " — probably flatly also. At Coney Island one of the " thrillers " is known as the " old Virginia reel "; and one of the fixed backgrounds for the make-it-while-you-wait photograph galleries is the " old plantation home." On the billboards that adorn our highways or fringe our vacant lots, there suddenly appears an advertisement of a famous cigarette, an ambitious presentation in colors of a typical plantation scene. It is not uncommon for the costume parties of more pretentious social or artistic circles to exemplify some such plantation pageant as appears on the billboard and to employ the various plantation songs and dances as diversion. The potency of the concept in our general thinking is indicated in certain phrases drawn from that old life, phrases accepted as self-explanatory; thus to refer to a man as " a Southern gentleman " connotes a clear-cut image, if not the most definitive certainly the most impressive.

To such surface manifestations as have been mentioned there must be added other evidence. The literary tradition, as we shall see in a later chapter, is now more a reflection than a determinant of public taste. The actual current of the fictional romance runs less vigorously than it did a quarter of a century ago, indeed it runs but in a wee little trickle; yet it does persist. One might make a case for a meager artistic tradition, apart from literature, musical treatments like MacDowell's *From Uncle Remus* and John Powell's *Rhapsodie Negre,* paintings like Winslow Homer's *Sunday in Virginia* and Eastman Johnson's *My Old Kentucky Home.*

Without further enumeration of the traces of the conception in contemporary civilization, let us turn to a consideration of what the popular conception actually is. A somewhat detailed analysis of the prevailing idea will be the theme of other chapters in this study. In the present connection we may most clearly suggest the popular conception in terms of the principal points of concentration, around each of which an indeterminate number of associations cluster. These focuses are, roughly, the following ideas: the plantation setting, usually a central splendor flanked by picturesqueness; a scale of life, not strictly distinguishable from setting, yet social rather than physical; a mode of gaiety, invariable in both races; vivid characters, white and black, sometimes mere caricatures but not less spectacular; idealized relations between the races.

Concerning the setting, the scale of life, the mode of gaiety, the popular conception is not meticulous; it is aware of the gesture of magnificence in all these matters and cares for little more. What is the size of the estates, as commonly conceived? Simply large enough to supply illimitable sweeps of white cotton — cotton must always be in the open-boll state — to provide stamping ground for hordes of blacks, to support the masters in a prodigality of luxuriant idleness. The image of the mansion is usually clear-cut: " a stately house on a wooded hill, the huge white pillars that supported the porch rising high enough to catch the reflection of a rosy sunset, the porch itself and the beautiful lawn in front filled with a happy crowd of lovely women and gallant men, young and old, the wide avenue lined with carriages, and the whole place lit up (as it were) and alive with the gay commotion of a festival occasion." This description by the creator of Uncle Remus must be taken as typical; and it is specially significant for one important fact; the popular conception hardly thinks of the big house as distinct from human characters and activity. If this vague notion could become articulate, it would insist that the mansion was the Mount Vernon type, white, rectangular, two-storied, with wide porch, great columns, out-houses, either regularly or irregularly arranged in attractive manner, perhaps a separate kitchen. Beyond these larger details, the popular conception is not certain; grounds are accepted as decorative, as spacious, but the general public does not carry in its sentimentalizing a catalogue of the precise flora of plantation landscape gardening. Similarly the conception of the scale of life is rather indefinite. It is agreed that social life was colorful, marked by hospitality without stint, by epicurean insouciance almost to the point of recklessness, by a whole program of festivity for white and black alike. Just what was the precise schedule of this merry-making is not obvious to the public conviction; dancing and music and vivacious conversation in indoor recreation, horsemanship and hunting in outdoor sport; everywhere a good deal of courting; refreshments, always important concern of the democratic imagination, representing ultimate perfection in daintiness and adequacy; these large details are in the popular mind and not much else. But if the conception is not definite as to what was done, it has no doubt whatever of the ubiquity of mirth. Everybody was happy; the old planter with a julep, the young cavalier with horses, dogs, and slaves, the plantation beauty in the first ecstasy of romance, the old servants grinning with pleasure from multitudinous favors, the mass of slaves in some frenzied break-down, — all are pictured as in a sort of unparalleled rapture of joy.

Concerning plantation types the popular conception is more explicit. When former Governor Taylor of Tennessee proposed a monument to the Old South he suggested some of the generally recognized characters: " a trinity of figures to be carved from a single block of Southern marble, consisting of the courtly old planter, high-bred and gentle in face and manner; the plantation 'uncle,' the counterpart in ebony of the master so loyally served and imitated; and the broad-bosomed black mammy, with vari-colored turban, spotless apron, and beaming face, the friend of every living thing in cabin or mansion." But there are other types which "Fiddlin' Bob" did not include. The gay girl from Dixie is assuredly a romantic figure; the young cavalier has his place; and there is yet another typical darkey, not the butler or mammy, but the prototype of minstrelsy.

Plantation characters are the subject of a somewhat fuller treatment later in this study; it is not necessary to do more here than to suggest in barest outline the dominant ideas concerning these figures. The old planter, as he exists in the popular conception, is the embodiment of inconsistencies, not to say contradictions, but the unity of the delineation is not vitiated, for he is accepted as autocratically capricious, in contra-distinction, let us say, to the traditional Puritan who most dependably " talks like a log of wood and acts like a poker," as Walter Pritchard Eaton says. In the main, however, the planter is regarded with affection. The abolition idea of a rich and idle nabob, reveling in luxury gained from the misery of his bondmen and steeping himself in licentiousness, has given way. The old gentleman is in high and not unattractive relief; clad in the archaic habiliments of the gentleman, frock coat, ruffled shirt, trousers of high visibility, hat of gently curving lines; endowed with the graces of the gentleman, hospitality, courtesy, ease of deportment, self-contentment, honor; endowed, too, with the vices supposed to be peculiar to gentlemen, hot temper, profanity, intemperance, intolerance, obstinacy, unchastity — all forgiven him because they, it is believed, redeem his character from stupidity and add to the color of personality.

The young lord and heir stands in the shadow of his

more picturesque father, in spite of a cycle of stories, including many by Page, presenting this young man as "the pink of courtesy, courage incarnate, and honor's self." The mistress of the plantation is a dim figure, as though matrimony faded womanhood into rapid indistinctness. The plantation belle, however, is one of the delights of popular fancy. She is the Juliet of our national romance; not even the war could alter sentiment concerning her, for many a Northern soldier married the Southern girl. Beautiful, graceful, accomplished in social charm, bewitching in coquetry yet strangely steadfast in soul, she is perhaps the most winsome figure in the whole field of our fancy. The loveliness of her costume is a part of the image, not visualized, of course, with the accuracy of a scientific historian of fashion, but apprehended in general outline. The hair may be brushed back in pompadour style and covered with snowy powder, as in colonial days, or may fall in curls; the neck may be bare in the manner of evening or may be covered in a pretended way by fine lace of *point de Venice;* the bodice is white or else some delicate shade as — let us fall into the mood of the romance — pale yellow much like the sunset glow and is trimmed with blue and silver while the upper edge is like a line of foam on the sea beach; the sleeves are large and full, embroidered in unusual designs; the skirt must be the hoop effect; a flounce may be admitted but the hoop is more dearly cherished; a big thing with furbelows within which the dainty bit of humanity appears a mere wisp; the little feet, the little mice-like feet, are caged in velvet slippers with radiant buckles and with heels several inches high; bracelets, rings, jeweled brooches, and spangles of one kind or another complete the picture of the plantation belle as she is seen by the popular mind.

The negro is of all plantation types most firmly lodged

in public consciousness. It is not, moreover, the "uncle" of Harris' stories or the mammy of a thousand lullabies who has penetrated most deeply. These are valuable pieces of the decoration and they are symbols of a spirit of adulation and self-effacement. But the negro who has most completely captivated the public is the clownish black, the pure "Jim Crow." A recent writer, C. S. Johnson, has described with some bitterness this conception: "He is lazy, shiftless, and happy-go-lucky, loves watermelon, carries a razor, emits a peculiar odor, shoots craps, grins instead of smiles — is noisily religious, loves red, dresses flashily, loves gin, and can sing. On the stage he is presented lying easily, using long words he does not understand, drinking gin, stealing chickens, and otherwise living up to the joke book tradition." It is this negro who is most vivid in the popular conception of all the personnel. Because of the rigid convention, even a light-hued Ethiopian comedian must paint his face black and adhere to the generally accepted role. Other plantation blacks are less importantly in the tradition but this figure is conspicuous. If the popular conception is certain of one thing, that confidence is that "it knows a nigger"; the fruit of such knowledge is the character here suggested.

The popular conception thinks of race relations, as we shall find out later on, as always happy. For a season the onslaught of abolitionism provoked an outcry but it was hushed in the period of glorification, beginning about 1880. From that time on, public imagination has recognized that, on the whole, the white was benign, the black happy in the peculiar status of plantation society.

CHAPTER II

THE DEVELOPMENT OF THE CONCEPTION IN LITERATURE

I. *The Beginnings of the Tradition* (1832–1850)

THE plantation conception in literature must not be likened to a plant which grew out of dry ground and at definite dates or even at periodic intervals put forth the shoots of new ideas. Specific elements of the material cannot be placed in precise chronological sequence. Thus the notion of the devoted slave is found as early as Defoe's *Colonel Jacque* (1722) and again in Simms' *The Yemassee* at the beginning of our period. More accurately the plantation in literature may be thought of as originally a rough outline made increasingly distinct as successive writers illuminated its various phases, and brought to the fulness of light in period of post-bellum romance.

The plantation makes its first important appearance in American literature with the work of Kennedy and of Carruthers, the one picturing in Irving's style a contemporary estate, the other looking backward with eyes of affection to the days of the early cavaliers. For purposes of convenience we may accept 1832, the date of *Swallow Barn,* as marking the beginning of the literary tradition. The same year, it happened, saw Paulding's *Westward Ho!,* a significant work which linked Virginia and Kentucky, favorite fields of romance. It was at almost the same time that T. D. Rice first "jumped Jim Crow," an eccentric gyration which proved the introduction of negro

18

minstrelsy.   Not much later abolition literature began in earnest to focus attention upon the actual plantation.

The rise of this literature is thus identified chronologically with a period of importance in general plantation history.   In the decade of the thirties there were at least three developments which sharply gave re-direction to this history.   The first of these facts was political in effect, however moral in origin: the rise of a vigorous abolitionism, which, to the Southerner, was fraught with such possibilities as the Nat Turner insurrection.   The second was economic: the increasing agricultural opportunity of the lower South which produced a new type of plantation and greatly modified plantation policy in the older states.   The third was both political and economic and something more: the assumption by the South of a definitely defensive attitude marked by a solidification of political action if not of thought, by the death of pronounced emancipation sentiment which had previously been considerable, by the repudiation of Jefferson's philosophy as expressed in the Declaration of Independence, and, what is most important, by the rapid growth of intense sectional consciousness. Properly to relate these three developments, one of the most delicate problems in our history, is not the task of the student of the literature of the period.   The point of consequence is that plantation literature was powerfully stimulated by political and social conditions and became more and more a forensic weapon.

We have suggested that before the time of *Swallow Barn* there was already in the country a wide-spread, though dim, conception if not of the plantation in full detail at least of certain distinctive modes of life.   To some extent, of course, a basis of fact underlay the opinion.   When Cooper, for example, introduced into *The Spy* (1821) the cavalier Captain Lawton, he bodied forth imaginatively a

type actually existent in such a figure as John Laurens
who years later appeared in Gertrude Atherton's *The Con-
queror* (1901). Charles Dudley Warner has attempted to
analyze [1] the fact that " Southern society has always enjoyed a certain prestige in the North," a condition which
he attributes to the leisure of Southern life, allowing social
cultivation, to the ardency of temperament and the soft-
ness of manners resulting from climate, and to the Southern
appreciation for charm of manner as opposed to Northern
emphasis on wealth. To a minor extent, the prevalence of
the " prestige " may be attributed to display made by
Southerners while in the North. An interesting comment
may be found in the sixteenth of the *Salmagundi Papers*
(Oct. 15, 1807); the behavior of Southern aristocracy at
Northern resorts is the theme. Ladies appeared with the
annual produce of a rice plantation in their clothing, or
with hogsheads of tobacco on their heads, or with a bale
of cotton trailing at their heels; gentlemen drank, gambled,
and " sported " generally — one poor fellow lost his equi-
page, being reported to have eaten the horses and " drank
the negroes." [2] In the late ante-bellum period leaders of
Southern thought, like DeBow and Simms, deplored the
practice of trailing clouds of social glory over the North
and encouraged a " See-the-South-First " movement.

By way of further caution, let it be said that 1832 must
not be considered an absolute *terminus a quo* for plantation
literature. This resource had been employed by many
writers before *Swallow Barn*. Defoe was captivated by

[1] *Society in the New South, New Princeton Review*, 1:13 (Jan.,
1886).

[2] Postl, writing before 1827, confirms the report of Southern
planters who made processions of ostentation through the North
(*Die Vereinigten Staaten*) and Mrs. Hale affirms in *Northwood*
(1827) that in New England all Southerners were reputed " immensely wealthy."

the idea of Virginia as a land of beginning again for unfortunate Englishmen and his plantation, though wholly unlike the later literary image, contained certain romantic figures and episodes. The literature of travel of the period reflects much plantation life and custom.[3] Early American novelists were not unaware of the value of the material. Isabel Drysdale's *Scenes from Georgia* (Phila., 1827) uses this background freely and introduces in Aunt Chloe a typical mammy of the plantation tradition. Better known at the time was Mrs. Sarah J. Hale's *Northwood: a Tale of New England*[4] (Boston, 1827) which treats fully, though at long distance, the South Carolina estate on which the Northern hero was reared and develops with care the character of the lovely Dixie heroine. Mrs. Anne Royal in *The Tennesseean* (New Haven, 1827) elaborates, in a few preliminary chapters which precede the story of wild adventure, many qualities afterward recognized as typically plantation. Cooper's *Spy*,[5] to which reference has been made, though in no sense a plantation novel draws freely upon Southern characters, particularly in Captain Lawton and the devoted slave, Caesar. Most conspicuous of all plantation novels before 1832 is George Tucker's *The Valley of the Shenandoah* (New York, 1824), a story of a tide-water family which carried its habits of life to a valley home. This novel is fairly rich in plantation

[3] Notably in Crevecoeur's *Letters* (London, 1782), in Paulding's *Letters from the South* (1817, New York) and in Carl Postl's (Charles Sealsfield) *Die Vereinigten Staaten* (Stuttgart, 1827, London, 1828).

[4] This novel launched its author on her long and varied career. It was reprinted several times, the fifth edition (New York, 1852) appearing in the wake of *Uncle Tom's Cabin* as *Northwood: Life North and South*.

[5] Cooper was interested mildly in negro character; witness *Wyandotte* (Philadelphia, 1843); Poe said of this novel (*Graham's*, Nov., 1843); "The negroes are, without exception, admirably done."

themes, notably hospitality, prodigality, festivity. It is, however, franker than most novels of the later tradition; the master of the place admits an unhappy feudalism in society and recognizes that slavery, whatever its influence upon the blacks, is not to the best interest of the whites.

The tradition which persisted, however, began with *Swallow Barn*, published in 1832 and again in 1851.[6] That the method of work was borrowed directly from Irving, that Kennedy sometimes had his eye on the model rather than the material, these facts do not minimize the importance of this work as the first appearance of the plantation solely for its own picturesque qualities. Here the setting, the types, and the customs become everything. Kennedy's significance lies in the fact that he fixed the attitude toward plantation material. He threw the glamour of romantic coloring over all: over the century-old brick mansion with its ornate approaches, its wings, its doors, its great hall, its spacious rooms, its antique furniture; over the characters, their dress, conversations, points of view; over the meals from the bowl of iced toddy an hour before dinner to the iced wine that followed the dessert; over the negro quarters, that " attractive landscape," the patches for melons and 'taters; over the whole conduct of life, designed for the attainment of happiness, characterized by thriftless gaiety and by the flood of hospitality which " knew no retiring ebb "; over quaint merrymaking and elaborate social functions, over magnificence of manner and all outward expressions of an inner grace. Kennedy brought out the first literary representation of the plantation " as open as an inn and as rich as a castle,"

[6] Both editions were fairly well received by the North; and the work was accepted by the South as just (see review in *Southern Literary Messenger*, December, 1851).

of plantation gentry as marked by a hearty companion-
ableness and by a personal charm which made that com-
panionship worth while, of a society which if made up of
gradations was permeated with joy from top to bottom.
He also fixed an attitude of romantic sentimentalizing
as the point of view in literary treatment of this material.
To the modern reader the revelation of a feudalistic society which made Frank Meriwether lord not only of his
black chattels but of a host of nominally free white vas-
sals may resemble social satire; the account of Meriwether's training for the pursuit of agriculture is ironic;
the story of the negro mother approximates tragedy. But
Kennedy meant to portray no more unfavorable foibles
and conditions than might have marked, let us say, good
Sir Roger and his circle and nothing more depressing than
a little pathos. In the main, the end sought was realized;
to idealize with his own culture and art an example of
plantation life at its best. Doing so, he gave matter and
method for a literary tradition.

It was not enough for the tradition to color with romantic hues the contemporary plantation; the romancers expanded their field to include the founders of the system
so that the light of other days might add to the glory of
the present. This element was first added to the tradition by W. A. Carruthers, author of three novels, *The
Cavaliers of Virginia* (New York, 1834) being most significant. The importance of this work is not in its plot,
the usual mysterious romance with midnight parleys,
prophetic dreams, weird figures, and the recluse like a
deus ex machina; it is not in the style, which is stilted
and grandiose, nowhere more so than in the courtship of
Virginia Fairfax by Nathaniel Bacon. Its value is in the
glorification of the men and women of early Virginia history and the emphasis upon the richness of life even at

that date. These cis-Atlantic nobles, says Carruthers,
fixed permanently the tone of Virginia life, were " the
founders of the aristocracy which prevails in Virginia to
this day. These were the immediate ancestors of that
generous, wine-drinking, duelling, and reckless race of
men which gives so distinct a character to Virginians
wherever they may be found." Carruthers does more than
exalt character. He sets forth in bright perspective the
home life; the ball and the reception at the governor's
mansion attended by the Virginia gentry; the fox hunt,
a social event, led by Berkeley himself with a picturesque
negro, Congo, as master of hounds; and a duel between
Bacon and Beverley. A later novel, *The Knights of the
Horseshoe* [7] (Wetumpka, Ala., 1845) concerned with the
days of Spotswood, is even fuller in detail, but its ante-
bellum vogue was limited and it had little influence.

Like *Swallow Barn* in portrayal of more modern times,
Paulding's *Westward Ho!*, a literary reflection of the westward exodus of many Virginia planters, contains plantation characters much as the later tradition interpreted
them. Colonel Dangerfield, in particular, is precisely the
type of portraiture developed by subsequent writers;
aristocratic in lineage; prodigal beyond all fancy and
therefore overwhelmingly in debt; charmingly ignorant of
business detail, size of estate, amount of income, number
of slaves; sensitive in respect to honor, as witnessed by
his challenge to a creditor who dared present a dun; fas-
cinated by blooded horses and by the race-course; a gambler by nature; horrified at even a suggestion of economy;
generous in his greatest emergency, offering, upon one occasion, freedom to his bodyguard, Pompey, a freedom

[7] Republished, 1882, in Harper's Franklin Square Library.
Carruthers' other novel is *The Kentuckian in New York* (New
York, 1834).

which Pompey as cordially refused; in short, almost the ideal of a traditional type.

Of the remaining literature of the thirties, Virginia is best represented in the novels of Beverley Tucker, *George Balcombe* (New York, 1836) and *The Partisan Leader* [8] (1836, Washington). These are not plantation novels but they reflect in traditional fashion Southern figures. In the former novel, true tide-water gentlemen exhibit, even in remote Missouri, marks of gentility which act like pass-words to other members of the aristocratic order. Many plantation traits are exemplified, courtesy, hospitality, honor, and culture — Balcombe bestows upon his dog the name of a character in the *Orlando Furioso*. In *The Partisan Leader*, curiously prophetic of the disunion epoch, we have again specimens of highly bred ladies and gentlemen,[9] representatives, according to the author, of "a class peculiar to a society whose institutions are based on domestic slavery."

In addition to this early Virginia literature, there was a gradually increasing treatment of other Southern states, though not on the same scale of luxury or of romantic glory. One of the first studies of a South Carolina estate is Asa Greene's *A Yankee among the Nullifiers* [10] (New York, 1823), a reply to Thomas Cooper's *Memoirs of a*

---

[8] The first edition bore the fictitious date of 1856 in order to increase the effect of verisimilitude. Poe called *George Balcombe* "the best American novel" (*Southern Literary Messenger*, Jan., 1837) but his judgment was probably based on other than artistic considerations.

[9] T. W. White, reviewing this novel (*Southern Literary Messenger*, Jan., 1837) points out that the women are peculiar products of rural Virginia.

[10] Both of these novels were reprinted in the North at the outbreak of the Civil War, as was *The Partisan Leader*. The work of Cooper and of Tucker was considered evidence that the South had conspired years before to dissolve the Union.

Nullifier of the preceding year. Though he was writing a polemic work, Greene included much plantation material for its own interest, specially interesting being his pictures of slave frolics. Some traces of plantation life may be found in Henry Junius Nott's *Novelettes of a Traveller*[11] (New York, 1834). The single work which stands out as best of all interpretations of Carolina plantation life is Mrs. Caroline H. Gilman's *Recollections of a Southern Matron* (New York, 1837), a chronicle of reality thinly concealed under the guise of fiction. For a real understanding of the customs, for a sympathy with the characters, for a sense of the significant detail, Mrs. Gilman takes a place with the foremost early plantation writers. It is significant, moreover, that her portrayals of cordial home life, of plantation festivities, of beautiful race relations, fit harmoniously in the general tradition.

Chief of Southern writers of fiction, the novelist Simms manifested little interest in the contemporary plantation as a social unit. Absorbed in antiquarian interests as he was, however, Simms employed minor aspects of plantation life, particularly whenever he approached realism in the sweeping tales. In *The Yemassee* (1835) he visualized in Hector the faithful house slave of the Southern estate; elasticity of temperament expressing itself in true negro melody and in cheerful optimism, loyalty that scorned a proffered freedom, such traits are well within the tradition. The famous Captain Porgy, regarded by some as a " vulgar imitation of Falstaff," is in certain respects a [12] " typical Southerner, brave, high talking, careless in money matters, fond of good living, and last, but

---

[11] A story of abused hospitality suggesting A. C. Gordon's *Sinjinn Survivin'* (Harper's, Jan., 1918) though the motives are widely different.

[12] W. P. Trent, *William Gilmore Simms*, 109.

not least, too frequently inclined to take his own common-places as the utterance of inspired wisdom." It is in the collection of stories entitled *The Cabin and the Wigwam* (New York, 1844), however, that Simms deals most spe-cifically with the actual plantation. *The Lazy Crow* is a keen study of superstition, potent element in the psy-chology of the blacks, and *Caloya, or, The Loves of the Driver* [13] traces the somewhat bombastic amours of the negro foreman, Mingo, with real penetration into negro character and with interesting side lights upon plantation customs. *The Snake of the Cabin*, another plantation story, elaborates the theme of slave loyalty.

Georgia, a state of broad and burly democracy, failed to receive treatment in the plantation writings of the period. Longstreet's " brutally exaggerated bits of real-ism," *Georgia Scenes* [14] (New York, 1840), enjoyed some popularity but had no connection with the romantic tradi-tion. The lower South soon found representation. Ingraham brought out by 1835 his *The Southwest* [15] (New York), a descriptive volume offered as fiction. It was a fairly popular work and it was a favorable picture, al-though a few plantation barons took offence. The prin-cipal plantation chronicle of the lower valley, however, is the work of a foreigner, Carl Postl, who came to this country in 1823 and within a decade produced several works which, his biographer [16] tells us, had a continental

[13] It is important to remember that in plantation literature this word may mean, as here, the negro foreman, or, as in the writings of Page, the driver of a carriage.

[14] Original published in Augusta, 1835.

[15] Reference should be made to Ingraham's *The Quadroone* (New York, 1840), one of the earliest novels to utilize as motive the agony of a beautiful slave girl whose single drop of black blood condemned her.

[16] See A. B. Faust, *Charles Sealsfield* in *Americana Germanica*,

vogue rivalling the successes of Scott and of Cooper. He
did not impress America before 1844 when there appeared
in New York two of his more famous works, *Life in the
New World* and *The Cabin Book*. The former volume,
or rather part 3, *The Planter's Life*, is a work of uncommon realism.[17] He records in great detail the plantation
customs of the Mississippi Valley, presenting social life
and race relations much in the conventional pattern. He
undertakes thus early to differentiate the peculiar character of Kentucky planters. One distinction may safely
be urged for Postl's work; it excels in a pitiless analysis
of the ignorant, shirking, primitive slave of the lower
South, different from the house slave of other sections.
Sealsfield's portraiture is to the idealizations of the abolitionists much as Mark Twain's skit on *The Noble Red
Man* is to Cooper's eulogies. It is a sufficient illustration
of this quality merely to refer to old Pompey, a pious
darkey who had for many years been loving Jesus under
the impression that He was a woman and who, disillu-
sioned by his master, doubted his ability to love a male
deity. *The Cabin Book* belongs in the large to the literature of the pioneer age when the plantation frontier was
being extended into rough and remote zones; but it shows
the appeal of the plantation to men of all professions, it
presents something of the entertainments and recreations
of plantation life, and it illustrates the devotion of slaves
for their masters.

It is remarkable to note how many of the writers thus
far considered were not to the plantation manner born, —
Paulding, Greene, Ingraham, Mrs. Gilman, Sealsfield, for

Jan., 1897; the same writer has a life of Postl (Baltimore, 1892); see
also *Bibliographical Notes* by Otto Heller in *Modern Language
Review*, III, no. 4, July, 1908.

[17] He even attempts a German equivalent of negro dialect.

example. A companion fact of interest is that the greatest
body of plantation literature in this period was the work
of another group of aliens, actuated, however, by a widely
different motive.

Foremost among the factors which promoted a wide dissemination of the plantation concept, and strikingly consistent in many respects with the tradition as already
established, was the manifold propaganda of abolitionism.
When we consider the multitudinous forms of expression
employed by this movement, novels, poems, essays, autobiographies, songs, sermons, orations, newspaper writings,
lectures accompanied sometimes with vaudeville features,
we begin to comprehend something of its reach into American thought. When, moreover, we scrutinize closely the
plantation as it appears in most of these portrayals, we
recognize that in spite of much distortion there is a considerable confirmation of the elements of more sympathetic literature. The purpose of the abolitionist, apart
from philosophical or ethical discussion, was to awaken
for the slave a moving pity; the general plan was to focus
on the individual instance; and the frequent artistic
method was the old device of contrast. To brighten the
light of the planter's life deepened the shadows of slave
existence. The defenceless and pious black was therefore
placed side by side with the haughty and sometimes dis-
sipated ruling class. The arduous toil of field or gin or
curing house was balanced against the idleness and the
recreation of white lords who, toiling not and spinning not,
subsisted by the sweat of other men's brows. Cramped,
dirty, miserable huts were placed beneath the wings of
mansions. The grind of labor and its ceaselessness, work
from daylight till dark, work on Sunday, work for pregnant women and for newly-made mothers, work for whin-
ing children, work for the sick, all under the restless eye,

and sometimes under the lash, of the overseer — this condition was opposed to gay music or vivacious laughter from spacious halls or to the merry shouts of hunting parties. The chief specific items in the indictment brought by reformers were brutality and unchastity; these were spectacular features utilized with largest possible dramatic appeal. But the background was rarely missing, an emphasis for each incident. When the literature of apology undertook to refute the charges, it, too, utilized the happier aspects, endeavoring to prove that the contrast, if it existed at all, was one of degree and not of kind. Thus the curious result happened: the two opposing sides of the fiercest controversy that ever shook national thought agreed concerning certain picturesque elements of plantation life and joined hands to set the conception unforgettably in public consciousness.

Now this note of abolitionism had been early sounded in our literature. Pastorious wrote in 1688 what is probably the first public protest; Sewell brought out *The Selling of Joseph* in 1700; Crevecoeur recorded some of the horrors of slavery in 1782; Freneau attempted poetic expression of the anti-slavery mood and Barlow made dire prophecies of evil in his *Columbiad* (1807). But it was in the decade of the thirties that the apostles of freedom began to visualize the definite slave in his definite plantation environment. This fact appears even in the verse. Whittier's *The Hunters of Men* (1835) and his *Farewell of a Virginia Slave Mother* are more clearly localized than the rhetorical effusions of Atlas in Barlow's cumbrous epic. Longfellow, normally content with academic denunciation, narrates what he considers a real plantation horror in *The Quadroon Girl* (1842) and Lowell strikes at many an assumed plantation custom.

The exaggeration of true propaganda is, of course, in

all this writing, but it served in certain essential respects to reenforce the tradition. The sharpest deviation from the established conception is in the idealization [18] of the plantation negro, the process that ultimately gave to the world saintly Uncle Tom. It was not long, however, before this canonization of the black, a portrayal diametrically opposed to the more appealing figures of minstrelsy, was emphatically rejected. This departure from the tradition is, moreover, of little significance compared to the service of abolitionism to the plantation idea as a whole. For in general anti-slavery writers chose the plantation as the stage of their narratives and corroborated many of the major elements of the tradition.

The most effective piece of abolition fiction of the early period was *Archy Moore* [19] (Boston, 1836), the work of the historian, Richard Hildreth. Over this typical specimen of its kind we may linger for a moment. Large attention is paid to the character and mode of life of the whites, to the conduct and psychology of the blacks, and to race relations. The greater part of a lengthy chapter is concerned with Colonel Moore, a Virginia planter, by blood and breeding a member of the landed aristocracy. Full justice is done his courtesy, his affability, his courage, his generosity, his sensitiveness to honor, his fairly

[18] Wendell says of one of Longfellow's poems: "One may fairly doubt whether in all anti-slavery literature there is a more humorous example of the way in which philanthropic dreamers often constructed negroes in the simple process of daubing their own faces with cork." (*Literary History of America*, 388.) This spirit is found in extreme representation in Miss Martineau's *The Hour and the Man* (London, 1841).

[19] Republished the next year in London as *The White Slave*. Howells says (*Literary Friends and Acquaintances*, 97) that this novel enjoyed prestige because of "imaginative verity." Hart curiously lists it in the bibliography of *Slavery and Abolition* among authentic slave narratives.

radiant personality, his wide social contact; but the master quality of his life is a profound, though hidden, sensualism, a result of the effect of slavery upon him and men of his class. The life that centers in his home is one of gaiety, in spite of the menace of bankruptcy. The negroes suffer greatly — not even the master's own half-blood daughters are safe from paternal lust — but are credited, nevertheless, with a stolid happiness, the stupid, temporizing joy of those whose finer sensibilities are dead. In general, much of the picture coincides with the traditional view. An interesting point in connection with this work is the occurrence of many elements that later become fixtures in abolition novels: the cruel Yankee overseer, Jonathan Snapdragon, returns in scores of treatments, notably *Uncle Tom's Cabin* and *The Octoroon;* the analysis of the unreality of Southern religion, strangely indifferent to negro agony, is seen again in *Dred;* and the spectacle of negroes, waiting for a sale, engaging in the slave warehouse upon a characteristic frolic, recurs over and over, specially in post-bellum drama.

A popular form of campaign material was the slave autobiography. One of the earliest was Charles Ball's *Slavery in the United States* (New York, 1837). More ambitious was the work of W. W. Brown, whose *Narrative* (Boston, 1848) was almost immediately republished in London, where, the following year, he brought out a second volume.[20] This fugitive slave also attempted to portray in fiction plantation life as he knew it. Best known of all writings of former slaves of the period was Frederick Douglass' *Narrative* (Boston, 1844). Douglass,

[20] Brown's second volume was *A Description of William Wells Brown's Original Panoramic Visions of the Scenes in the Life of an American Slave.* The novel referred to was *Clotelle; a Tale of the Southern States.*

a man of considerable intelligence, made his story effective by the use of some proportion and restraint. Nowhere in abolition writing is there more skilful application of the method of contrast. Josiah Henson's *Life* (Boston, 1849) is well known for its influence upon *Uncle Tom's Cabin*.

Meanwhile there was in Southern literature a movement for defense, at first merely aggressive expression of sectional pride, later professed rebuttal. As most of this writing prior to 1850 appeared in Southern periodicals, or from Southern publishing houses, its effect upon the popular conception was negligible. But it is worthy of mention. If one runs through the files of a representative journal, as *The Southern Literary Messenger*, one is impressed with the number of such efforts. As early as 1835 an anonymous novel, *Lionel Granby*, emphasized slave happiness and devotion. By 1839 another story, *Judith Bensaddi*, was deemed worthy of even second publication because, presumably, it recorded the conversion of the abolition heroine. Best of these local studies was Philip Pendleton Cooke's *The Two Country Houses*[21] which appeared just before the death of the author and which John R. Thompson called one of the truest descriptions of the agreeable and hospitable life of rural Virginia.

In any consideration of the plantation in literature, passing reference should be made to the rather extensive writings of travel.[22] These included many observations of, and comments upon, Southern life and its institutions. Some of this work was provocative of wide discussion,

[21] Serial in *Southern Literary Messenger*, 1848; Thompson's praise, *ibid.*, June, 1858.

[22] A list of some more important travelers will be found in Bibliographical Notes. Bryant was guarded concerning points of controversy, Lyell saw both sides; most of the other visitors were unfriendly.

particularly the accounts of such authors as Mrs. Trollope and Miss Martineau, but none of it was of great moment in building the plantation tradition.

Toward the close of the period under consideration, the plantation had so penetrated the American artistic imagination that its echoes are found in unexpected places. Poe is commonly thought of as the author who, more than any other of our native writers, let his fancy indulge in some ethereal dream by some weird, eternal stream. At the same time, however, he brings Jupiter into *The Gold-Bug*. However justly this black may be criticized as to dialect or characterization, the fact is before us that Poe realized the appropriateness of placing in his mystery tale a typical devoted house slave on the Southern estate. Stedman hints [23] at another connection between Poe and the plantation: " I have a fancy that our Southern poet's ear caught the music of ' Annabel Lee ' and ' Eulalie,' if not their special quality, from the plaintive, melodious negro songs utilized by those early writers of ' minstrelsy ' who have been denominated the only composers of a genuine American school." Melville with his romance of southern seas and cannibal pardises is removed as far as possible from the Southern plantation; yet in *White-Jacket* (New York, 1850) there are suggestions: his experience with officers which convinced him that Southern-bred men made best commanders; Rose-Water, who boasted that his mother had been the mistress of a planter; John Randolph's comparison of plantation brutality with that of a man-of-war; hints of negro song. Even Hawthorne in *The Marble Faun* (1860) offers among the conjectures concerning the origin of Miriam a rumor that

[23] *Poets of America,* 251. C. Alphonso Smith in *Edgar Allan Poe* makes a similar suggestion. The present writer records the statment for what it may be worth; it would be hard to prove.

she is the carefully nurtured daughter of a rich planter, driven from her section by the fearful taint of African blood.

By 1850, at which time the plantation and its social connotations began to loom larger in American thought, this concept had already received a moderate treatment in literature resulting in a fairly well defined tradition, a tradition that through the instrumentality of friend and foe alike magnified somewhat the scale of plantation luxury, intensified the color of plantation life. This treatment was most frequently the result of an earnest point of view; even Postl as he wrote was experiencing a transition in feeling from abolitionism to sympathy with slavery. But the tradition suffers little from conflicting attitudes. Whether a kindly romancer, prompted by love of his section, sought to present its chief social unit in most favorable aspect, or whether the zealot, prompted by pity for the slave, endeavored to increase pity for him by augmenting the weight of regal splendor which rested on his weary shoulders, the effect was the same: the noblest plantation to be found, or perhaps one that never was by land or tidewater, was proposed as typical.

CHAPTER III

THE DEVELOPMENT OF THE CONCEPTION IN LITERATURE

II. *Arraignment and Apology* (1850–1870)

So far as plantation literature is concerned, the period from 1850 to 1870, from the tenseness of feeling occasioned by the fugitive slave agitation to the graciousness of national reconciliation when North and South kissed each other, may be roughly considered the epoch of Mrs. Stowe and John Esten Cooke, of Uncle Tom and Squire Effingham. More exactly, however, there were three types of literature which were of consequence in fixing the plantation in popular thinking. Most varied was the literature of slavery, *pro et con*, which commonly employed the plantation in rather free fashion; most widely read, perhaps, was the romance of domestic sentiment, the nation's "most tender, most tearful classics," which not infrequently utilized the plantation as setting; most serious in purpose was the work of a school of which Cooke and Porte Crayon may be taken as representative, who regarded the plantation principally as material for a purely artistic treatment. In the latter group we may include a small body of fairly significant writing which, coming immediately after the Civil war, began dimly to apprehend the glamorous possibilities realized by the following age.

A. *The Plantation in Polemic Writings*

The preceding period had been marked by the beginning of literary hostilities between the opponents and the defenders of slavery but the fifties and the early sixties were notable for a contest more voluminous and more bitter. The Fugitive Slave Law sent a tentacle of the slave system into many Northern communities and awakened from its lethargy a colossal sentiment which shortly made itself felt, in literature as elsewhere. Southern apologists, moved by the sudden onslaught of fury, made desperate efforts to roll back the tide of opinion engulfing and annihilating their civilization. Looked at from the vantage point of time, the contest appears singularly one-sided; a single product of the reformer's urge, like *Uncle Tom's Cabin* or the famous Beadle dime novel, *Maum Guinea's Children*, reached larger audiences and stirred more effectually popular imagination than the entire output of slavery's vindicators. Yet by one of the curious reversals of history, barely a generation was to pass before, in literature at least, this spirit of defence was to achieve a retribution and sweep from the field of fancy most of the attackers.

Further analysis or interpretation of *Uncle Tom's Cabin*, reputed to be the most widely read novel and most frequently presented stage offering in American history, seems inadvisable if not impossible. It is important, however, in consideration of plantation literature to call attention to the oft-neglected sub-title of this work; for as a study of *Life among the Lowly* it takes rank with the foremost plantation documents. A modern Southern critic has said: [1] " It was the first attempt to portray in vivid colors the social and institutional life of the South." Whether first or not, it is certainly the most influential before the Civil War. The history of the work, rooted

[1] C. Alphonso Smith, *The Historical Element in Recent Southern Literature, Publications of the Mississippi Historical Society,* II, 8; see also Wendell, *Literary History of America,* 384.

in impressions received as early as 1839, planned definitely in 1850, and offered to an applauding world in the
National Era, beginning with June, 1851, has been recorded by the author's best biographer, her son;[2] the
simplicity of plot devices, consisting principally of inter-
weaving the pathetic themes of breaking family ties and
of pursuing fugitives, has been demonstrated by Professor
Erskine;[3] and the adherence of the work in spirit to "the
established native tradition, as old as *Charlotte Temple*
and as new as *The Wide, Wide World,* the tradition of
sentimental, pious, instructive narratives written by women
chiefly for women and largely about women" has been
made clear by Dr. Van Doren.[4] The point of moment
here is that this was a plantation novel; that through its
enormous appeal the plantation, as Mrs. Stowe saw it,
was lodged more strongly in the imagination; and that
Mrs. Stowe's plantation, in certain important respects,
was congruous with that already presented in literature.
Here is the traditional hospitality, munificence of life,
luxuriant idleness, prodigality, thriftlessness, the pursuit
of happiness as the end of being. Southern character of
the higher stratum receives rather sympathetic treatment;
the supreme villainy is charged to a Yankee, the supreme
satire directed against another Yankee. The affectionate
and the happy, not less than the terrible and the revolting,
race relations are elaborated, particularly in the home of
St. Clare, too lenient not only for the welfare of his
household but even for the good of slaves themselves.
Little Eva, intended for the ideal of sentimental romance,
is in many ways the sweet spoiled child of the slave-
holding family, as absolute in her whims as Henrique.

[2] C. E. Stowe, *Life of Harriet Beecher Stowe,* chap. 7.
[3] *Leading American Novelists,* 292.
[4] *The American Novel,* 118.

Mrs. Stowe did not utterly idealize black character. A Southern scholar has made a list[5] of negro traits displayed in this work in comparison with the character generally accepted and finds the fictional treatment lacking only in the absence of " appropriativeness," the natural propensity to steal. In spite of the hero's unreal piety, this story exhibits the negro's gregariousness, his love of finery, his childish irresponsibility — Topsy is one of the most famous examples in literature — the variations in conduct that result from difference of blood content, and many other qualities which run true to form.

In *Dred*[6] (1856) Mrs. Stowe shifted the setting from Kentucky and the lower South to North Carolina, the emphasis from the injury of slavery upon the blacks to its vicious effects upon the whites; but many elements are thinly disguised repetitions of what she had used in the the former novel. The principal points of divergence in the later work are the enlarged dissertation upon the ethical insensibility of Southern society, the less favorable treatment of white character, the keener consciousness of the tragedy of mixed blood, the richer and more poorly

[5] T. P. Bailey, *Race Orthodoxy in the South,* 192.

[6] Passing reference should be made to the vitality of this work, for its influence has extended into other periods than the one under consideration. Nehemiah Adams called Mrs. Stowe " not only the foe but the Defoe of slavery." " The book," says Dr. Van Doren, " met with a popular reception never before or since accorded to a novel " (*The American Novel,* 118); according to C. E. Stowe, the story quickly went through 20 editions. Five years after the publication of the novel it was asserted that even in the South there were few people who had not read it (*Russell's Magazine,* May, 1857). The claim is made that over the United States as a whole it has been read more widely than any book save the Bible (F. S. Arnett, *Fifty Years of Uncle Tom, Munsey's,* August, 1902).

organized assemblage of plantation material — for *Dred*
has the stuff of several novels. Old Tom is subdivided
into two characters, his religious mantle falling upon Dred,
his gentle temperament persisting in expanded manner in
Tiff. The Gordon mansion of colonial brick and the life
that centered in it are typical of the traditional plantation home. The types of character are consistent. Nina
Gordon, the heroine, is the usual plantation paragon plus
abolition tenderness; John Gordon is a specimen of kindness and incompetence which marked the conventional
plantation master; Clayton is St. Clare fitted more intimately into the plot. The Legree of this story, however,
is a highly bred Southern gentleman, Tom Gordon, the
personification of that viciousness which Mrs. Stowe
thought was made almost inevitable by the ownership of
humanity. Mrs. Stowe enlarged her range of negro types.
Dred has little of the truly African, if we except a certain supernaturalism, but Milly manifests negro religion
at its best, Aunt Kate, the cook, and Old Hundred, the
coachman, are standard plantation functionaries, and
Tomtit is representative of the comic slave popularized
by minstrel treatment. Best of the darkies, though, is
Tiff, with his veneration for his family and with that
devotion which passed from generation to generation and
had no winter in it.

There appeared during the decade many other abolition
narratives of significance in developing the plantation idea.
Some of these enjoyed noteworthy popularity. A year
before the appearance of *Uncle Tom's Cabin*, Mrs. Emily
C. Pierson brought out *Jamie Parker the Fugitive* (Hart-
ford, 1851), a characteristic anti-slavery presentation of a
Virginia plantation that emphasized the darker aspects,
such as the heartlessness of the master, the cruelty of the
overseer, the separation by sale of members of the slave

family. In 1853 there appeared *Cousin Franck's Household* (Boston) the fourth edition of which, published in
1864, bore the title of *Ruth's Sacrifice*.[7] Plantation life in
this rather bitter forensic is closely in line with the tradition, though such unpleasant features as racial unchastity
and slave breeding as a business are made unusually prominent. F. C. Adams' *Manuel Perira* (Washington, 1853),
an indictment of the laws of slavery operating in Southern
states, contained little direct plantation material. More
important for the tradition was Mary Langdon's *Ida
May*[8] (Boston, 1855) depicting the adventure of a little
Pennsylvania girl kidnapped and sold into slavery on the
South Carolina rice estates. The splendor of plantation
life for the whites and the misery of existence for the
negroes receive the largest elaboration which the author
could give. Differing in point of view is another story
of the rice plantations, *Wolfesden* (Boston, 1856) by
" J. B.," in which a haughty planter is almost enslaved
himself because his mother, it developed, had a drop of
negro blood. In the same year Boston saw the dramatic
spectacle, later turned into fiction, *Neighbor Jackwood,* by
J. T. Trowbridge, which, without direct plantation scenes,
depicted certain plantation elements as New England
understood them.

Among the followers of *Uncle Tom's Cabin,* two novels
deserve special mention. Mayne Reid's *The Quadroon*
(London, 1856; New York, 1857) is important in its own
right, for it passed rapidly through several editions, and
has further significance as the probable source of Boucicault's drama, *The Octoroon*. Reid based his work, he

---

[7] The 1853 volume was credited to Mrs. C. H. Pearson, the
1864 edition to Mrs. Emily C. Pearson; the same author, probably, wrote all.

[8] Of this novel 50,000 copies were sold in a few months.

tells us, on actual observation; and though in true abolition fashion he reveals luridly the pits and pendulums
of slave existence, there are bright glimpses of redemptive features: a happy home life, fidelity of slaves, reasonable care for the blacks, including a plantation physi-
cian, and the prevalence of fairly cordial race relations.
The central theme is known to all who are familiar with
Boucicault's adaptation; the beautiful quadroon, the
bankruptcy, the agony of the sensitive quadroon held up
to the bidding of sensual overseers, and, unlike the drama
here, the rescue by the hero with wedding bells in England. More valuable, measured by popularity, was Mrs.
M. V. Victor's *Maum Guinea's Children* [9] (New York,
1861), a publication in the Beadle series of dime novels.
Mrs. Victor indicates in her sub-title an intention of giving merely a narrative of " a holiday week on a Louisiana
estate," but the point of view is emphatically abolition.
Like much of Louisiana literature, this novel treats principally the tragedy of beautiful quadroons. Interwoven
into the main plot are reminiscences of slaves, tales which
bring out frightful examples of cruelty, impurity, family
separation. As material for one story, the Nat Turner
insurrection is dragged in, that striking episode in the
history of slavery which from the time that Warner rushed
from the New York press, even before Nat was captured,
his *Authentic and Impartial Narrative* (1831) has been a
fruitful theme. The memorable features of Mrs. Victor's
work are, however, the pictures in the tradition; the
Christmas festivities, the rollicking songs like interludes
from minstrelsy, the intimate reflections of life in the
mansion or in the cabin.

[9] The vogue of the little book was remarkable; incidentally
it is said that Lincoln himself enjoyed this story (Harvey, *The
Dime Novel, Altantic,* July, 1907).

In conventional pattern and without any real distinction, came other plantation novels inspired by opposition to slavery.   James R. Gilmore, writing under the pseudonym of Edmund Kirke, brought out during the Civil War several works, the best known being *Among the Pines* (New York, 1862) and *My Southern Friends* (New York, 1863).   Gilmore had actually traveled in the South and he obviously tried to be fair.   The earlier story presents South Carolina society, rich and idle, a sort of beautiful flower growing out of the muck of slavery; negro traits are analyzed with considerable attention to the frenzied emotionalism as expressed in frolic or worship.   *My Southern Friends* transfers the scene to North Carolina and introduces a contrast between the relatively happy estate of Colonel Preston and the unimaginable inferno of lust and cruelty that was Dawsey's plantation.   Stephen G. Bulfinch brought out in 1863 *Honor; or The Slave-Driver's Daughter* (Boston); Trowbridge returned with *Cudjo's Cave* [10] as his second offering (Boston, 1863); and the anonymous *Daingerfield's Rest* (New York, 1864), without plantation locale, exhibited the sins of slavery persisting unto the third and fourth generation.   The vintage of more grapes of wrath was trampled out in Epes Sargent's *Peculiar*, a story almost wholly unrelieved by bright customs or pleasant portraiture.   Of more than ordinary interest is the work of an English writer of multiplied romance, Miss M. E. Braddon, whose *The Octoroon,* [11] written during the Civil War, was almost immediately republished in this country and enjoyed a popular reception.   It is in the main a less accurate and more lurid study of the same form of plantation life that had

[10] Northrup (*A Manual of American Literature,* 171) calls this novel a good second to *Uncle Tom's Cabin.*

[11] This conjecture is based on internal evidence.

appeared in Reid's *Quadroon*. Four years after the Emancipation Proclamation, Mrs. Lydia M. Child brought out a collection of short stories, *Fact and Fiction* (New York, 1867), of which at least two [12] presented aspects of plantation life as seen in the reformer's fancy.

During this period there appeared many real or supposititious slave autobiographies. [13] The diversity of the places of publication illustrates the wide-spread vogue of this kind of writing; everywhere there was the slave story prepared for the Northern audience, sometimes for the local audience. The most interesting type of this literature is the rather sensational female autobiography, of which class Mattie Griffin's *Autobiography of a Female Slave* (New York, 1857) may be taken as representative. This work is a compilation of all the assumed baser qualities of plantation life as they worked dread misery to the heroine who, however, was sustained by a shy, virginal chastity. Illustrative of the author's attitude is the account of a terrible whipping which she endured without murmur because she kept her mind fixed on the passion of Christ. A similar work is Harriet Jacob's *Incidents in the Life of a Slave Girl* (Boston, 1861), a work for which Mrs. Child assumed editorial responsibility.

Manifold forces outside the realm of imaginative writing were at this time enlarging and enforcing the plantation conception. One can hardly estimate, for example, the influence of the Nast cartoons which appeared in *Harper's Weekly,* many of them representations of plantation scenes. Works of travel and description increased in power. Of this type the most conspicuous were the work of Olmsted and of Fanny Kemble Butler. Frederick

---

[12] *The Quadroon* and *Black Saxons*.

[13] Several of these works will be found listed in Bibliographical Notes.

Law Olmsted brought out in the late fifties three books, all resulting from his tour of the South, the most important being his *Journey through the Seaboard Slave States* (New York, 1856). His picture of life in the slavery zone was ranked [14] by so careful a critic as Lowell as second to none in formulating Northern opinion. Olmsted, as Professor Trent points out,[15] did not have access to the plantations which typified Southern civilization at its best; but he did see much of the rural life on estates of medium grade and he recorded carefully. His skill in observation, his apparent freedom from prejudice, his journalistic power, all combined to give his books peculiar weight. Less dispassionate is the work of Fanny Kemble Butler, *A Journal of a Residence on a Georgian Plantation in 1838–39*. The English actress went to her husband's rice estate a staunch abolitionist and there saw much that confirmed her convictions; she achieves, however, some power of description, particularly in her account of the hardships of slave women, and her influence upon Northern thought was considerable.[16]

The abolition spirit in its varied expressions did not, however, preempt the field of literature. Not small in bulk, though of no real influence, was the pro-slavery writing. The year of the publication of *Uncle Tom's Cabin* saw six pro-slavery novels brought out by Northern publishers; the following season the output was little diminished. Some of these novels were direct rejoinders to Mrs. Stowe's volume. Most of them employed the plantation as demonstration plot for some story exemplifying the truth of the argument proclaimed by the leaders of contemporary Southern thought. But the effect of this

[14] See review in *Atlantic*, November, 1860.
[15] See preface to 1907 edition (New York).
[16] See review, probably by Curtis, *Atlantic*, August, 1863.

body of work on the tradition was insignificant. If we except for the moment the romances of domestic sentiment, we may simply affirm that the work of the artisans of apology was refused a hearing. Ingraham's *The Sunny South* had a fairly extensive run during the season of 1853–54 in the Philadelphia *Saturday Courier* and Mrs. Eastman's *Aunt Phyllis' Cabin* [17] attained a sale of 18,000 copies in a few months, but none of the others did so well. Not even the South itself manifested any active interest in the roseate pictures of life on its estates.

Not all this fiction, it should be remembered, utilized the plantation. A favorite device was to carry the war into the enemy's country and there resort to the analogy of the glass house. This scheme accounts for many stories depicting the suffering of the poorer classes in the North or in England, suffering sometimes contrasted with the happiness of Southern blacks, sometimes standing alone in its woe. Caroline E. Rush opens her story, *The North and the South; or, Slavery and its Contrasts* (Phila., 1852), amid scenes of squalor in New York and then moves the setting in a transition of glory to a Mississippi plantation where even the " servants have bread enough and to spare." J. Randolph Thornton follows a similar plan in his reply to Uncle Tom,[18] and so does J. W. Page, the title of whose work suggests its method and its literary obligation: *Uncle Robin in His Cabin in Virginia and Tom without One in Boston* (Richmond, 1855). The suffering of Northern poor whites contrasted with the merriment of Southern slaves is prominent in *Mr. Frank, the Underground Agent* (Phila., 1853), by " Vidi," in *Liberia* (New York, 1853), Mrs. Sarah J. Hale's colonization novel, in

[17] Erskine, *Leading American Novelists*, 297.
[18] *The Cabin and the Parlor; or, Slaves without Masters* (Phila., 1852).

White Acre vs. Black Acre (Richmond, 1856), an allegorical rendering of the pro-slavery argument, in *The Black Gauntlet* (Phila., 1860), by Mrs. Mary H. Schoolcraft. Some of the novels which omit entirely plantation background, centering interest in foreign wretchedness are L. B. Chase's *English Serfdom and American Slavery* (New York, 1854), Marion Southwood's *Tit for Tat* (New York and London, 1856), S. H. Elliot's *New England's Chattels* (New York, 1858) and, most remarkable of its class, W. T. Thompson's *The Slave Holder Abroad* (Phila., 1860), a labored compilation by the Georgia humorist demonstrating the profligacy, immorality, and brutality that marked English society. Variations of this theme are found in Mrs. H. E. Wilson's *Our Nig* (Boston, 1859), a dissertation on the suffering of free negroes in the North, and Mrs. G. M. Flanders' *The Ebony Idol* (New York, 1860), a satire upon an abolition organization which undertook to care for a fugitive slave.

The plantation was, however, the chief reliance of the defenders, a setting of reality and a motive of charm. Thompson realized this value and introduced even into his English scenes a Southern slave, Billy Buck, in order that characteristic negro stories and conduct might brighten the pages of rather dull reading. The pattern of such novels as employ the plantation is constant: a joyous life for both races, the gaiety of the whites being, however, subordinated to a stern sense of responsibility for the welfare of the blacks; Southern character glorified with ethical and cultural perfection; tender feelings of both sides of the race relations, with special emphasis on the happiness of the slaves. This was the chief message, that the slaves were gloriously happy. This formula explains the plantation as found in novels already mentioned by "Vidi," J. W. Page, Caroline Rush, Mrs. Schoolcraft,

and Mrs. Hale. The same general theme is in Ingraham's
Sunny South which after its run in the periodical appeared
in book form in 1860. This is the method, too, of Robert
Criswell's *Uncle Tom's Cabin Contrasted with Buckingham Hall* (New York, 1852) in which the social radiance
and moral firmness of a Southern home bring about the
conversion of an ardent Yankee "bobolitionist"; of Law-
rence Neville's story of the Virginia plantation, *Edith
Allen* (Richmond, 1856); and of Reverend E. W. Warren's
scriptural novel, *Nellie Norton* (Macon, Ga., 1864). Occasionally the monotonous sequence of argumentative tab-
leaus is broken by bits of characterization that stand
apart, such, for example, as old Bacchus, the waiter in
Mrs. Eastman's *Aunt Phyllis' Cabin*, gifted alike in pray-
ing or in drinking. The most curious history of these pro-
slavery novels is attached to a work by a North Carolina
educator, C. H. Wiley, which in a few years appeared in
as many as six editions under four different titles, the
best known being *Utopia; a Picture of Life at the South* [19]
(Phila., 1852). The best defence from a Northern pen
was Nehemiah Adams' *The Sable Cloud* (Boston, 1861),
a kind of miscellany extending from the contemporary
plantation backward to the church of Philemon.

If the importance of these works justified our lingering,
we might give special consideration to three novels. J. R.
Thornton's *The Cabin and the Parlor* is perhaps most
typical of pro-slavery stories. Every device of the abolition fiction is introduced and turned to purposes of charity; for example, the bankrupt sale takes place, but the
negroes, instead of being "sent to Georgy" remain with
kind neighbors until their own "white folks" can pur-

[19] Partial consideration of this work may be found in a note,
Pub. So. History Ass'n., 6:67 (Jan., 1902), which does not, however,
refer to the 1849 edition, probably the first.

chase them again. T. B. Thorpe, the humorist, in *The Master's House* (New York and London, 1854) comes closest to realism of all the pro-slavery novels. Overseers, slave-traders, and certain " po' whites " are presented in almost abolitionist manner; certain evils of society, as duelling, are confessed with frankness; the cleavage between planters and smaller farmers is suggested as ominous. In the main, however, the treatment is one that justifies domestic slavery. J. S. Peacocke's *The Creole Orphans* (New York, 1856) includes such conventional themes as the conversion of abolitionists who visit the actual estates but deals candidly with the strange results from the too frequent mingling of white and black blood in the society of the Louisiana plantations.

B. *The Plantation in Domestic Romance*

In American fiction on the eve of the Civil War it was "the domestic sentimentalists who held the field." [20] This type is of prime importance in a consideration of the plantation conception, for in the work of many of these writers the plantation is the setting. The worthlessness of the representations here made of Southern life has been repeatedly pointed out; the novels were, so far as accuracy of background is concerned, out of time, out of space. But this truth must not obscure the fact that the hungry millions who devoured this brand of fiction accepted the plantation as here presented, accepted the shadowy exaggerations of character as typically Southern. It is reasonable to assume that nothing in print more influenced bourgeois minds, emphasizing and popularizing, if not defining, than the tenuous romances of Mrs. Southworth, Mrs. Hentz, and others of the same school.

[20] Carl Van Doren, *The American Novel*, 114.

For sheer immensity of production and for popularity, Mrs. E. D. E. N. Southworth, born in the North but a resident of Virginia most of her life, is entitled to a position of priority in the group. Bitterly denounced by Southern critics [21] as untrue, her pictures of plantation life were repeated in scores of novels, generally after the same pattern. Of her many works, the most interesting from the point of view of background are *Retribution* (New York, 1849), one of her earliest, *Shannondale* (New York, 1850), *Virginia and Margaret* (Phila., 1852), and *The Mother-in-Law* (New York, 1857), all of which have since appeared in numerous republications. Everywhere plantation life is depicted in strong lights and shadows, and the light is not less than gorgeous. Houses are almost palatial; social activity is ceaseless, cultured, idyllic; men are gallant, courtly — princely is a favored adjective — prodigal in the uncalculating Southern fashion; the heroines are beyond description in beauty, sentimentality, and ineffable sickliness from which the maid of romance often languishes; carefully nurtured hothouse creatures, educated by tutors, a custom which affords the romance of *Shannondale*, these dainty damsels are tender and true. Local color is sought by the introduction of negro characters, speaking a crude dialect and performing comic tricks. The closest approach to tragedy is in the story of the quadroon, Henny, of *Retribution;* reared in luxury and experiencing no effects of slavery until the death of her father, she suffers much because of the jealousy of the young plantation mistress, Juliette Dent.

Hardly second to Mrs. Southworth in popular esteem, and closer to plantation reality, was another Northern

---

[21] See review of *The Mother-in-Law, So. Lit. Mess.,* Jan., 1852; see also Page, *Authorship in the South before the Civil War, Lippincott's,* July, 1889.

lady who wrote chiefly from Alabama, Mrs. C. L. Hentz. The sale of her novels went early into the hundreds of thousands, and within a few years after her death a complete edition of her works appeared in Philadelphia. In practically all of her better known romances the charm of plantation life is given large emphasis. Two of these novels may be classed as pro-slavery propaganda: *Marcus Warland* (Phila., 1852) and *The Planter's Northern Bride* (Phila., 1854). The former work illustrates reciprocal devotion between the races, especially in the case of the old mammy and the young hero. In the later work,[22] a reply to *Uncle Tom's Cabin*, Mrs. Hentz allows a lovely young New England heroine, and even her rampant abolitionist father, to become converted to pro-slavery views through actual experience on the plantation.

For such distinction as mere popularity confers, surely the name of Mrs. Mary J. Holmes is an illustrious one. Her *Tempest and Sunshine* (New York, 1854), we may infer from the sub-title, undertook to present " Life in Kentucky " but succeeded chiefly in giving to fiction two of its most distorted figures. It is probably true, however, that hosts of readers accepted " sunshine " Fanny as the embodiment of the devoted Dixie maid, " tempest " Julia as evidence of the fact that " bright and fierce and fickle is the South," marveled at the gay hospitality, and shed tears over such scenes as the rapture of the old mammy, ready to depart in peace when once she had seen her young " marster " again. In *Meadow Brook* (New York, 1857) Mrs. Holmes shows us a Georgia estate as seen through the eyes of a young New England governess who is astonished by the culture of the whites and by the happiness

---

[22] The style of this work exemplifies the pure essence of sentimentality; a birth is recorded thus: " The crowning grace of maternity had humanized the celestial loveliness of Eula."

of the blacks. True to form, the pretty abolitionist becomes converted to the plantation view-point and marries a plantation Bayard.

Page accords Marion Harland a higher rank than the writers just considered; her early works,[23] however, belong in the same category. In these stories piety of purpose reduces to very subordinate relations any local color; but the plantation life and characters are unmistakable: a rich social regime with such distinctive features as the hiring of tutors for the young ladies; cultured personages; influential and dignified house servants; happy rural recreations. Mrs. Harland's *Sunnybank* (New York, 1866) is historically important as one of the very first of the "Civil War romances," that is, a love affair between a Southern girl and a Northern soldier. Page calls this work "the first novel to utilize without gross partisanry the material of the war." It is a plantation novel, prophetic of the type of glorification which developed rapidly after the close of the War.

The list of domestic romances involving some elements of plantation material is a long one. Miss Eliza Ann Dupuy, at one time under contract to furnish one thousand columns annually to the New York *Ledger*, was a rival of Mrs. Southworth in popularity. Her most widely read novel, *The Planter's Daughter* (New York, 1857), a story of the Louisiana estates, moved even the kindly disposed Davidson, writing in 1869, to protest.[24] Miss Maria J.

[23] Within six months after the appearance of her first book, *Alone*, which was published in New York in 1856 (it seems to have appeared first in Richmond in 1854), it had passed through six editions, including one in England. By 1860, if we may accept a publisher's statement as found on the cover of Miss Warfield's *The Household of Bouverie*, 500,000 copies of her books had been sold.

[24] *Living Writers of the South*.

McIntosh, a prolific writer, is best represented in this connection by *The Lofty and the Lowly* (New York, 1853), a highly colored picture, made all the more splendid by reason of contrast with the base commercial society of the North. Similarly glowing accounts are in Lizzie Petit's *Household Mysteries* (New York, 1856), in the anonymous *Home and the World* (New York, 1857), which contains, among other features, the plantation story-teller of the Uncle Remus nature, and in Rose Jeffrey's *Woodburn* (New York, 1864). Plantation setting appears in most incongruous relation in Catherine Warfield's *The Household of Bouverie* (New York, 1860), a kind of sensational and mysterious terror story. The piety which often marks this kind of work receives its maximum emphasis in such plantation stories as Mary E. Bradley's *Douglas Farm* (New York, 1858), in the anonymous *Dew Drop of the Sunny South* with its pictures of "that happy race of beings *called*[25] the slaves," and in John H. Caldwell's evangelical novel, *The Thurstons of the Old Palmetto State* (New York, 1861). If certain of these works were to be singled out for rather serious and relatively just treatment of plantation material, the distinction would belong to Mary E. Wormeley Latimer's *Our Cousin Veronica* (New York, 1855) and to the anonymous *Woman's Faith* (New York, 1856).

This hasty consideration of a really consequential type may be appropriately concluded with reference to Mrs. Dorsey's[26] *Lucia Dare* (New York, 1867), a marvel of inclusiveness, covering geographically England, France, and America, and extending historically from the contemporary estate back to the Phillip Noland[27] episode.

[25] Italics are the author's.
[26] Miss Warfield's niece.
[27] Mrs. Dorsey insists that this is the proper spelling.

Its chief interest lies in the fact that, written after the war, it includes the retrospective attitude toward the plantation epoch; already the life of that regime begins its transmutation into that of a golden age.

C. *The Plantation in Serious Art*

In the period from 1850 to 1870 the plantation received limited treatment at the hands of a group of writers differentiated by attitude from the slavery debaters and by artistic method from the makers of insipid sentimental romance. These artists are, in the truest sense, though not in the most popular significance, the maintainers of the tradition. Judged by importance in the transmission of this tradition, and by his own contribution to the historical perspective, John Esten Cooke [28] is probably the most notable figure between Kennedy and the post-bellum masters.

Cooke brought to relative perfection the glorification of the past, attempted by Carruthers twenty years earlier; he crystallized in a few novels all the sentiment entertained by highly bred Southerners, particularly Virginians, concerning the magnificence of the plantation in its colonial aspect; he supplied a scale of operation and some structural material to innumerable writers who have since entered the field. He was, in short, the central figure of a literary triple pass. Cooke's memorable year was 1854 when there appeared in New York, all from different publishers, *Leatherstockings and Silk*, *The Virginia Comedians*, and *The Youth of Jefferson*. In 1856 *The Last of the Foresters* (New York) with its picture of Virginia gentility

[28] The present writer acknowledges obligations to Professor Beatty's admirable biography of Cooke and to critical comment in Dr. Van Doren's *The American Novel* and in Professor Pattee's *American Literature since 1870*.

on the border, enlarged the field of his imaginative effort, and in 1859 *The Youth of Jefferson* completed the cycle of his chief novels.[29]   *The Virginia Comedians* remains his foremost work,[30] both for vogue and for use of the material. It is worthy of note, in passing, that Cooke's use of setting, a reflection of a spectacular plantation regime, has given to his novels a vitality which his archaic plot method could never have earned.

They are plantation novels. It is a rural civilization that Cooke portrayed. Henry St. John voices the spirit of the works: " To be a country gentleman seems to me a grander ambition than to bow my knee before the grandest royalty in Europe." This, then, was Cooke's most successful exercise of the art of fiction and his greatest contribution to the tradition: the portrayal of the rich social life that marked the plantation society of an earlier age, the affectionate, sometimes penetrating, appraisal of the romantic figures who moved across the spacious stage. Great mansions, like Effingham Hall or the Vanely home, imposing brick structures set in gracious landscapes and furnished with elaborate interiors; gay parties assembled almost uninterruptedly; meals; games; dances; picnics; hunts; everywhere the vivacious, if sometimes forced, dialogue; everywhere beauty of costume, reminiscent of court society, — these are the unforgetable backgrounds which Cooke brings into the consciousness of his readers. His presentation of character is valuable, though many of his critics feel that he failed with the plantation girl. In the figure of this Virginia belle, Cooke probably recognized the greatest challenge to his art; certainly he labored lov-

[29] Cooke's post-bellum novels have some plantation material; but they do not equal the earlier works.

[30] A review in the *Southern Literary Messenger*, August, 1855, says that this work " met with a favor almost unprecedented in the annals of American fiction."

ingly to exhibit a radiant creature of charm and winsome-
ness, of accomplished personality, of coquetry, of courage,
of independence, of love of the open life, of tenderness and
devotion. That the picture went beyond reasonable bounds
is not, after all, surprising, for the heroines of romance
are usually rather visionary. In his treatment of men,
Cooke is surer of his visualization. We have, therefore,
in Squire Effingham, in young Champ, the embodiment
of certain aspects of the traditional plantation gentry; in
Henry St. John we see typified the best of the colonial
nobility, knightly, courageous, generous, kind to servants,
gallant, and, as good Virginians ever are, a loyal descend-
ant of Pocahontas. Even in his delineation of negro character, Cooke succeeded better than has been asserted. He
developed many of the types, as Cato the driver and the
old mammy, which became popular in the tradition, and
he suggested the attitude of many subsequent writers. In
the chapter of *The Last of the Foresters* dealing with the
song of the negro harvest hands there is more than a hint
of the power of slave melodies, one of the appealing themes
of the tradition.

Linked with Cooke by similar artistic purpose and talent,
as well as by personal relations, but differing widely in
chosen period and in method is Porte Crayon, under which
name General D. H. Strother did his work. *Virginia Illustrated*, his sketches of current life, appeared serially in
Harper's Magazine from December, 1854, to August, 1856,
was brought out in book form the next year, and shortly
afterward was republished in London. Page refers to this
work as " that early and delightful chronicle of Virginia
life "; [31] and the tribute is a just one. Strother was more
of a realist than most of the plantation writers but his
choice of detail was always happy and his pictures har-

[31] Preface to *Pastime Stories*.

monized with the general tradition. He was, perhaps, of all plantation writers of his day most completely free from any kind of thesis to maintain. While white character is given suggestive treatment, the major charm of the work is in the interpretation of the negro. This volume contains the plantation negro not to prove anything about him or by him, but just as he was. The burly, good-humored servant, Little Mice, whose name is a memorial of his habits resembling those of the tiny thieves, exemplifies many of the traditional elements, love of frolic, love of finery, superstition, optimism, and is one of the prize-men of plantation literature. Not the least impressive feature of the work is found in the illustrations, drawn by the author.

The plantation finds a certain interpretation in individual works by a number of miscellaneous authors. Foremost in literary importance is Thackeray's *The Virginians* (1857–58) which was based on his observations and conversations in this country. The blending of romance and history has been criticized and the characterization is said to be not wholly true; yet the novel reveals at least a surprising richness of detail in its account of the customs on the tobacco estates of the eighteenth century. Here are suggested with some care the large scale of economic operation with its relatively meager income, the organization of labor, the caste structure of society approximating the English order of which Virginians felt themselves a part, the pretentious social recreations and the joy in social activity, the hospitality, the feasts of food and drink, the multiplied duties of the mistress. Thackeray evidently gave some care to his representation of negro life and though his success in this respect was not absolute, he revealed certain traditional elements of slave psychology, particularly the musical temperament, the religious ecstasies, the mastery of easy lying, and a devotion to the master; even the grape-vine telegraph is found in this novel. Another English writer, G. P. R. James,[32] brought out in *The Old Dominion* (New York, 1856) a closer, though less famous, study of plantation locale. The phase of James' story which has largest significance for the tradition is the magnifying of the culture and the hospitality of the rural South, quite the equal of that which marked good English society. James was not realistic in his treatment of negro character, though he gets close to the traditional feeling of the negroes in the chapters dealing with the Nat Turner insurrection. Among native writers, St. George Tucker most closely follows the tradition with his *Hansford* (Richmond, 1857), a tale of Bacon's rebellion. This story is laid chiefly upon the colonial estate, Windsor Hall, described as "a little independent barony," limited only by blue horizon walls, a principality in which the feudal lord, his family, his indented servants, and his slaves led a life of splendor fashioned on the plan of a patriarchal epoch. George W. Bagby [33] deserves mention for his plantation writings. He was not widely known outside Virginia, however, and he was, certainly in ante-bellum time, far more of a realist than the majority of the makers of the tradition. In the line of the tradition Edward A. Pollard brought out in 1859 his *Black Diamonds* (New York) a kind of imaginative rebuttal to H. R. Helper's slashing attacks on slavery. Variations of the theme occur in such a work as H. W. Herbert's *The Quorndon Hounds* (Phila., 1852), in which the author of sporting manuals writes a novel demonstrat-

[32] Similarly sympathetic was a little non-fiction essay, *Life in Virginia, Knickerbocker's*, Sept., 1858.

[33] See, e.g., *Blue Eyes and Battlewick, Southern Literary Messenger*, beginning January, 1860; note the elements of realism in this story.

ing the at-homeness of Virginia gentlemen in high circles of foreign society. Most comprehensive in detail of all plantation records since *Swallow Barn*, obviously the model for the present work, is James W. Hungerford's *The Old Plantation* (New York and London, 1857). This record of life on an eastern Maryland estate lacks the literary art of Kennedy's work but it remains the most complete picture of plantation life, at its best, while that institution was yet in existence.

The miscellany of plantation literature is large, including a few prominent writers, even such divergent figures as Simms and Whitman, and a host of less consequential workers.[34] Simms, in addition to much writing which had only a Southern vogue, treats directly plantation material in *Home Sketches*, a series of descriptive essays which appeared serially in the New York *Literary World*, beginning January, 1852, noteworthy for its account of plantation festivities, especially Christmas. Simms placed the epilogue of his Revolutionary romances, *The Sword and the Distaff* (Phila., 1853) in the disorganized and devastated plantation life of post-revolutionary times; and such material as shows the difficulty of rehabilitation, and episodes demonstrating the fidelity of slaves and the viciousness of low-born whites forecast much literature of the reconstruction period following the Civil War. Whitman's plantation connection is undoubtedly remote; but in his " Song of Myself " or " I Sing the Body Electric " there are echoes of distinctive plantation customs. Among minor writers we may note J. B. Cobb who in his *Mississippi Scenes* (Phila., 1851) brought out a tame imitation of the work of his friend Longstreet, and Charles E. Whitehead

[34] Attention should be called in this connection to the republication of earlier works, notably *Swallow Barn* (New York, 1851) and Mrs. Gilman's *Recollections* (Phila., 1859).

who included in his *Wild Sports in the South* (New York, 1860) a chapter on " The Plantation Home of ' Far Away.' "

The brief stretch of time between the close of the war and the opening of what we call the national period, between the overthrow of the plantation in fact and its re-establishment in sentiment, produced only a few works. The two most worthy novels which touched the South at all were not precisely plantation stories: Baker's *Inside* [35] and DeForrest's *Miss Ravenel's Conversion from Secession to Loyalty* (New York, 1867). Both of these works, moreover, exhibited a kind of severe realism which the nation later refused to tolerate in plantation treatments. Yet these two works, both by writers who were later to add something to the tradition of glorification, showed some qualities at once of the old attitude and of the new. Baker's story, an attempt to analyze Southern character during the war period, placed large emphasis on the really fine gentlemen of the Southern estates. DeForrest's [36] novel was even more valuable for its appraisals of character; Colonel Carter, embodying much of the lovely and the unlovely of traditional plantation gentlemen, appealed to Mr. Howells as " a most symmetrically molded figure," Miss Ravenel is a conventional Southern beauty, and certain negroes, particularly those whom Dr. Ravenel sought to make industrious, are genuinely of the popular stripe. Within a few months after Appomattox there appeared W. H. Peck's *The McDonalds; or, Ashes of Southern Homes* (New York, 1867); and the ashes were hot. This work represents a defiant glorification of plantation life and correspondingly darkens the fame of Gen-

[35] Serial in *Harper's Weekly,* 1866; book form, New York, 1867; both appearances under pseudonym G. F. Harrington.
[36] *Mr. DeForrest's Novels, Atlantic,* Nov., 1873.

eral Sherman's companions on his trip through Georgia. Mary Louise Cooke brought out in *Ante Bellum* (Phila., 1868) what is in many respects purely a domestic romance with, however, a suggestive quality of that dreamy retrospect which became popular a few years later. John S. Page's *Abraham Holt, Esq.* (Phila., 1868) is a specimen of the apologetic novel; it is dignified and far more finished artistically than either of the two just cited; but it never made great appeal to the reading public. Suggesting an entirely different theme which is far removed from the plantation yet echoes plantation attitudes and reflects plantation sins is Anna Dickinson's *What Answer?* (Boston, 1868).

For the piece of literature which in these years most accurately foreshadows the dominant taste of the subsequent period, we turn again to DeForrest. In a little story, *A Gentleman of the Old School* (*Atlantic*, May, 1868), he suggests the attitude and brings forth many of the elements which were later to be almost stock conventions. In the figure of the immaculate South Carolina gentleman, proud, obstinate, cultured, violent, generous; in his resolute consideration for the slaves, who happen to be also his children; in their hundred-fold return of his kindness, — in these matters we recognize prominent features of the literary method of the next period.

CHAPTER IV

THE DEVELOPMENT OF THE TRADITION IN LITERATURE

III. *The Haze of Retrospect* (1870–   )

THE conviction has been expressed in the last two chapters that the literary tradition of the plantation began, in effect, with Kennedy; that it was a broad tradition including many elements and enriched from time to time with new ones; that writers worked busily upon one or more of these elements and expanded or fixed more firmly in public consciousness the aspects of their special concern. It would be a mistake to suppose, and the purpose of the preceding survey has not been to pretend, that there was any great body of writers who treated plantation material solely for its own value; Kennedy did, and Hungerford, and, to a certain extent, Cooke; but most of the authors were seeking some other literary objective and took account of plantation life incidentally.

We come with 1870 to a new age. There is not a new tradition. There is a new appreciation for the old tradition, there are striking enlargements of it. What makes this age new is a two-fold fact: the surprising increase in the number of writers who turn to the plantation or some characteristic representation exclusively for the value of the material; and the prevalence among these writers of as romantic an attitude as ever characterized the most rapturous of the early sustainers of the tradition.

There are few more interesting episodes in the history

of American literature than the shift to sentimentality in the attitude toward Southern life and its typical institution. Various explanations are suggested: it was but one manifestation of the wide-spread hunt for local color in distinctive phases of national life; it was a representation in literature of the increasing kindliness of Northern thought in general, caused in part by a perception of the extremes to which Reconstruction leaders had gone. Whatever the cause, the effect stands in almost amazing relief. Abolitionism was swept from the field; it was more than routed, it was tortured, scalped, " mopped up." A popular literary device, repeated again and again, was to hand down the legend of splendor and joy through the mouths of the slaves themselves, " those upon whose labor the system was founded and for whose sake it was destroyed." [1] In spite of proclamations and amendments, the old slave, remembering happier days, wails: " Marse Lincoln gun me freedom. Whar' my Chris'mus? " Tourgee and his kind carried on for a season the custom of the earnest Northerner pointing out the error of Southern ways; but they were belated specimens of a vanishing race, for most of the Northern writers were in the chorus of magnification. Even more indicative of the shift was the reception given Southern writers, treating their own native material; and the cordiality of the audience heartened the performers. By 1880, when Harris introduced to a grateful populace his sable curator of folk-lore, all restraints were declared off and the romancers of plantation life were allowed any measure of romantic abandon.

The plantation underwent, then, in the ebullient writings of authors who never knew it or of those who remembered it in a passion of loyalty, a sea-change " into something rich and strange." The horrible visions of abolition

[1] Review of Page's *In Old Virginia* in *Nation*, Sept. 22, 1887.

frenzy were largely forgotten. Slavery was softened until
whatever may have been evil was regarded as accidental.
Even writings of serious nature aided in the amplification
of the estates that were no more; Charles Dudley Warner,
dazzled by the sheen of life in the Carolina rice districts,
exclaims "nowhere in this leveling age . . . so much
splendor." But it was the imaginative fancy that most
thoroughly utilized this resource as the stuff of which
dreams are made. The scale of life was steadily enlarged, the colors were made increasingly vivid. Estates
swelled in size and mansions grew proportionately great.
Gentlemen were perfected in courtly grace, gay girls in
loveliness, slaves in immeasurable devotion. Parties were
more and more elaborate, hunts more frequent and spectacular. Christmas holidays grew apace. Swords flashed
more brilliantly the gleaming arbitraments of honor.
Down in cozy quarters as twilight fell, melodious and
tender voices lulled into drowsiness little heads that lis-
tened to wonderful yarns or to the increasing volume of
mammy's lullaby.

It must not be overlooked that the shift moved slowly
at first. A contemporary reviewer [2] of DeForrest's *Kate
Beaumont* admitting the power revealed by the story won-
dered whether the old life should ever, even on the pages
of fiction, be resurrected. DeForrest himself was a realist
and mingled some satire with his rather unusual character-
izations. Miss Woolson, according to Page,[3] failed to
"find the treasure of the inner life which lies deeper than
her somewhat scornful gaze penetrated." Cable was not
romantic in his stories of the seventies; indeed, he never
was. A good illustration of the relatively cautious manner of the first writers of the new age may be had by

---

[2] *Harper's Magazine*, May, 1872.

[3] *Literature in the South since the War, Lippincott's*, Dec., 1891.

comparing two works of G. C. Eggleston, *A Man of Honor*
(New York, 1873) and *Dorothy South* (Boston, 1902).
Both are stories of tide-water Virginia, both concern the
return of a native aristocrat, both introduce characters
and conventions peculiar to plantation society. Here the
resemblances end; and the differences are more striking
because of the fundamental similarity. The earlier work,
as if not quite sure of its reception, touches lightly characteristic things, attempts, as it were, an impartial point
of view. The later work, with utter confidence, throws
glamour riotously. " Never," is the unabashed declaration,
" anywhere in America a country life like that of Virginia
before the war."

There are in connection with this new and rather impressive literature many features which tempt to lingering
analysis. One might consider the reality of local color,
varying all the way from a mere varnish to the serious
painting of writers who knew by instinct the section depicted. One could make interesting classification of the
varieties of treatment: fictional narratives of the old
regime; reconstruction literature including much of the
old-time material; literature of travel, of reminiscence;
humorous treatment of the negro; the folk-lore stories;
studies of typical Southern characters, as Bret Harte's
Colonel Starbottle, in distant environment; the sweep of
negro song. One could catalogue certain stock elements by
which the plantation effect is sought, the devoted slave,
the beautiful heroine whose love clashes with her sectional
loyalty, the motive of mixed blood, the symbols including
flask, horse, duel, and, for the " coon " melon, 'possum,
'tater, banjo. But in the present consideration chief consideration must be given merely to the general current
of treatment which, in some way or another, entered into
the aggregate glorification of the plantation as a whole.

A. *The Preliminary Seventies*

The romantic interpretation did not make complete conquest of literature before the eighties. There was, however, during the preceding decade, no small body of treatment, appearing principally in the work of a few authors who carried in modified form the earlier methods, in miscellaneous and scattered bits of fiction, and in the work of a small group of authors, chiefly new ones, of considerable importance.

A persistence of the domestic sentimentalist is found in the work of Francis C. Tiernan (Christian Reid) whose romances of Southern life, poured out in astonishing abundance during the early seventies, met with large popular favor. Her novels [4] pretending to depict plantation society were accepted by her readers as chronicles of the spirited charm of womanhood and the gallantry of manhood. The portraiture was, of course, simply the exaggerated characterization of unreal romance where life is " forever in chronic nervous tensions of hating or loving — usually hating with a vehemence," and the figures at their best do not differ from well-bred men and women the world over. Page passed a charitable judgment when he said [5] that if she had utilized her knowledge of character as she did her familiarity with Southern scenery, " she might have led the way into the untried domain of Southern literature." To the literature of the period many other women contributed this kind of romance in which reality and often vitality are sacrificed to overwrought emotionalism. Mrs. Dorsey resumed her languid

[4] For example *Valerie Aylmer* (New York, 1870); *Morton House*, serial in *Appleton's*, beginning March 18, 1871, book form New York, same year; *A Daughter of Bohemia*, beginning in *Appleton's* Oct. 25, 1873 (New York, 1874).

[5] *Literature in the South since the War, Lippincott's*, Dec., 1891.

stories [6] of the Mississippi Valley, Mrs. Sallie Chapin
sounded the fiercest note of unreconstructed sentiment in
a vindication [7] of the Carolina plantation, and Elizabeth
W. Bellamy began her literary career with a novel [8] of
Maryland plantation life just after the war. An illustration of the manner in which plantation material was incorporated into fiction of popular appeal is afforded by
many volumes of the " Elsie " series of Martha Finlay.

Something of the abolition tradition persists in the work
of a small group of which A. W. Tourgee is most conspicuous. *Toinette* (New York, 1874), which appeared under
the pen name of Henry Churton, treats in the style of the
earlier reformers a South Carolina plantation. The master's cruelty, as in Hunter's sale of the black nurse's babe
so that she may give attention exclusively to his own, the
horror of family separation, the prevailing unchastity, all
of these are standard elements of anti-slavery portrayals.
Some details suggesting the affluence of life, the occasional
kindness of masters, and resultant happiness of slaves, are
introduced. Tourgee's famous work, *A Fool's Errand*
(New York, 1879), can not be reckoned a plantation novel,
but its purpose was to show the vitality of slavery in the
new regime, not as a " formal state of society " but as " a
moral entity." The suffering produced by racial mixture,
a kind of pall which the plantation throws over its blacks
even after they have escaped to free countries, is the central theme of *Hot Plowshares* (New York, 1883). Though
the best known, Tourgee is only one of a class [9] of writers
who reflect this attitude.

[6] For example, *Athalie; or, A Southern Villeggeturia* (Phila.,
1872).

[7] *Fitz-Hugh St. Clair* (Phila., 1872).

[8] *The Little Joanna,* serial in Appleton's, 1875; book form New
York, 1875.

[9] See, for example, the anonymous *Other Fools and Their Doings*

Some writers who had already produced plantation literature took up the material anew in this decade. Baker followed up *Inside* with a woefully tame ecclesiastical story, *The New Timothy* (New York, 1870), in which, however, the patriarchal estate of General Likens is used as background, and then brought out *Mose Evans*[10] which presented in some fulness the old regime in and around Charleston. His best plantation novel is probably *Colonel Dunwoddie, Millionaire* (New York, 1878) which contains many echoes of the ante-bellum civilization, particularly in the person of the old Colonel himself, and in the character of Anderson Parker, a former slave. More significant than Baker in the development of the tradition is DeForrest, best represented in this connection by *Kate Beaumont*,[11] a story of a feud between two prominent South Carolina families, which was culminated by the wedding of the lovers. DeForrest is not wholly sympathetic with a society of " hard drinking and easy shooting," as he shows it, but his work includes tribute to the spectacular qualities fixed in the tradition, the courage, the frankness, the ease of deportment, the affluence, the kindness to dependents, all traits of the men of his story. His study of plantation women is more penetrating and less conventional.

The Northern writer who manifests surest grip upon a mood of plantation life, the bewildering numbness of that

---

(New York, 1880), bitterly anti-Southern, and *John and Mary* (Lancaster, Pa., 1873) by Ellwood Griest.

[10] Serial in *Atlantic*, beginning Jan., 1874; book form, New York, same year.

[11] Serial in *Atlantic*, 1872; book form, Boston, same year; this novel is the subject of a chapter in Howell's *Heroines of Fiction*. DeForrest's later novel, *The Bloody Chasm* (New York, 1880) also contains studies of Southern character.

civilization after the full import of the change was realized, is Miss Woolson. Her imagination was struck by
the contrast between what was and what had been. Southern character and atmosphere are in several of her novels,[12]
but her significant work in this connection is a group of
short stories collected under the title of the leading narrative, *Rodman the Keeper*.[13] Miss Woolson does not de-
fine the plantation as the romantic symbol of the next
literary generation but she depicts the courage of that
society with real sympathy. Even a modern reader recognizes in her stories artistic conscience, a true sense for
the important detail, and a particularly intelligent treatment of Southern womanhood.[14] Negro character receives,
at her hands, consideration both in its best and its worst
aspects.[15]

Other Northern writers [16] found plantation material attractive but the largest volume of work is by native
authors. Some major writers of the South began in this
decade to treat in subordinate fashion the general theme.
Lanier, for instance, not only brought out dialect verse [17]

[12] For example, *East Angels* and *Jupiter Lights,* serials in
Harper's in 1885 and 1889, respectively.

[13] The volume appeared in 1880 (New York). The title story
was first published in the *Atlantic,* March, 1877.

[14] Particularly in *Rodman the Keeper* and *In the Cotton Country,* the latter appearing in *Appleton's,* April 29, 1876.

[15] Compare Pompey in *Rodman the Keeper* with types introduced in *King David, Scribner's Monthly,* April, 1878.

[16] For example, F. H. Underwood of Boston brought out a
fairly popular novel of Kentucky in 1874; see review in *Atlantic,*
Sept., 1874. The lights and shadows of slavery, the caste system
of slave society, and specially the Kentucky gentleman, are all
fully presented.

[17] See *The Power of Prayer* and *Uncle Jim's Baptist Revival
Hymn,* originally published in *Scribner's Monthly* for June, 1875,
and May, 1876, respectively.

but produced at least one plantation poem, *Corn*,[18] in which he pictures the Southern estate, mutilated by the one-drop system of agriculture, baring to the sun " a piteous aged crest " like " a gashed and hoary Lear." The theory has been advanced [19] that Lanier owed something of his melody to the influence of negro song.

The plantation as a definite locale is largely missing from the work of George W. Cable; yet the social manifestations of the life that characterized the institution, particularly in its caste structure and its race relations, are all through his early works. In *Posson Jone*[20] and *Jean-Ah-Poquelin*[21] the theme of slave loyalty is prominent. In such stories as *Tite Poulette*[22] and *Madame Delphine*,[23] Cable utilizes with power the agony of race consciousness as it operates in the hearts of those who are almost white yet condemned because of the small percentage of African blood. *The Grandissimes*,[24] hailed on its appearance as " one of the great novels of our times," is notable chiefly for the mingling of races and race interests; but throughout this mingled society there is the dominance of customs and attitudes associated with, usually produced by, plantation life. It is safe to assume that Cable strengthened the tradition by the diversity of themes which interplay in this novel. Emphasis is laid on the feudalistic nature of society, on an almost universal im-

[18] Appeared first in *Lippincott's*. Feb., 1875.

[19] Moses, *Literature of the South*, 371.

[20] *Appleton's*, April, 1876.

[21] *Scribner's Monthly*, May, 1875.

[22] *Scribner's Monthly*, October, 1874. These three stories were included in *Old Creole Days* (New York, 1870).

[23] *Scribner's Monthly*, May, 1881.

[24] Appeared first as a serial in *Scribner's Monthly*, beginning Nov., 1879. The criticism referred to appeared in *Harper's*, 77:801; the same attitude characterized most of the contemporary notices.

purity, on much brutality, on superstition, casting its shadow over white as well as black, on the musical temperament of the slaves.

The current of plantation literature was swelled during the decade by an increasing company of writers, North and South, who did not greatly aid in popularizing the tradition. A claim for priority, together with a tragic life history, has set Irwin Russell somewhat above the other local colorists of the period. He is regarded by some as the first not only in successful negro dialect but in " utilizing for literary purpose the social and institutional conditions in which he had lived." [25] Page, writing in 1891, called *Christmas Night in the Quarters* " the best delineation of negro life yet written." Sherwood Bonner, another Mississippian whose life was pathetically short, was esteemed by Longfellow, and has been given attention by later investigators.[26] Her short stories reveal occasional

[25] C. A. Smith, *Historical Element in Recent Southern Literature, Pubs. Miss. Hist. Soc.*, II, 9–10. For other estimates of Russell, see Page's article in *Lippincott's*, Dec., 1891; Mims, *South in the Building of Nation*, vol. VII, 39; Baskerville in *Southern Writers* I, 21; Pattee in *Century Readings in American Literature;* Joel Chandler Harris' opinion as recorded in the life by Julia Harris, page 163; remember, too, Page's dedication of *Befo' de War*. All of these writers agree that Russell was, in a way, the pioneer. Somewhat similar claims have been advanced for others, including Porte Crayon and Miss Bonner; the question cannot be accurately settled, or at least not before some careful defining has been done. But Russell's poems, most of which appeared in *Scribner's Monthly*, beginning Jan., 1876, are of real significance historically.

[26] See lengthy article in vol. II of *Southern Writers*. Miss Bonner (Mrs. Meadowell) is the author of two volumes of stories, *Dialect Tales* (New York, 1878) and *Suwanee River Tales* (Boston, 1884). Her novel is *Like unto Like* (New York, 1878). Some of her most important stories were never collected; for example, *From '60 to '65* (*Lippincott's*, Oct., 1886), a bit of reminiscence,

flashes of insight into types and customs and her one
novel differs from the sentimental romance in at least more
accurate characterization. George C. Eggleston wrote not
only fiction but many sympathetic studies of the types of
the old regime and one of the very finest of all non-fiction
reminiscences.[27]   A. C. Gordon [28] began in this decade a
career that has continued down to the present time, an
honored career in plantation writing; Stockton [29] turned
to his interesting studies of plantation material; and
writers as far apart as Thomas Dunn English [30] and Emma
Lazarus [31] attempted some kind of plantation writing.
Varying widely in sympathy of attitude and in manner
of approach, a large number [32] of less important story

---

and *A Volcanic Interlude* (*Ibid.*, April, 1880) a sharp study of the
consequences of plantation immorality.

[27] This essay is *The Old Regime in the Old Dominion*, *Atlantic*,
Nov., 1875; for one of his type portrayals, see *My Friend Phil*,
Galaxy, Dec., 1875.

[28] *Kree*, a little dialect poem, appeared in *Scribner's Monthly*,
Oct., 1876.

[29] Most of Stockton's work came later but *That Same Old
Coon* was published in *Scribner's Monthly*, Jan., 1878.

[30] See, *e.g.*, poems in *Scribner's Monthly*, July and Nov., 1871.

[31] See poem in *Lippincott's*, Jan., 1878.

[32] A complete list would be tedious reading, even if it were
worth the effort. Among the more prominent stories were W. J.
Flagg's novel, *A Good Investment* (serial in *Harper's*, beginning
Dec., 1871, book form, New York, 1872); the anonymous *Military
Ball at Goulacaska* (*Atlantic*, March, 1870); Annie Porter's *Told
by an Octoroon* (*Galaxy*, Dec., 1870) and *Ninon* (*Scribner's
Monthly*, Jan., 1878); Alice Dutton's *The Castlewood Tragedy*
(*Atlantic*, Feb., 1872); such slave autobiographies as *Aunt Eva
Interviewed* (*Harper's*, March, 1873) and *Story of a Contraband*
(*Atlantic*, June, 1875); Jennie Woodville's series of half a dozen
stories in *Lippincott's*, beginning April, 1875; Mary Wyeth's *Moses
an' Aaron* (*Scribner's Monthly*, Aug., 1877); W. L. Murfree's (father
of Miss Murfree) *How Uncle Gabe Saved the Levee* (*Scribner's*

tellers brought out scraps of fiction which fitted into the general pattern.

The awakening of larger interest in plantation life is attested by the vogue of travel or descriptive writing. In this class the work of Edward King, whose *The Great South* began to appear in *Scribner's Monthly* in 1873, is of foremost significance. Though most of such treatment was at the hands of Northern visitors, no inconsiderable portion was the work of Southerners. Cooke,[33] Porte Crayon,[34] E. A. Pollard,[35] John R. Thompson,[36] even Paul H. Hayne,[37] furnished to Northern journals sketches of life at the South including many reflections of the old regime. More important as evidence of the hunger of Northern readers for accounts of plantation conditions is the journalistic work of many Northern reporters [38] who came South for the specific purpose of recording their impressions.

Monthly, October, 1878). Specially notable in this decade is the gathering momentum of negro humor; see, for example, humorous columns of newspapers and magazines.

[33] Several articles, the best being one drawn from memories of his youth, *Mistletoe Hall* (Appleton's, Sept. 13, 1873).

[34] *A Visit to the Shrines of Old Virginia* (*Lippincott's*, April 23, 1879).

[35] *The Romance of the Negro* (*Galaxy,* Oct., 1871).

[36] *Southern Sketches* (*Appleton's,* July and August, 1870).

[37] *A L'Outrance,* society of the Ashley River district (*ibid.,* Feb. 8, 1873).

[38] Conspicuous among many writings are articles by Geo. W. Nichols, S. G. W. Benjamin, and Chas. R. Dashler in *Harper's;* by H. C. Woods, A. Webster, Jr., and Marie Williams in *Appleton's;* the long series by R. B. Elder which appeared in *Lippincott's* in 1872-73; and the book by Charles Nordhoff, *The Cotton States in 1875* (New York, 1875).

B. *The Great Outburst*

The dawning light had brightened throughout a decade but the perfect day of plantation literature was ushered in by Uncle Remus. Harris, it seems, stumbled unconsciously upon a delightful field of folk-lore and, incidentally, recorded with unusual accuracy of feeling a unique dialect; but what charmed the public was not a new expression of fables, not a new treasury of linguistic values, but the winsome figure of the old darkey and the associations of his personality. Uncle Remus did more than tell stories; he reflected a regime; and in so doing, he opened a door widely, completely, to a spacious chamber of literary values, the wealth of which was made available for those who had the capacity to use it. Encouraged by his first success, Harris spread more Uncle Remus over the pages of many magazines and of a dozen volumes, meantime reproducing the old epoch in other forms of stories. Four years after Uncle Remus came the first of Page's stories, *Marse Chan;* and in the next three or four years the Virginian brought out some of the most significant plantation fiction. In 1886 Harry Stilwell Edwards published his *The Two Runaways,* sufficient in itself to establish a reputation but merely the beginning of a long list of writings. Other Georgia contemporaries of Harris, like Richard Malcolm Johnston, were already in the field. By the nineties, Allen, F. Hopkinson Smith, and many others had brought out more plantation writings. Northern authors began to use the material directly, as did Stockton, Miss Jewett, Miss Wilkins, or to play upon its fringes, as Mark Twain, Bret Harte, and a great company of others. Humorists drew increasingly upon the plantation; authors, especially Cable and Page, gave readings from their own works; lecturers amused audiences with anecdotes of the old regime; cartoonists, minstrel managers, touring companies of jubilee singers, all assisted in making vivid the general conception. The vogue persisted into the twentieth century; as late as October, 1901, a single number of a magazine [39] carried Page's *Bred in the Bone,* Harris' *Rosalie,* and Mrs. Virginia F. Boyle's *The Triumph of Shad.*

Among masters of plantation literature, Harris must be given high rank. When Page called the work of the Georgian "the most valuable contribution to Southern literature that has yet appeared " he passed a judgment which so far as the plantation is concerned seems true for all time.[40] The popularity of the cycle of story tellers, Uncle Remus, Daddy Jake, Aunt Minerva Ann, and the others, has sometimes obscured a fact that is, in the present connection, of supreme importance. This fact, which cannot be stated too emphatically, is that in Harris the whole plantation appears, not with the glamour of Page but with a completeness of understanding not equaled by any other writer. Harris knew the plantation from one end to the other, and in his several stories has reconstructed for us, bit by bit, the entire institution. With a sweeping inclusiveness running from the very structure of society, from the great problematic aspects, down to the single lovable personality, Harris' work is the literary history of the plantation.[41]

[39] *The Century.*

[40] James W. Johnson, in the preface to *The Book of American Negro Poetry* (New York, 1922) lists Uncle Remus as one of the four original artistic creations of this country.

[41] Harris is generally thought of as Uncle Remus; let it be repeated that he did not merely play in one of the eddies of plantation literature, however charming, but was all over the stream. The dominance of caste is in *Mingo* (*Harper's,* Dec., 1882, book form, same title, Boston, 1884), in *The Baby's Christmas*

So far as the truly popular conception is concerned, however, Harris is most significant for the revelation of the plantation darkey. Every trait of African temperament receives at the hand of Harris the treatment at once most interesting and convincing: the strange musical sensitiveness and genius; the resilient humor of his disposition, reflected in conversation and in conduct; [42] the homely wisdom, expressing in unforgetable metaphor some aphorism or drawing some parable-like moral from the animal fables; the contempt of the well fed slave for the free negro; the simple dependence of the serf upon, and his unswerving devotion to, his master. Harris was far from blind to the darker aspects of plantation life, such as the suffering of fugitives and the tragedies resulting from

---

(*Century*, Dec., 1893, book form, *Tales of the Home Folks*, Boston, 1898). The size of plantation and the magnificence of the mansion are suggested in *The Old Basom Place* (*Century*, Aug., 1889, book form, *Balaam and His Master*, Boston, 1891); the hunger of the planter for more land is in *A Piece of Land* (book form, *Mingo and Other Sketches*). Southern manhood may be studied in *The Old Bascom Place* or in *A Run of Luck* (book form, *Tales of the Home Folks*) and the loveliness of womanhood is in most of the stories; see, *e.g.*, *Aunt Fountain's Prisoner* (*Scribner's*, March, 1887, book form, *Free Joe*, New York, 1887). Hospitality is one of the charms in *Little Compton* (*Century*, April, 1887, book form, *Free Joe*) and the Christmas holidays fairly jingle in *How Whalebone Caused a Wedding* (*Scribner's*, Nov., 1894, book form, *Tales of the Home Folks*). The cruel overseer, rich and vicious in postbellum times, is found in *The Bishop and the Boogerman* (New York, 1909) and the loyal negro foreman is met with in Uncle Shadrach of *The Colonel's Nigger Dog* (*Tales of the Home Folks*); economic self-help of slaves, mooted point of historians, is real at least in *Aunt Fountain's Prisoner*.

[42] See, for example, Uncle Remus' account in *Preaching that is Preaching* (*Uncle Remus and His Friends*, Boston, 1892) of the negro preacher's gestures which, we are reminded, were but rehearsal for the more serious gymnastics of chicken-lifting.

mixed blood.[43] The most casual or most partisan reader
cannot escape the great question raised by *Free Joe*,[44] the
question as to how real was the assumed happiness of
slave life.   In the main, however, the contribution of
Harris to the tradition is a comprehensive and charming
presentation of the romantic elements.

Thomas Nelson Page has brought to the tradition a
body of writing which, like that of Harris, is considerable
in quantity and marked by high artistic ability.   The
Virginian is, however, far more passionate in the main-
tenance of a hypothesis of departed glory, paints in more
glowing colors, is uniformly more idealistic, descends less
frequently — if ever — from the heights of romantic vision;
in short, he expresses the supreme glorification of the old
regime, he " wrote the epitaph of a civilization."   He
accomplishes this end with such felicity of manner that
though the forensic purpose is but thinly veiled the reading public has yielded itself easily to the illusion.   Such
work as this of Page,[45] rather than the labored effort of

[43] For some hint of the emotions of fugitives, see *Blue Dave*
or the pursuit of Mink in *On the Plantation* (New York, 1892).
The problem of mixed blood is in *The Case of Mary Ellen* in
The Chronicles of Aunt Minerva Ann (New York, 1899) and in a
fierce, almost enigmatic story, *Wher's Duncan?* in *Balaam and His
Master* (Boston, 1891).

[44] Mr. Roosevelt considered *Free Joe* one of the two greatest
American short stories; see Julia Harris's life of Joel Chandler
Harris, 509.

[45] His first appearance was a little poem *Uncle Gabe's White
Folks* in *Scribner's Monthly*, April, 1877.   This piece, as Roswell
Page says in his memoir of his brother, is an epitome of all his
subsequent writing.   Wider recognition came with the publication
of *Marse Chan* in *The Century* for April, 1884.   His most notable
year was 1886 when there appeared *Unc' Edinburg's Drowndin'*
(*Harper's*, Jan.), *Meh Lady* (*Century*, June), *Ole 'Stracted*
(*Harper's*, Oct.), and *Polly* (*Harper's*, Dec.).   These stories were
collected under the title *In Old Virginia* (New York, 1887).   From

scholars or the lurid melodrama of later literature, is the
final reply to the onslaughts of abolitionists, the final and
the sufficient reply.

Less comprehensive than Harris, Page achieves a glamour, a mellow light the like of which no other author can
command; he is, therefore, of the largest significance in
the tradition. One story alone, *Unc' Edinburg's Drowndin'*, crowds into its few pages virtually all the significant
elements of the social rapture which marked the old epoch;
all of life's splendor, its joy, and, at the same time, the
unique cordiality that marked race relations. Page produced not such distinct figures as did Harris but he emphasized types even more powerfully, and his portrayals
remain as the standard of plantation literature, particularly for the aristocratic old gentlemen and the lovely
heroines, most delicate of the creatures springing out of
the regions of plantation enchantment. Perhaps his greatest contribution to the tradition is his portrayal of the
benignity and the steadfast kindliness of race relations.
The motive is, of course, an old one in literary procedure;
but Page adapted it most happily to the plantation setting
and demonstrated in appealing fashion the integration of
the " chattel " into the very family circle itself. He reveals the intimacy between mammy and her charges; but
he goes beyond this and shows an almost brotherly love,
strengthening through the years, between young master
and young servant. Thus he softens the inevitable hard-
ship of slavery by linking in uncommon fraternity master
and man, and thus he gives to the serf a not incongruous
dignity and a sense of importance in being a member of
that social institution which was the plantation family.

----

that time till his death, Page continued to produce plantation
literature, including novels and several prose essays, a few of which
are collected in *The Old South* (New York, 1892).

Harris and Page are the principal names but by no means the only ones of importance. Georgia contributed several authors, a state that had been conspicuously lacking in ante-bellum writers. Richard Malcolm Johnston wrote his *Dukesborough Tales* in the tradition of Longstreet, with no plantation significance. He never idealized the great planter or the picturesque darkey — Page chides him for failure to write of the beautiful old South — but he did draw some pictures of conditions and characters which, on a lowered scale, harmonize with the general pattern. Maurice Thompson, like Johnston, made no effort to present the gorgeous plantation image, but he, too, treated many characteristic features.[46] He brought out early in the decade three novels more or less directly connected with plantation life and came closer to the accepted type in several short stories, one of which, *Ben and Judas,* is a member of a trinity of stories dealing with fraternity between owner and slave, the other two being Allen's *Two Gentlemen of Kentucky* and Edwards' *The Two Runaways.* Closer to the tradition than the two other Georgia writers just mentioned, Harry Stilwell Edwards followed the rather curious custom of producing at

[46] In Johnston's work, the clash of caste is suggested by *Ogeechee Cross-Firing* (*Harper's,* May, 1889); the worthless overseer is in *Mr. Neelus Peeler's Condition* (*Scribner's Monthly,* June, 1878); a typical Southern colonel may be found in *The Expensive Treat of Colonel Moses Grice* (*ibid.,* Jan., 1881); and the extreme devotion of which slave nature was capable is presented in *Moll and Virgil* (*Harper's,* Sept., 1887) and *Travis and Major Jonathan Wilby* (*Century,* May, 1890). The three novels by Thompson are *A Tallahassee Girl* (Boston, 1882), *His Second Campaign* (Boston, 1883), and *At Love's Extreme* (New York, 1885). Among his short stories which have plantation significance are *The Balance of Power* (*Harper's,* April, 1895) and *Rudgis and Grim* (*Century,* July, 1892). *Ben and Judas* appeared in *The Century,* Oct., 1889).

the outset of his career a few stories which remain unexcelled by any thing in the voluminous work of later years. At least three [47] of these stories deserve a high rank among all plantation literature.

No single book in this period was more influential in forming the conception of certain plantation types than F. Hopkinson Smith's *Colonel Carter of Cartersville*.[48] The fact that the hero of this story was of a type virtually non-existent upon the actual plantation cannot minimize the importance of the work upon the public, particularly the Northern imagination. This was accepted as the portrait of the Virginia cavalier of ante-bellum days: proud of his section and his stock, hospitable to the verge of beggary, careful in dress, accepting the head of the table as a sort of throne for the dispensing of epicurean royalties, a connoisseur of drink, hopelessly unadaptable to modern conditions, regarding the credit system as a personal compliment, challenging and then, convinced of error, insisting upon the right of public apology, courtly in thought of, and bearing toward, women, in every way the beau ideal of a charming and quixotic civilization. Perfection is given the picture by the introduction of Chad, not less a member of "de fambly" than his master, capable manager, dusky philosopher, dedicating himself to that master who regards his sable companion as "a bawn gentleman" who will "never get over it."

James Lane Allen, prose laureate of the blue-grass, and Mark Twain, author of the epic of the Mississippi River, are not plantation writers, yet each in his way reflects

[47] *The Two Runaways* (*Century*, July, 1886), with its delightful pair of vagabonds, one master, one slave; *De Valley and De Shadow* (*Century*, Jan., 1888) with its blending of plantation joy and sorrow; and *Ole Miss and Sweetheart* (*Harper's*, July, 1888), which has been called "as exquisite as anything in Daudet."

[48] Serial in *Century*, 1890; book form, New York, 1891.

elements of the old regime. Allen went so far as to answer Mrs. Stowe and to describe plantation life in several
essays; [49] he hints at, rather than develops, plantation
distinctions in more than one novel; and he has written
two famous stories of race relations. [50] Mark Twain introduced in several connections what at least were accepted as plantation features. [51] *The Gilded Age* (New
York, 1873) concerns chiefly Beriah Sellars who, though
a great planter only in his dreams, is a kind of burlesque on the Virginia planter who emigrated; old Daniel [52]
of this story is typical in many ways of the plantation
darkey. *Tom Sawyer* (New York, 1876) and *Huckleberry
Finn* (New York, 1885) exhibit some of the common plantation material, varying from negro character to duels.
Not far removed from the main current of plantation fiction is *Pudd'nhead Wilson* with many reflections of slave
life, particularly the cruelty of some masters, the flight
of fugitives, the tragedy of tainted blood.

The enlargement and the emphasis given the plantation
in popular fiction cannot be thought of as the work of
a few authors, whatever their significance may be. The
most impressive thing about the vogue of this writing

[49] *Uncle Tom at Home* (*Century*, Oct., 1887); see also *The
Blue-Grass Region of Kentucky* (*Harper's*, Feb., 1886) and *The
Home-Steads of Kentucky* (*Century*, May, 1892).

[50] These stories are *Two Kentucky Gentlemen of the Old
School* (*Century*, April, 1888) and *King Solomon of Kentucky*
(*Century*, June, 1889). Note that in *A Kentucky Cardinal* (New
York, 1894) the heroine is of " the rose-order of Southern women "
and that Mrs. Falconer of *The Choir Invisible* is the Virginia
gentle-woman transplanted.

[51] Gertrude Atherton in *Geographical Fiction* (*Lippincott's*,
July, 1892) calls *Huckleberry Finn* " a wonderful picture of the
Old South."

[52] Compare the prayer of this old darkey with Lanier's poem,
The Power of Prayer.

is the number of authors who fed to the public fancy some variety of plantation material. There was, for example, a group of Northern writers, most of them with reputation already established, who availed themselves of this fresh resource. Stockton, best representative of this class, found in the old regime, notably in negro character, material pleasing to his fancy and in a few short stories and one novel [53] revealed with uncommon insight the spirit as well as something of the spectacle of plantation life. Miss Jewett,[54] Miss Spofford,[55] and Thomas Bailey Aldrich [56] brought out etchings of familiar types. Stephen Crane [57] transplanted the humor and the loyalty of darkey temperament to remote settings; Bret Harte introduced a typical Southern gentleman in a series of stories [58] placed far from plantation settings; numerous [59] other Northern writers gave consideration to plantation material.

[53] See, for example, such stories as *A Story of Seven Devils* (*Century*, Nov., 1885) and *The Cloverfield's Carriage* (*Century*, Jan., 1886). The novel, *The Late Mrs. Null* (New York, 1886) is full of plantation background, particularly in negro traits; the religious orgies at which Aunt Patsy enjoyed the " Jerusalem Jump " have been often cited.

[54] *The Mistress of Sydenham Plantation, Atlantic*, Aug., 1888.

[55] *A Guardian Angel, Harper's*, May, 1897, with a devoted mammy.

[56] *My Cousin the Colonel, Harper's*, Dec., 1891, not complimentary.

[57] See *The Monster, Harper's*, Aug., 1898, and *Whilomville Stories, Harper's*, 1899 and 1900.

[58] The stories of Colonel Starbottle appeared in *Harper's*, 1901.

[59] Octave Thanet developed plantation features as they occurred on the western fringe of the slavery zone; see *Half a Curse, Scribner's*, Jan., 1887, and *Expiation*, a serial in *Scribner's* in 1890; book form, New York, 1890). Robert A. Boit's *Eustace* (Boston, 1884) and R. M. Bache's *Under the Palmetto* (Phila., 1884) are two novels by authors of smaller literary renown glorifying the estates of the Carolina rice district. The well known agricultural editor, H. W. Collingwood, brought forth a novel,

A large body of plantation writing, much of it consistent with the romance of domestic sentiment, is the work of Southern women. Some of these writers developed a power which makes them compare favorably with the best of their masculine contemporaries. Mrs. M. J. Preston, "poet of the Confederacy," turned to retrospective [60] sketches of the old life. Marion Harland continued her remarkable literary activity with novels [61] in which the attitude of glorification is more pronounced. Mrs. Virginia Frazier Boyle in manifold writings represents the charm of the old days. Although her novels are of more than passing interest, her most important work has been in the field of the short story. Her portrayals of the humor, the loyalty, the superstition of negro temperament rank with the best of their kind. It is not unlikely, in fact, that her *Devil Tales* [62] will remain the best exposi-

---

Andersonville Violets (Boston, 1889), as his contribution to the spirit of good will. Much poetry appeared from the pen of Northern writers; for example, James Whitcomb Riley dropped Hoosier dialect long enough to attempt negro in such poems as *Gladness, Century,* July, 1890, and Harrison Grey Fiske wrote a little *Mammy's Lullaby* for the Christmas, 1890, number of his New York *Dramatic Mirror*.

[60] For example, *Aunt Dorothy's Funeral, Harper's,* Oct., 1889.

[61] *Judith* (Phila., 1883) is in essential respects a typical plantation novel. *His Great Self* (Phila., 1892), a fictional treatment of the legendary romance between Evelyn Byrd and Lord Peterborough, treats fully the social life of Westover in the days of its glory.

[62] These tales appeared in *Harper's,* 1899; book form in 1900, New York. *The Taming of Jesrul* has been likened to Rossetti's *Sister Helen* and *The Devil's Little Fly* to an African version of the Faust legend. Other stories of plantation life which deserve mention are *A Kingdom for Micajah* (*Harper's,* March, 1900) and *How Jerry Bought Malindy* (*Century,* Oct., 1890). Of her novels, *Brockenburne* (New York, 1897), an old mammy's narrative, is probably most significant.

tion of the last named quality.   Ruth McEnery Stuart
is at her best in the delineation of the psychology of
the modern negro, but her work is full of the traits recognized as belonging to the plantation tradition.   In the
large school of Virginia writers, Mrs. Burton Harrison has
perhaps been more successful than any of her sister workers, certainly in her presentation of plantation women.
Mrs. Harrison's contribution is large and is, in many ways,
valuable; but in the group of stories of which *Crow's Nest*
may be taken as typical, she almost preempted the field
of feminine psychology.[63]   The Louisiana tradition, which
has been a fairly distinct one, was materially enriched
by the work of Grace King and of Kate Chopin, two
writers of real power.   Neither confines herself to the
plantation but both utilize many of its elements.   A sort
of mob slave action is introduced with telling effect in
Miss King's *Bayou L'Ombre*,[64] while the loyalty of the
slave is the central theme of *Monsieur Motte*.   Mrs.
Chopin is most impressive in her delicate studies of the
tragedy of mixed blood.[65]

The great volume of plantation literature by women is
not distinguished for quality but for quantity, for conformity to the tradition, and frequently for popular ap-

[63] *Crow's Nest,* which appeared in the *Century,* Sept., 1885, is
one of the collection of stories, *Belhaven Tales,* New York, 1892.
Her novel, *Flower de Hundred* (New York, 1890) is one of the
fullest studies of plantation life just before the Civil War.

[64] *Harper's,* July, 1887.   *Monsieur Motte, New Princeton Review,* July, 1885.

[65] The best of Mrs. Chopin's writing is in her *Bayou Folk,*
Boston, 1894.   See particularly *The Beritous' Slave* and *Desiree's
Baby.*   Pattee (*Camb. Hist. Amc. Lit.,* II, 390) praises highly the
latter story.   Many novels of no great consequence treat this same
theme as it obtained in Louisiana life; *e.g.,* the anonymous *Toward
the Gulf* and A. L. Jones' *Beatrice of Bayou Teche,* popular, sensational romances of the eighties.

peal. Most of this work is post-bellum domestic romance;
but sometimes the feeling for real local color sets aside a
particular novel. Miss Mary Tiernan's *Homoselle* [66] Boston, 1881), a story of the Virginia plantation at the time of
Gabriel's insurrection, is relatively rich in detail and is
valuable for its analysis of the negro's attitude. Molly
Elliot Seawell has written much concerning the old regime,
her most successful work being *Children of Destiny* [67] (New
York, 1893), a sort of triangle story in which the rich
rejected suitor wages a duel with the poor husband — own-
ing only 1200 acres — with race horses as weapons.

The list of these women authors is a long one. Miss
M. G. McCleland [68] produced various novels of the old
regime, one, *A Self-Made Man* (New York, 1887), emphasizing the caste feeling of Virginia rural society. Frances
C. Baylor in *Claudia Hyde* (Boston, 1895) drew a picture
of an estate after the war when only the relics of departed splendor remained. Louise C. Pyrnelle adopted
the method of the story-teller, popularized by the narratives of Uncle Remus, for her *Diddie Dumps and Tot* [69]
(New York, 1882). Amelie Rives, center of a slight controversy because of *The Quick or the Dead,* [70] which, it

[66] Miss Tiernan also wrote *Suzette* (New York, 1885), laid in
Richmond.

[67] Besides short stories, as *Unc' Ananias, Lippincott's,* July,
1892, Miss Seawell has brought out other novels of the Virginia
plantations, as *The Berkeleys and Their Neighbors* and *Hale-
Weston,* New York, 1888 and 1889, respectively.

[68] Her *Princess* (New York, 1886), was a popular novel of the
old epoch.

[69] Page in his article in *Lippincott's,* Dec., 1891, on *Literature
in the South since the War* ranks this work high for "tenderness
and humor."

[70] This novel appeared in *Lippincott's,* April, 1888, book form,
Phila., same year. *Virginia of Virginia* appeared first in *Harper's,*
Jan., 1888.

may be noted in passing, had a plantation setting, had previously brought out in *Virginia of Virginia* a closer study of plantation life. Even in the juvenile [71] literature of the period, plantation themes are freely employed. Somewhat in the manner of Mrs. Susan Dabney Smedes' *A Southern Planter* (Balto., 1887) came many other volumes [72] of reminiscence by women of the old plantation society.

Since we are considering here the development of a popular rather than an artistic tradition, we must glance for a moment at another type of plantation writing, that which we may call the people's own library of plantation romances. This literature was distinctly of the masses and not of the literati; it was essentially plebeian; and it was cherished by readers. None of this class made any pretension to art; most of it gathered copiously and recklessly the conventional plantation elements and served them scrambled, while they were hot. But it was an influential kind of writing if for no other reason than its popularity. Thus while, as M. D. Conway records ruefully, such conscientious studies as his own *Palm and Pine* (New York, 1887) and Virginius Dabney's *Don Miff* (Phila., 1886) were not very successful, two lurid melodramas, as fervidly sensational as anything in our history, Elizabeth Meriwether's *The Master of Red Leaf* (New York, 1880) and *Black and White* (New York, 1883) sold in a fashion

[71] See, *e.g.*, Mrs. Jamison's *Toinette's Phillip* (New York, 1894), a work which developed the theme of slave loyalty.

[72] For example, Mrs. Mary Ross Banks' *Bright Days in the Old Plantation* (Boston, 1882), a glorification of everything including even the overseer who does not often receive such treatment. Another specimen is Mrs. M. J. Bacon's anti-Uncle-Tom story, *Lyddy* (New York, 1898). Elizabeth Johnson's illustrated *Christmas in Kentucky* (Washington, 1892) ran quickly through several reasonably large editions.

that is not less than astonishing. Similar in tone are such
novels of Kentucky life as Opie Read's *A Kentucky
Colonel* (Chicago, 1890) and Tom Johnson's *A Blue-Grass
Thoroughbred* (Chicago, 1889). The anonymous story of
the Mississippi plantations, *A Prince of Good Fellows*
(New York, 1891) and Charlotte M. Clark's [73] *The
Modern Hagar* (New York, 1882) represent the lowest
expressions of the theme, while higher in literary value
but none the less melodramas are E. P. Roe's *Miss Lou* [74]
and John Haberton's *Brueton's Bayou* (New York, 1886).
Martha Holley's *Samantha on the Race Question* [75] (New
York, 1892) is typical of the pretended humorous novel
of plantation life.[76]

Justice cannot be done in this hurried survey to many
really consequential divisions of plantation writings. The
influence of the short story has been great, not only in
the work of such leading authors as have been mentioned
but also in a host of minor writers. It is doubtful, to
cite one example, whether the interest of the plantation
in the horse has been more effectively utilized than in the
brief narratives of J. J. Eakins [77] and Harrison Robert-
son.[78] More than passing attention should be paid to the
work of a few negro writers, notably Paul Laurence Dunbar and Charles W. Chesnutt,[79] who have contributed

[73] Wrote under the name of Charles M. Clay.

[74] This novel, the last one written by Roe, appeared first as
a serial in the *Cosmopolitan,* beginning March, 1888.

[75] Really a sort of late abolition story.

[76] The best work of this group is Jeannette Walworth's *On the
Winning Side* (New York, 1893), in many respects a strong work,
though still a lurid melodrama.

[77] See *Century,* November, 1891.

[78] See *Scribner's,* July, 1889.

[79] Dunbar has introduced virtually every element of the plantation tradition into his poems, of which a dozen volumes appeared,
and his stories. Chestnutt handled his plantation material with

some rather artistic evaluation of plantation material. The vogue of travel and descriptive literature, and particularly the volumes of reminiscence,[80] should be noted. Essays have appeared in increasing numbers, Dr. Gildersleeve's *The Creed of the Old South* [81] and Walter H. Page's *A Study of an Old Southern Borough* [82] ranking among the best. An interesting survey might be made of the appearance of plantation elements as found in literature not at all in the direct current of the tradition. Hearn's *Youma* [83] is laid in *Martinique* but the theme is that of a slave who preferred her white charge above her lover; Bunner's *Story of a New York House* [84] is entirely metropolitan but the devoted darkey butler and the hospitable Southerner who appears at the close of the story are plantation types; Fox's *The Kentuckians* [85] is post-bellum and political in major interest but the aristocratic characters are lineal descendants of plantation society; Charles B. Lewis' humorous volume, *Brother Gardner's Lime-Kiln Club* (Chicago, 1882) is remote from the South but its exposition of negro psychology is in terms of dialogue and symbols familiar to the plantation tradition. The fact is apparent in any literary study of our writings as a whole that during this period the plantation was cen-

---

considerable self-discipline; see the stories in *The Atlantic: The Goophered Grapevine* (Aug., 1887), *Dave's Necklace* (Oct., 1889), and *The Wife of His Youth* (July, 1898). The first two stories are in *The Conjure Woman* (Boston, 1899); the last-named story gives the title to the volume of 1900 (Boston).

[80] See Bibliographical Notes.

[81] *Atlantic,* July, 1887.

[82] *Atlantic,* January, 1892.

[83] Serial in *Harper's,* beginning Jan., 1890, book form, New York, 1890.

[84] Serial in *Scribner's* and book form in New York, 1887.

[85] Serial in *Harper's,* 1897, book form, New York, 1898.

tral in a large body of work and that it lent many values to much literature not ostensibly concerned with its life.

C. *Abiding Elements in the Present Century*

As the century came in, the plantation tradition was at the height of a prosperity which continued well into the first decade. Even after this most romantic of the local color modes had given way before the severe realism of our own day, there was no dearth of writers who, maintaining the old methods, continued to court a shifting public favor. But neither the initial momentum in this century nor the gradual slowing down of the tradition is quite so significant as that fact that after the plantation had ceased to be a kind of literary passion, various derivations of the tradition persisted as permanently fixed in literary craft. Though the unit broke up, it seems, some of the fragments were salvaged and used over and over again.

The conventional treatment of the plantation continued without material modification. Harris and Page, their best work done, persisted in more of the same thing. Cable, never directly in the tradition, approached it as closely in his later novels [86] as at any point in his career. A. C. Gordon persevered well through the second decade with a series of short stories,[87] perhaps the best plantation memories recorded in this period. George C. Eggleston brought out several novels; Edna Turpin [88] and Eleanor

---

[86] For example, *The Flower of the Chapdelaines* (New York, 1918).

[87] Among the best are his stories of the Kingsmill plantation, notably *The Shunway* (*Scribner's,* March, 1915), *The Cockatrice Den* (*Scribner's,* Dec., 1916), and *Sinjinn Survivin'* (*Harper's,* Jan., 1918). *Maje,* a serial in *Scribner's,* 1914, ranks high.

[88] See *Abram's Freedom, Atlantic,* Sept., 1912.

Gibbs,[89] among others, contributed short stories of a rather high degree of excellence; John Charles McNiel, before death cut short his promising life, caught up the mantle of John Henry Boner — North Carolina has had few writers of plantation literature; John Trotwood Moore [90] celebrated the old Middle Tennessee society of fast horses; Frank L. Stanton furnished almost daily to the Atlanta *Constitution* poems of humor or of gentle sentiment, many of which were copied by columnists all over the country; A. E. Gonzales brought out in 1922 an interesting series of tales in Gullah dialect.[91]

The vogue of the purely historical novel gave a slight re-direction to the tradition in the fashion of including larger epochs of time, wider sweeps of the old life, than had appeared in the typical local stories of the preceding generation. The list of writers who utilized the historical materials of the South is a considerable one. Foremost in the group is Mary Johnston who not only entered the treasure house of Colonial life in such novels as *Prisoners of Hope* (New York, 1898) but also availed herself of the wealth of several other periods. One of the most significant of her works is *Lewis Rand* (Boston, 1908) with its portrayal of the caste structure of Virginia society in the late Jeffersonian period. Mary E. Wilkins Freeman in *The Heart's Highway* (New York, 1900) caught something of the spirit of the pre-revolutionary plantations. Emerson Hough introduced the Missouri plantation into his story of the period of the Fugitive Slave Law, *The Purchase Price* (Indianapolis, 1910); John U. Lloyd incorporated much of Kentucky color in *Stringtown on the Pike* [92] (New York, 1901); and Norval Richardson set

[89] For example, *Conjur' and Suasion, Atlantic*, Dec., 1921.
[90] See *Uncle Wash, His Stories* (Phila., 1910).
[91] *The Black Border* (Columbia, 1922).
[92] Serial in *The Bookman*, beginning March, 1900.

against the background of the Natchez district his life of
Sargent Prentiss, *The Lead of Honor* (Boston, 1910). In
connection with the historical novel, it is interesting to
note that one of the most lucid and restrained of all plan-
tation chronicles is the work of an author who was a
distinguished historian in the field he treated, W. G.
Brown's *A Gentleman of the South* (New York, 1903).
The Civil War romance proved a popular theme; Cyrus
T. Brady's *The Southerners* [93] and Frederick Palmer's *The
Vagabond* are typical of this class.[94]

There are other expressions of the old tradition which
have marked the literature of the twentieth century. The
tide of reminiscent writing has not yet ebbed [95] and
throughout the two decades there has been a stream of
reconstruction fiction, of which Thomas Dixon's *The
Leopard's Spots* (New York, 1902) and Walter H. Page's
Nicholas Worth [96] may be taken as representative of extreme attitudes. Most significant is the recurrence of certain themes, devices, or problems, which are sharply detached from the plantation setting and yet are but
disguised repetitions of some of the elements. The literature of the negro question as it appears today, whether
in the vigorous statements of such apostles of their race
as W. E. B. Dubois or Claude McKay or in the work of

[93] New York, 1903.

[94] It was in the historical novel that the first hint of a new
realism appeared. This attitude is best reflected in the works of
Miss Glasgow. The plantation is often found in traditional aspects, as in the opening chapters of *The Battle-Ground* (New
York, 1902) but her interest was principally in the extinction
of the plantation and the cavalier types in the face of new conditions, in the tragedy of a great transition, in the clash of a
new democracy with what remained of the old aristocracy.

[95] One of the best, Mrs. E. W. Pringle's *Chronicles of Chicora
Wood* appeared in 1922 (New York).

[96] Serial in *Atlantic*, beginning in July, 1906.

such white authors as T. S. Stribling [97] or H. A. Shands,[98] is concerned primarily with modes of thought not with romantic background; yet this problem is rooted in plantation life and much of the soil inevitably clings. The theme of the agony of mixed blood, the tragedy of racial consciousness on the part of those who are socially outcasts, has been used often; it is in Howells' *An Imperative Duty* (New York, 1892), in Mrs. Atherton's *Senator North* (New York, 1900), in Dorothy Canfield's *The Bent Twig* (New York, 1915), in Don Marquis' little story, *Mulatto,*[99] in Margaret Deland's *The Black Drop;* [100] in each of these stories the action is laid far from the old folks of the plantation home; yet the problem everywhere grows out of plantation sins, is everywhere made acute by what is generally considered the plantation point of view.

The negro as conceived of under the plantation system has become one of the most commonly utilized resources of fiction. The captivating comedy of his disposition and his procedure has been made the theme of innumerable scattered fragments of writing and has been consistently employed by a school of rather successful writers best represented by such names as Irvin S. Cobb, Harris Dickson, O. R. Cohen, E. K. Means, Hugh Wiley, and Dorothy Dix. The old plantation theme of slave loyalty comes over into much modern literature transmuted into the motive of the faithful and sometimes humorous servant; O. Henry's *A Municipal Report* and *The Guardian of the Accolade* introduce the faithful retainer; he is also in Tarkington's works, some of Mrs. Deland's writings, and a large body of American fiction. Something of the kindli-

[97] *Birthright* (New York, 1922).

[98] *White and Black* (New York, 1922).

[99] *Harper's,* April, 1916; the final scene of this story is in Atlanta.

[100] Serial in *Collier's Weekly,* beginning May 2, 1908.

ness of African temperament occurs in so unexpected a
place as Sherwood Anderson's *The Triumph of the Egg* [101]
(New York, 1921). The religious intensity of the darkey's
character, often the theme of burlesque, is treated with
an almost mystic interpretation, which materially heightens
the dramatic effect, in Moody's *The Faith Healer*. Superstition, favored theme of plantation writers, may be found
in forms of art not at all akin to plantation romance, as,
for example, Wilbur Daniel Steel's *Clay and the Cloven
Hoof* [102] or Joseph Hergesheimer's *Ju Ju*. [103]

It is hardly necessary to add that plantation song, its
distinctive lilt and its picturesque image, may be now
reckoned among the fixed conventions of American poetry.
Multitudes of the jingle makers have rattled off dialect
verse in such quantity and such variety, running from
the coon song which may be heard on today's vaudeville
stage to the attempt at mammy's lullaby which may appear in this month's magazine, that the din is not entirely
pleasing to sensitive ears. All this clamor of mingled
melody and jazz does little more than keep alive in general
consciousness some remembrance of plantation life. But
from an artistic point of view, this poetic material and
this poetic method, " this sure growth of the cis-Atlantic
muse," promises to prove most permanently influential in
the work of a few writers of ability to whose lines it has
given color or tone. To call the roll of this group is hardly
essential; one need think only of such figures as Alice
Corbin, Lindsay, Sandburg, [104] Untermeyer, Clement Wood,

[101] See the story *I Want to Know.*

[102] Serial in *Harper's,* beginning October, 1919.

[103] *Saturday Evening Post,* July 9, 1921.

[104] Writing in *The Bookman* for March, 1922, " J. F." suggests
that Sandburg has learned something of his method from negro
jazz. This hint may be compared with theories concerning the
obligation of Poe and Lanier to negro music.

Mary Johnston,[105] to realize that the theme has been productive of high results. It may come to pass, in fact, that through its singing, which has already had effect upon music, the plantation will most vividly, most popularly, most artistically make its permanent entry into our literature.

[105] Not commonly thought of as a poet; see, however, a quotation of real power in *The Literary Digest*, Feb. 25, 1922.

CHAPTER V

THE DEVELOPMENT OF THE CONCEPTION ON THE STAGE

THE stage has been a conspicuous factor in the development of the popular conception of the old plantation. This fact can hardly be over-estimated, though it must not be inferred that the theme has been, in any measurable degree, the subject of a real dramatic art. As a matter of history, the old regime has appeared in a few plays exceedingly significant because of the popular response, and in a great body of pageantry of low degree, much of it marked by a similar popularity. The lack of a real plantation drama, as distinguished from ephemeral spectacle, has been commented upon. "The truth is," says a critic [1] writing in 1882, "no true picture of the period (the ante-bellum regime in the South) has ever been presented in dramatic form." Twenty-one years later another dramatic writer observed: [2] "It is strange that so little should have been made of the only real caste our country has ever known — that found in the relation of master and slave." But the absence of authentic drama has been more than compensated for by the vogue of a few plays and even more largely by the immense influence of the black-face artists, conquering knights of minstrelsy. No fact is more obvious to the student than the remoteness of the connection of such minstrelsy with, indeed its utter

[1] Review of *The White Slave, New York Dramatic Mirror,* April 8, 1882.

[2] Review of *Colonel Carter of Cartersville, Munsey's,* March, 1903.

dissociation from, plantation darkies. Few of this type, save in the early years, ever made a real effort to offer more than the baldest travesty on the supposed original setting. "A representation of negro life and character," Mr. Harris writes [3] with spirited scorn, "has never been put on the American stage, nor anything remotely resembling it." But however inaccurate the form, the sweep and efficacy cannot be gainsaid. For several decades companies of professional minstrels were lodged permanently in various theatres of our larger cities; other troupes swung out perennially on triumphal tours over the whole theatrical circuit; the circus, the street carnival, the "patent medicine show," and many other agencies aided in carrying to the very doors of the people the world of burnt cork. Not without weight, moreover, was the incalculable number of amateur and private performances of some kind of minstrelsy for which various publishing houses have through the years been busily engaged in preparing librettos.[4]

A. *The Plantation in Minstrelsy*

The vogue of negro minstrelsy may be said to have begun on November 12, 1832 when T. D. Rice, whom Joseph Jefferson [5] calls the "first and best knight of the burnt cork," with his famous song and dance of *Jim Crow* made his debut at the Bowery Theatre, New York, where he attained a popularity unequaled by anything of the kind before [6] or since." [7]

[3] Quoted by Baskersville, *Southern Writers*, I, 63.

[4] As late as 1906 one New York house was advertising over 200 of these sketches.

[5] Autobiography, p. 6 (New York, 1889).

[6] The exact date and the statement concerning Rice's success are from Ireland's *Records of the New York Stage*, 55–56, which further asserts that Rice is "generally regarded as the founder

The work of Rice was not, of course, the first appearance of the negro in comic role. By 1769 New York witnessed[8] Isaac Bickerstaff's comic opera *The Padlock*, in which a negro slave, Mungo, played by Lewis Hallam, got gloriously drunk — to the great delight of the audience. In 1796 *Robinson Crusoe and Harlequin Friday* pleased another New York audience with an elaboration of the humorous black, and a sequel to this drama, *The Bold Buccaneers, or, The Discovery of Friday*, was popular in 1817.[9] As early as 1795 a company of negro comedians had been objected to in Boston and in the following year Joseph Tyler appeared in the same city with a pathetic ballad of the misery of slave life.[10] In 1814 a certain Tatnal sang in the Mount Pitt circus a darkey jingle commemorative of the battle of Plattsburg.[11] In 1824 James Roberts, a black-face in continental uniform, was render-

---

and father of Ethiopian minstrelsy." The New York appearance of Rice has been given as 1831; see, *e.g.*, article on Negro Minstrelsy in Chambers' *Encyclopedia*.

[7] A singular uncertainty exists as to the source of Rice's inspiration. Nevin (*S. C. Foster and Negro Minstrelsy, Atlantic*, Nov., 1867) says Rice heard a Cincinnati stage-driver sing the song and that he gave his first performance in Pittsburg. Hutton (*Curiosities of the American Stage*, 115–119) records two theories, one to the effect that Rice used as a model a Cincinnati slave, Jim, property of Mr. Crow, the other that he used a Pittsburg negro, Cuff. Jennings (*Theatrical and Circus Life*, 368) affirms that the inspiration was a Louisville negro and that the first performance was in that city,

[8] Hutton, *Curiosities of the American Stage*, 95–96. The chapter of this work called " The Negro on the Stage," from which quotations here used are drawn, appeared first in *Harper's*, January, 1889.

[9] *Ibid.*

[10] I. J. Greenwood, *The Circus*, 105.

[11] Greenwood, *The Circus*, 105.

ing [12] *Massa George Washington and Massa Lafayette.*
About 1820-21 an unknown company presented [13] in New
York *Tom and Jerry, or, Life in London,* which included
with fine geographical irrelevance a scene from the
Charleston slave mart, not for its pathetic effect but as
an opportunity to present much negro singing and dancing. Of more than passing significance was the appearance of Edwin Forrest as the Kentucky negro, Cuff, in
The Tailor in Distress, Louisville, 1823. [14] He is reputed [15]
to have been " the first actor who ever represented on the
stage the Southern plantation negro with all his peculiari-
ties of gait, accent, dialect, and manners." The most important of the predecessors of Rice was probably George
W. Dixon who seems to have originated the favorite
melody *Coal Black Rose* in Albany, 1828, and to have
enjoyed unusual popularity when he appeared the following season in New York with an entertainment which
approximated negro burletta. [16]

Rice was evidently not the pioneer [17] in comic representation of the negro. He cannot even be called the first

---

[12] Hutton, *Curiosities of the American Stage,* 121.

[13] *Ibid.,* 97.

[14] Greenwood, *The Circus,* 106.

[15] Hutton, *Curiosities of the American Stage,* 103-4.

[16] This appearance was at the Chatham Theatre; see Ireland's
Records of the New York Stage, 585 and 633. Dixon claimed to
be the author of " Old Zip Coon " one of the most popular of all
the early minstrel songs; see Hutton, page 121.

[17] There are many other reputed appearances of black-faces in
the years before Rice; see, *e.g.,* Edward L. Rice's *Monarchs of
Minstrelsy,* 5-6; the list herein submitted is merely a compilation
that seems reasonably well authenticated. The appearance of a
certain Young in the Federal Street Theatre, Boston, has been
called the first black-face performance of the established model;
and the same honor has been accorded an appearance of Graupner
in a circus at Taunton, Mass., 1809.

minstrel, if we think of the ornate form of that art as later developed. He is unquestionably, however, the father of minstrelsy, an honor which must be accorded him because of a three-fold significance. His was, in the first place, the first important sketch " in which the darkey performer was sufficient to himself and was deprived of any support from persons of another complexion." [18] His *Jim Crow*, again, was essentially dramatic, perhaps "more than anything else ever staged depending on the actions and mimetic power of the performer." [19] His popularity, finally, was a kind of economic revelation and established minstrelsy as a dramatic fact of first magnitude, certainly from the box-office point of view. He drew more money to the Bowery Theatre, it is said, than any other actor; and in England, whither he went in 1836, he further enlarged his fortune. Imitators of Rice, many of them relatively competent actors, sprang up in great numbers. Thomas H. Blakely was singing *Jim Crow* by 1833.[20] Within a year or two after Rice's first metropolitan appearance, the vogue of black-face attraction was fixed. In the late thirties, Barney Williams gained fame as a dancer of negro steps, and about the same time Barnum included in his circus a popular Ethiopian " break-down " in which Jack Diamond was featured; it is said [21] that Barnum himself blacked his face for more than one appearance. In December, 1841, John Smith and " Mister " Coleman, a famous vaudeville team, executed negro dances and sang comic " coon " songs at the Chatham Theatre, New York, and the same pair with the addition of Dia-

[18] Matthews, *Rise and Fall of Negro Minstrelsy, Scribner's*, June, 1915.

[19] Anon., *Negro Minstrelsy, Putnam's*, Jan., 1855.

[20] Ireland in his *Records of the New York Stage* gives Jan. 1, 1834.

[21] Hutton, *Curiosities of the American Stage*, 111

mond and T. E. Whitlock returned in 1842. In the following year, 1843, the Virginia Minstrels appeared at the same theatre, apparently the first regular performance of this nature in America.[22]

In spite of the uncertainty of the records,[23] it seems safe to consider this company, composed of individuals all of whom had previously won some personal renown in negro character sketches, as initiators of formal minstrelsy. The group, composed of Dan Emmett, Frank Brower, "Billy" Whitlock, and "Dick" Pelham, sang, played various instruments, danced jigs singly and doubly, and did *The Essence of Old Virginia* and *The*

---

[22] See Ireland, *Records of the New York Stage*, II, 377, 396, and 418.

[23] This is another of the disputed points in the confused history of minstrelsy. Ireland names in the company Whitlock, T. E. Booth, H. Mestayer, and Barney Williams, and suggests September as the month of their appearance. The four players mentioned above are listed by Greenwood in *The Circus* and by Hutton in *Curiosities of the American Stage* and are accepted by Professor Matthews in *The Rise and Fall of Negro Minstrelsy*. Hutton names February 17 as the date of the first performance. Jennings (*Theatrical and Circus Life*, 361) enumerates the same company but insists on 1841 as the date. A memorial article to G. S. Buckley (*New York Dramatic Mirror*, July 5, 1879) states that "the first band of negro minstrels organized in this country was formed in 1843 by Frank Brown." The claims to priority of the Christy organization, said to have been founded in 1842 though it did not appear in New York City until 1846, are recognized by several authorities as valid. The assertion that Christy is "the originator of Ethiopian minstrelsy" appears on the title page of the Christy song-book, *Christy's Plantation Melodies* (Phila., 1851). This view is vigorously combated by E. L. Rice in his *Monarchs of Minstrelsy;* and in an editorial in the new York *Sun,* January 30, 1918, on the origin of minstrelsy, the Christy company is named as third on the list. Both of these authorities, it may be mentioned, name the four actors cited above as the original company.

Lucy Long Walk-arounds. Most famous in this cast was Dan Emmett, for a long time one of the leaders of American minstrelsy, who early began to devise new tunes and songs, producing in the course of his career "Old Dan Tucker," one of the greatest of all minstrel songs, *The Boatman's Dance, Walk Along, John, Early in the Morning,* and the world-famed *Dixie* which became the war song of the Confederacy but was, according to Mr. Lincoln, recaptured by the entire country. Other companies soon followed the pioneers, particularly the Christy Minstrels, White's *Kitchen Minstrels,* Nelson Kneass' company, G. S. Buckley's *New Orleans Serenaders,* and Harrington's Minstrels, all in the forties; and scores, if not hundreds, of other organizations took the field in the next few decades. Among the prominent actors who at one time or other had minstrel connection were Joseph Jefferson,[24] Edwin Booth,[25] Francis Wilson,[26] and Chauncy Olcott.[27]

By the decade of the Civil War minstrelsy was at the height of its vogue with an almost unimaginable grip upon popular fancy. This form of entertainment held permanent possession of theatres in half a dozen American cities, three companies being settled definitely in New York City, and more than a dozen great enterprises were traveling from town to town.[28] Astute critics saw some indications of a wane in the seventies, yet we learn from a Philadel-

[24] Jefferson when just a little boy appeared with Rice in 1833; see *Autobiography,* p. 7.

[25] See sketch of Booth's life in *New York Dramatic Mirror,* June 17, 1893, and Hutton's *Curiosities of the American Stage,* 106.

[26] See " I remember —," *Lippincott's,* January, 1891.

[27] See *Munsey's,* March, 1899, and *New York Dramatic Mirror,* February 22, 1885.

[28] See Matthews, *Rise and Fall of Negro Minstrelsy, Scribner's,* June 1915, and anon., *The Decline of Orthodox Minstrelsy, New York Dramatic Mirror,* February 28, 1885.

phia report [29] as late as 1879 that " neither Modjeska, nor Clara Morris, nor Fanny Davenport, nor any other star that has flashed across the sky this season has drawn such a multitude of people as came to see Haverly's *Mastodon Minstrels*." Similar reports from every theatrical point confirm the persistence of public appreciation.[30] Through the executive ingenuity of certain producers minstrelsy in the eighties expanded into greater magnitude and magnificence. J. H. Haverly, who sponsored several companies at the same time, enlarged his most gorgeous production, the *Mastodons*, until the company included 100 people and elaborate settings.[31] In 1880 this company made " an unprecedented hit " in London and even invaded Germany. Other managements rivaled Haverly in grandeur and in popularity. The old Harrigan and Hart partnership, formed in 1871, offered many of the most cordially received sketches on the New York stage. The San Francisco players were highly praised [32] for a fairly successful struggle to be accurate in presentation of Southern darkies. Charles Frohman was by 1883 director of a company which included, according to its advertisement,[33] " the original Nashville Jubilee singers." McIntyre and Heath broke into the game by the mid-eighties.[34] Meantime Johnny Wild in the various performances of the Skidmore Guards of Harrigan and Hart earned a reputation as one of the foremost exponents of minstrelsy in the hodge-podge type

[29] *New York Dramatic Mirror*, January 25, 1879.

[30] One may find interesting corroboration of this fact by tracing out in the record of a single theatre, as Tompkins' *Boston Stage* (Boston, 1908), the large proportion of time in an annual program given to minstrel entertainment.

[31] *New York Dramatic Mirror*, July 3, 1880.

[32] *Ibid.*, September 4, 1880.

[33] *Ibid.*, December 15, 1883.   [34] *Ibid.*, May 8, 1886.

of show.[35] By 1893 Al. G. Fields had projected on great scale his Columbian Minstrels and at the middle of this decade his and the other major organizations, including Haverly's, Comstock's, Callender's, Barlow's, and Cleveland's companies, were in full swing, most popular of all being the 25-year-old Primrose and West combination, broken in 1898 when Primrose joined with Lew Dockstader. The immense vogue carried some of the leaders well over into the present century. In 1904 Fields had two groups on the road. Four years later " Honey Boy " Evans was disputing with the best for the leadership, while Dockstader's, Vogel's, and the Primrose minstrels, now managed by Decker, were all popular. But in the second decade of the twentieth century the doom of minstrelsy, foreseen by some thirty years before,[36] was sealed and today it " lingers superfluous on the stage with none to do it reverence." [37]

The immense magnetism of minstrelsy distorted many dramas of fundamentally serious nature; and the result was sometimes a queer compromise of pathos and comedy. No better illustration of this not uncommon practice of coloring heavier offering with minstrel hues can be cited than *Uncle Tom's Cabin*, which, having stirred righteous indignation now began to stir risibilities, slipping easily from the domain of the tear to that of the grin. By 1885

[35] It would be a mistake to think of all minstrel companies, even a majority as centering in the cities; a correspondent to the New York *Sun*, Jan. 23, 1918, cites a company that toured New England and New York State for 30 years without ever seeing Broadway; there must have been many of this class.

[36] See article by John P. Smith, well known manager, in *New York Dramatic Mirror*, August 7, 1880.

[37] Matthews, *Rise and Fall of Negro Minstrelsy, Scribner's*, June, 1915.

a famous revival [38] in New York advertised as special features Horace Weston on the banjo, Jasper Grew with a " hoe-cake reel," the Magnolia Quartette, and other plantation singers and dancers.   In 1890 a stock company took the road with a ballet of negro girls as added attraction.[39]   The role of Topsy was early regarded as a favorable opportunity for clog dance and comic song.[40]   In 1899 [41] the show carried as a new feature a monster cakewalk by a group of the slaves and by 1902 [42] a spectacular scene of Voodoo worship had been introduced as a kind of comic interlude.   This parable, dear to the abolitionists, degenerated in a great many cases into a laughable mingling of bathos and minstrelsy.   In June, 1889, *The Octoroon* appeared enriched with an elaborate company of *Georgia Jubilee Singers*.[43]   Other dramas more or less directly related to plantation life were given added charm by shrewd interpolation of minstrel features.   Among some of the more important supposedly serious plays which yielded to the popular fancy for minstrelsy were *The White Slave;* [44] Frank Chanfrau's famous *Kit* in which the professional banjoist, the *Black Diamond Quartette* and many plantation singers were prominently featured; [45] *Jack-in-the-Box*,[46] a melodrama not even remotely south-

[38] This was Smith's revival, presented in New York in February; see *Mirror* for February 28, 1885.

[39] *New York Dramatic Mirror,* Dec. 6, 1890.

[40] *Ibid.,* June 11, 1892.

[41] *Ibid.,* April 29, 1899.

[42] *Ibid.,* December 27, 1902; A. W. Martin's production, New Star, New York.

[43] *Ibid.,* June 8, 1889.

[44] *Ibid.,* May 2, 1891; this company steadily enlarged upon the minstrel idea until by its New York appearance in 1903 it was a great spectacle.

[45] *Ibid.,* December 19, 1885.

[46] *Ibid.,* February 13, 1886.

ern; *Old Lavender*,[47] a Harrigan production in which
Johnny Wild offered interesting but incongruous black-
face work; A. H. Spinks' famous racing melodrama, *The
Derby Winner*,[48] which punctuated the thrill of race-track
life with "a colored band, a group of plantation singers
and dancers, and a double colored quartette"; at least
two dramas located on the Swanee River;[49] *A Kentucky
Feud*,[50] a melodrama of mountains and moonshine which
had few of the elements of the blue-grass plantations;
I. N. Morris' *Jim Bludso*,[51] in which minstrelsy is introduced by the somewhat naive plan of having negro workers in a machine shop lay down their tools and render a
few "stunts" after the conventional methods.

The eventual waning of minstrelsy as a definite form
does not indicate a loss of popular favor so much as it
signifies the dissipation of the charm into other forms of
stage entertainment. At least one writer [52] has attributed
the decline to the increasing competition of briefer burnt-
cork features as offered in variety and vaudeville shows.
To consult the programs of leading vaudeville houses, between the seventies and the end of the century, is to be
convinced that the appearance of black-face comedians

[47] *Ibid.*, Dec. 18, 1893. This was not an uncommon practice
at Harrigan's for Wild's peculiar gift in burnt cork humor was
too valuable not to be utilized.

[48] *Ibid.*, May 26, 1894.

[49] *Down upon the Sewanee River*, Detroit, Aug., 1895, and *On
the Sewanee River*, New York, March, 1904. The spelling of the
word "Swanee" as used in the text is the form in which Foster's
song is most commonly written; and it was the song of Foster
that was in most minds, rather than any specific geographical
stream.

[50] See *New York Dramatic Mirror*, December 6, 1902.

[51] See *New York Dramatic Mirror*, Jan. 17, 1903.

[52] See *The Decline of Orthodox Minstrelsy*, *Dramatic Mirror*,
Feb. 28, 1885.

was the rule rather then the exception. In the spacious days of Harrigan and Hart there was almost unfailing blending of negro humor with Irish, German, Hebrew, and what not. The same policy marked the exhibitions of Tony Pastor. By this time the variety stage was crowded with individual performers who had established, within such circles, large reputations, including such figures as George Powers, himself from Kentucky, Dan Hart and Gussie his wife — the latter long enjoying prestige as Topsy — John P. Smith, Dooley and Tenbrook with their camp-meeting songs, W. H. Bray in the same specialty, and hundreds of others. As early as 1880, a dramatic writer protests [53] that " the old-time darkey on the variety stage is a bore "; but such objections were ineffectual. The practice continues with little modification to our own day.

Hardly less striking than the work of individual numbers is the absorption of minstrel methods and values, either partially or totally, by farce or musical comedy. Among the earliest of the typical negro musical comedies was *Africa*, produced on Christmas day, 1893, with George Thatcher in the cast. In the spring of 1898 there appeared a musical comedy, *A Trip to Coontown*, the work of the colored comedians, Cole and Johnson, which, largely a minstrel show in new guise, enjoyed great popularity. A rather notable pair of colored artists, Williams and Walker, was starred in another minstrel-like comedy, *The Policy Players*, in the fall of 1899. Another successful musical comedy of this season, *Three Little Lambs*, not modeled on minstrel lines, featured " a great cake-walk by Nellie Braggins and two little ' coons.'" Most famous of these comedies was *In Dahomey* with words by Paul Laurence Dunbar and music by Will Marion Cook, in which the principal role was taken by Bert Williams; this entertain-

[53] *New York Dramatic Mirror,* February 28, 1880.

ment had a good run covering several seasons. Cook repeated his original success with *The Southerners* which included, besides conventional minstrel features, a plantation plot with a villain made in the mold of Simon Legree. *Banana Land,* in 1907, featuring Williams and Walker, another triumph for this rather accomplished composer, is said to have won praise from Dvorak.[54] Before this time, McIntyre and Heath had presented their vehicle of black-face comedy, *The Ham Tree,*[55] and Eva Tanguay had with delightful irrelevance introduced a coon song into the Egyptian comedy, *The Chaperons.*[56] Other typical comedies employing minstrel elements were *A Girl from Dixie* in the season of 1903–04; *When Johnny Comes Marching Home,* which was popular through at least three seasons; and the rather farcical *Rufus Rastus.* Some of the most elaborate presentations of spectacles did not fall within the province of the regular theatre. To this class belongs the unusual entertainment of *Black Patti's Troubadours* which was remarkably popular for more than a decade. The program offered a curious blend of serious opera and minstrel amusements, and apparently delighted the public; more than 7,000 paid for the privilege of hearing this group on the opening night at Asbury Park in the summer of 1904 and when it concluded this run it went on a tour of triumph of over 30,000 miles.[57] Unique in the way of spectacle was Nate Salsbury's *Black America,* an enterprise at Ambrose Park during the summer of 1895 [58] which depicted on a relatively vast scale " the actual life of the plantation negro before the war." More than 200,000

---

[54] See *Munsey's,* May, 1908.
[55] New York, August 28, 1905.
[56] See *The Theatre,* July, 1902.
[57] *New York Dramatic Mirror,* Aug. 6, 1904.
[58] This organization later toured the country.

people witnessed this pageant during the first month.[59] Dunbar and Cook collaborated in a spectacle of somewhat different nature, *The Origin of the Cake-Walk*, which, exhibited by a cast of forty negroes, was a decided attraction at the Casino Roof Garden during the summer of 1898.[60]

The persistence of the minstrel in further modification is attested by the fact that the majority of the leading comedians of our own day have appeared in black-face or have sung many of the " coon songs." During the season of 1922–23 several " revues " elaborated a kind of reminiscence of the cake-walk. In one entertainment a Hebrew character comedian warbled " My Coal Black Mammy " to the great delight of an audience which resolutely refused to perceive any incongruity. Such recent theatrical successes as *Shuffle Along* and *Liza* represent the continuance in rather skilful fashion of the minstrel-comedy tradition.

A detailed study of the varying content of minstrel performances is forbidden here by considerations of space. It may be in order, however, to suggest that the material was less and less accurate in actual plantation portrayal. Obviously the general purpose of the founders of minstrelsy was to reproduce roughly the Southern darkey, preferably in his plantation environment. Rice, though responsible for the " dandy " character which later usurped the stage, gave some study to the true country negro; one of his more popular sketches, " The Virginia Mummy " was fairly representative of plantation blacks. The minstrel bands of the early forties generally followed the plan of introducing even if in spectacular exaggeration the traits of the actual black men. Real effort was made

[59] *New York Dramatic Mirror,* June 1 and June 29, 1895.
[60] See *Munsey's,* September, 1898.

to secure " the veritable tunes and words which have light-
ened the labor of some weary negro in the cotton field,
amused his moonlight hours as he fished, or waked the
spirits in the woods as he followed in the tracks of the
wary raccoon." [61]   Of these early performers Professor
Matthews says: [62] " The sole excuse for being was that
they endeavored to reproduce the life of the plantation
darkey.   The songs sung by the Ethiopian serenaders were
reminiscences of the songs heard where the negro was at
work, on the river steamboat, in the sugar field, or at the
camp-meeting — the hardest kind of labor to a negro was
religion.   These songs retained the flavor of slave life, with
all its pathos, its yearning, its hopelessness, its mournful-
ness."   But in this same decade of the forties minstrelsy
became corrupt.   *Old Dan Tucker* was probably the last
of the pure plantation melodies.   Henceforward the musical effort was devoted to parodies impossible to the slave
intellect, such as " Lucy did lam a moor," to excruciat-
ingly sentimental ballads celebrating " dead wenches " who
slept beneath willow trees or living girls with most romantic names and attributes; clog dances became in
mechanical precision unlike any of the reckless jigging of
the true darkey; comic dialogue strayed so far from pleasant Southern paths as to include Irish brogue or German
dialects; even plots brought from France to America were
seized upon for minstrel purposes.[63]   From time to time
certain leaders of the profession made rather feeble attempts to restore the plantation purity [64] and certain in-

[61] Anon., *Negro Minstrelsy, Putnam's,* January, 1855.
[62] *Banjo and Bones,* London *Saturday Review,* June 7, 1884.
[63] Professor Matthews records (*Rise and Fall of Negro Minstrelsy, Scribner's,* June, 1915) a minstrel plot that is merely " a
bold and more robust version " of one of the old French farces,
Maitre Pierre Pathelin.
[64] George Primrose and Lew Dockstader, for instance, announced

dividuals, like McAndrews, the "watermelon man," interpreted single roles with fidelity. But the unmistakable
tendency was away from the models.

By the middle of the century the minstrel performance
had fallen into a set program consisting usually of three
parts. The first act almost invariably presented the artists
seated, usually in a single row with the interlocutor in
the centre and the chief comedians as end men. These
interspersed comic questions and witty replies in the several performances of the balladists and dancers. The setting and costuming which at first were designed as a re-
production of the grotesque characteristics of negro habits
of finery and misfit grew more opulent until at last all
had something of oriental glitter. The second act, or
"olio," was a kind of variety program contributed by individual stars. The first part was not always true to
type, as witnessed by the inclusion of such songs as *Over
the Garden Wall* and the Sextette from *Lucia* in the
Thatcher, Primrose, and West show of 1882. But it was
in the third part that minstrelsy wandered farthest from
plantation life. Gradually this section came to be used
for comic opera, burlesque performances, appearances of
distinguished pugilists,[65] and the like. Sometimes a popular play would be burlesqued, as when Haverly's *Mastodons* offered in April, 1880, a "take-off" on *The Royal
Middy* and in September one of Bronson Howard's *The
Banker's Daughter;* and sometimes an opera would be simi-

---

the intention of reverting to more accurate plantation representations. Dockstader's experience led him to believe that the public
did not appreciate this purer form and he gave up the idea. (See
Mr. Dockstader's Policy, New York Dramatic Mirror, Feb. 25,
1888.)

[65] The association of John L. Sullivan with Lester and Allen's
minstrels in December, 1885, was one of the earliest of a long list.

larly treated as when the same company presented in 1881 a burlesque of *Il Trovatore*. In 1888 Thatcher, Primrose, and West had a Shakespearean burlesque with Malvolio and Mercutio as most charming singers; and the same year Dockstader closed his entertainment with a double barreled attraction: a satire on the keen political struggle of the year and a burlesque of *Othello* — justified in minstrelsy at least as far as complexion is concerned. Before the end of the century the minstrel stage had been used for a wondrous assortment of these burlesques, including such remote themes as *The Last of the Mohicans, Africanus Bluebeard, Hamlet the Dainty, Camille, Les Miserables,* and *De Octoroon.*

B. *The Plantation in Regular Drama*

Although sporadic attempts were made before 1850 to dramatize certain spectacular features of Southern life,[66] the plantation on the stage received no attention worthy of note until the appearance of Mrs. Stowe's *Uncle Tom's Cabin*, first exhibited in full form to New York City on July 18, 1853.[67] Its enormous popularity, which gives it

[66] For example, Morris Barnett's *The Yankee Peddler; or, Old Times in Virginia,* presented in St. Louis, 1841. This play and several others of no great moment are listed in Roden's bibliography, *Later American Plays.*

[67] The remarkable uncertainty attaching to much of our dramatic history is illustrated in the confusion concerning the origin and early career of this play. The fact stated above has been generally accepted; it has been agreed, too, that this version, Aiken's, sometimes referred to as the " official version," had been presented in Troy, September, 1852; and that it had been preceded by a fragmentary dramatization in New York, August, 1852. Brown (*A History of the New York Stage,* I, 311) locates this appearance in the Chatham Theatre; other authorities (Marlowe, *Uncle Tom's Cabin, New York Dramatic Mirror,* Christmas, 1905, and Arnett, *Fifty Years of Uncle Tom, Munsey's,* August, 1902)

foremost rank among all theatrical representations of the plantation, became apparent at once. It ran continuously until April 19, 1854 and then appeared three evenings a week until May 13. Meantime on January 16, 1854 another production appeared at the Bowery Theatre with none other than Rice himself as Uncle Tom.[68] Already in 1853 the play had begun its career of unbroken successes on the road.[69] From that time to this, especially to the end of the last century, the story of *Uncle Tom's Cabin*, certainly with respect to popular response, forms the most notable chapter of American dramatic history. One can hardly take up a trade-journal of the period without finding reference to the immense professional activity centering in this portrayal of old plantation life. Indicative of the vitality of the appeal is Augustin Daly's note from

---

place it in the National Theatre. The majority of writers credit this August version to C. W. Taylor, though Marlowe names A. H. Purdy as producer. Marlowe, who writes professedly to correct errors, makes Aiken the real pioneer by asserting that the original Troy version was not in September but in February and was witnessed by Purdy who employed the general idea in his subsequent production. Aiken's first presentation, Marlowe notes, went only as far as the death of Eva. The New York show of August was only an indirect adaptation; it did not have the names of the characters in the book, lasted just an hour, and was only one number of a variety program which included Rice in *Jim Crow in London*. An effort to summarize the case (*Literary Digest*, June 10, 1911) recognizes three early dramatizations: the New York version of August, the Troy version of September, and an independent Boston version of November, 1852, which had a run of 250 exhibitions. According to this source, the play reached London by September, 1853, where it proved immensely popular.

[68] Brown, *A History of the New York Stage*, I, 311 *et seq.*; elsewhere it has been said that the August, 1853, version went to 325 performances.

[69] Willard notes the enthusiastic reception in Providence in 1853 (in *History of the Providence Stage*, Providence, 1891, p. 150).

London,[70] October 14, 1878: " Five of the London theatres are playing *Uncle Tom* but no one place is hurting the others." Philadelphia witnessed the transfiguration of the play into an opera in 1882.[71] Two performances competed for New York's favor in 1900, one of them being William A. Brady's great revival with Wilton Lackaye and Theodore Roberts in the cast; and as late as 1906 there were six companies on the road all meeting with more than tolerable success.[72] To enumerate the distinguished stage figures who have at one time or another been a " Tommer " is virtually to call the role of prominent actors of the older generation — to say nothing of many who were not actors, as Peter Jackson, the colored pugilist, who once appeared as the leading character.[73] All in all, Uncle Tom's Cabin has been presented, it is estimated, 225,000 times, more often than any other play in English; two-thirds of the performances have been in America, distributed through practically all the theatres of the northern half of the nation.[74]

The history of this amazing stage career reflects interestingly the great romantic shift of the popular attitude. Presented first as abolition propaganda — though the vivid dramatic elements of plantation life were never absent — the play responded rather actively to the sentimental tendencies of the era of reconciliation. Reference has been made to the growing inclusion of minstrel elements, evident even in the operatic presentation of 1882. The sharp-

[70] *Life of Augustin Daly,* 277 (New York, 1917).

[71] May 22, 1882: the venture was not marked by great success.

[72] *New York Dramatic Mirror,* Nov. 17, 1906 (p. 9).

[73] Tompkins notes this fact in his *Boston Theatre.*

[74] The high rank of the play in certain theatrical conceptions is evident from the appearance of Uncle Tom as representative of the " old stuff " of negro drama in such a modern play as *Shuffle Along.* New York, 1921.

ness of the abolition motive has since the war been notice-
ably dulled. The increased care taken in the setting is
in itself a testimony to the managerial appreciation of the
picturesque values. From 1880 the play grew steadily
more spectacular with liberal use of the rich and mellow
environment of slave life. At the last the great plot over
which so many tears were shed, became little more than
a convenient thread on which were lavishly strung minstrel gems and rather sympathetic pictures.

Second in importance to Mrs. Stowe's story but even
closer to plantation life was the other memorable drama
of ante-bellum days, Boucicault's *The Octoroon; or Life
in Louisiana,* which began a remarkably successful career
at the New York Winter Garden on December 5, 1859
with Joseph Jefferson in the role of Salem Scudder. This
play, which may have been suggested by the fame of
Uncle Tom,[75] is significant for reception and for content.
It created " one of the greatest sensations;" [76] it was particularly rich in comprehensiveness of detail; and so skilfully were the good and the bad of slavery balanced that
it appealed alike to sympathizers with abolition and with
the " peculiar institution." [77] Southern character in its
most appealing guise was exemplified in such figures as
George Peyton, Mrs. Peyton, Sunnyside, and others; the
dog-like devotion of slaves even in most distressing circumstances — always a moving theme — was elaborated
with real art; [78] flashes of plantation humor relieved the

[75] Moses makes this suggestion in *The American Dramatist,* 46
(Boston, 1911). His reference is, of course, to the idea not the
plot which was adapted from Reid's *Quadroon.*

[76] Clapp and Edgett, *Plays of the Present* (Dunlap Soc., N. Y.,
1902).

[77] Jefferson notes this two-fold appeal in his *Autobiography*
(N. Y., 1889); see pp. 213–214.

[78] Note, for instance, the pathetic effort of the slaves to look

tragedy; yet the agony of the delicate Zoe, whom even
her father could not liberate while the estate was under
mortgage, the suffering of families disrupted through the
bankruptcy sale, the viciousness incarnate in McCloskey,
the Legree-like villain, all combined to form a powerful
indictment of slavery.

The subsequent career of Boucicault's drama, though insignificant as compared to *Uncle Tom's Cabin*, reveals its
abiding power in the development of the popular conception. The inherent value of the material, the artful mingling of various themes, the illusion of reality,[79] all united
to give the play a long and influential existence. Within
a short while after its appearance the Christy minstrels
put on a burlesque, called *The Moctroon*, written by
W. H. Peck.[80] Soon after its great success in New York
it began an equally prosperous road career.[81] Revivals
from time to time have met with considerable success.[82]

In the romantic epoch of American art, the plantation
has received at least incidental treatment in a surprising
number of dramas or dramatic efforts, none of which, however, approximates in influence upon public consciousness
the two earlier plays. The heterogeneous collection which

their best at the sale so that they might bring the largest possible
financial benefit to their owners.

[79] A famous anecdote concerning this play tells of a New York
state senator who while the bidding for Zoe was at its height
rose in the audience and cried, " Thirty thousand, by G——! "
(*New York Dramatic Mirror*, May 26, 1888).

[80] Author of *The McDonalds*, mentioned in chapter 3.

[81] See, *e.g.*, Willard's *Providence Stage*, 180, for success in that
city, 1867.

[82] Notable examples: at the Bowery Theatre, March 22, 1879,
with Frank Chanfrau as Salem Scudder; at the Third Avenue
Theatre, March 2, 1900; and at the Fourteenth Street Theatre,
June 12, 1905.

has utilized with varying advantage the plantation elements does not easily yield to classification. One group may, nevertheless, be certainly identified, the "Civil War" romance employing in the main conflict between love and sectional patriotism. Not often does the plantation in full detail appear in this type; but there is obvious struggle for Southern atmosphere and there is special emphasis on Southern character. The heroine is unfailingly the conventional Dixie beauty, commonly the young mistress of a great estate. Thus in the greatest of the Civil war plays, Bronson Howard's *Shenandoah,* the leading role, played first by Viola Allen, accentuated the coquetry, the charm, the devotion, and the horsemanship of the Southern maid.[83] Similarly in Gillette's *Held by the Enemy,*[84] Louise Dillon, who first interpreted the role of the heroine, was commended by critics for her success in impersonating "the pert and sassy Southern girl." In many of the plays the father of the girl, usually a volcanic old Southern gentleman, is the opposing force to love's sweet dream, and not infrequently the villain is a young Southern gallant. Great pains seem to be taken in elaboration of the plantation darkey, the treatment in this respect often veering toward the pure minstrel delineation. In a revival of *The Blue and the Gray,*[85] for example, J. W. McAndrews, long known as "the watermelon man" of minstrelsy, was generously applauded as Uncle Josh.

[83] Boston, Nov. 19, 1888; New York, Sept. 9, 1889. Dates recorded in this section will be understood as referring, usually, to public presentations. Little account can be taken of special or private performances which could not materially affect the popular conception.

[84] Brooklyn, Feb., 1886. The quotation is from the *Mirror,* Feb. 27.

[85] This revival was in September, 1889; the appearance referred to in the following paragraph was at Niblo's Garden, New York, May, 1884.

The list of these Civil War dramas is too long to allow more than the merest mention of certain representative productions.   The vogue was well established in the eighties.   Among the earliest was Elliot Barnes' *The Blue and the Gray* with a typical Southern heroine and with a typical plantation darkey played by Charles Bradshaw. The same year, 1884, witnessed the staging of J. K. Tillotson's *Lynwood*,[86] a revision of an older play, not especially characteristic of plantation life, though Maude Grainger earned high praise as the Southern girl, type dear to the heart of the Northern audience.   The following year, C. P. Dazey brought out *For a Brother's Life*,[87] a drama of Virginia notable chiefly for the negro character outlined in the persons of hosts of refugees to Federal camps.   In 1886 came Gillette's first play of this nature, *Held by the Enemy*,[88] with its popular story of the Southern girls, the old maiden aunt, and the negro servant, all within the hostile lines.   The marked success of this drama was attributed largely to the work of Miss Grainger and of John Woodward as the old family darkey.   Howard's *Shenandoah* began in 1888 its uncommonly successful stage career. By 1899 this interpretation of Southern character had expanded into a real spectacle "with 250 people and 50 horses in the cast." [89]   Other plays of this nature which in the decade of the eighties achieved a measure of fame were H. W. Ellis' *Loyalty*,[90] with echoes of the Kentucky plantation, and H. P. Mawson's *A Fair Rebel*,[91] which

[86] Union Square Theatre, New York, September, 1884.

[87] Third Avenue Theatre, New York, Oct., 1885.

[88] Brooklyn, February, 1886.

[89] See New York *Mirror*, Feb. 4, 1899.   Maurice Barrymore and Mary Hampden were in this cast.

[90] Park Theatre, New York, April, 1889.

[91] Presented at the Star, Dec., 1889, but not formally launched upon its career, apparently, until August, 1891.   Fanny Gillette was the heroine.

resounded with much banjo playing; this play was peculiarly acceptable to Southern audiences because the
villain-rival was a Frenchman and not a representative
of Southern manhood.

The nineties saw a swelling flood of this sort of production. Without significance other than conformity to type
and some popularity were George T. Ulmer's *The Volun-
teer*,[92] in which brothers of a Southern family join the
opposing forces, Pitou and Alfriend's *Across the Potomac*,[93]
which won a eulogy from Robert G. Ingersoll for its character delineation, John C. Webb's *After Twenty Years*,[94]
and Taylor and Meredith's *Maine and Georgia*.[95] More
earnest in an effort to reproduce distinctive phases of
plantation life was Margaret B. Smith's *Capt. Herne,
U. S. A.*,[96] including the ever popular octoroon, vainly
enamored of the hero, and including a particularly Spartan mother who in loyalty to the South disowns her son.
Similarly purposive was Russ Whytal's *For Fair Virginia*.[97]
The year 1895 brought forth two of the best known of
all Civil War plays: Belasco's *The Heart of Maryland*[98]
with Mrs. Leslie Carter as Virginia Calvert, which, with
its run of 208 consecutive performances, was probably the
season's leader, and Gillette's *Secret Service*,[99] laid in the
city of Richmond but elaborating what were regarded as
plantation characters. In 1896, James K. Collier's *Stone-*

[92] Hammerstein's, New York, 1891.
[93] Proctor's, October, 1885.
[94] Louisville, Sept., 1892; New York (Niblo's), December, 1892.
[95] Fourteenth Street, November, 1893.
[96] Union Square, New York, Jan., 1893.
[97] Fifth Avenue, New York, June, 1895.
[98] Herald Square, New York, Oct., 1895.
[99] Philadelphia, May 13, 1895. Note as an interesting departure on the theme of negro loyalty that Jonas' fidelity is to the
Northerners.

wall,[100] one of the few plays of this nature to originate in the South, opened its not particularly distinguished career. Kentucky — uncommonly popular with the dramatists — furnished the background for Franklin Fyles' *Cumberland, '61*,[101] which included a typical feud of that section and a hint of the tragedy of racial mixture; it was, however, brightened by the devotion of a characteristic mammy, and it made a fairly deep impression. Two plays,[102] leaning heavily on the plantation darkey for popular appeal, marked the season of 1898; and in the following year came the most ambitious and most comprehensive, though not most successful, drama of this class, James A. Herne's *Reverend Griffith Davenport;*[103] it included many aspects of the Southern plantation, all varieties of character, darkies suffering and darkies happy; it was marked by particularly good "sets;" but in spite of unanimous praise from critics, it did not make a great impression. One of the most successful of all Civil War dramas marked this year, however, Clyde Fitch's *Barbara Frietchie*[104] in which Julia Marlowe "flirted with easy grace."

The first years of the present century recorded little waning of public interest in this type. Early in 1900, Ed McWade's *Winchester*[105] drew large crowds. The following year something of plantation motive was adopted for the musical comedy, *When Johnny Comes Marching*

[100] Wilmington, N. C., April, 1896.

[101] Fourteenth Street, New York, Oct., 1897.

[102] J. K. Tillotson's *Report for Duty,* Fourteenth Street, New York, March, and F. G. Campbell's *Gettysburg,* Grand, New York, April, 1898.

[103] Herald Square, New York, Jan., 1899.

[104] See review in *Harper's Weekly,* Oct. 28, 1899. Fitch's play was made the basis of an interesting Weber and Fields burlesque, *Barbara Fidgety,* marked by specially good banjo playing; David Warfield was in the cast.

[105] American Theatre, New York, April, 1900.

Home,[106] with a particularly elaborate setting in a large Mississippi estate upon which darkies sang tuneful melodies. About this time, moreover, there came the vogue of dramatized war novels. Conspicuous in this class was Churchill's *The Crisis*,[107] prepared for the stage by the author and presented with a strong cast including James K. Hackett, Charlotte Walker, and Thomas A. Hall; this play was marked by effective " sets," as the moonlight dance before the Carvel mansion, and the powerful slave sale scene. Another example of this type was Cable's *Cavaliers*,[108] dramatized by Paul Kester and George Middleton, in which Miss Marlowe again had the role of a Southern heroine. The series of the great Civil War dramas closed with William C. DeMille's *The Warrens of Virginia* [109] which with the famous family interpreted by Frank Keenan, Emma Dunn, and Charlotte Walker proved a stage success of more than ordinary prestige.

The plantation has received since the shift to sentimentalism a fairly large treatment in numerous plays other than those on the war theme. Few of these would bulk large in any serious history of dramatic progress yet many had amazing vogue and were potent in shaping or emphasizing the popular conception. In this multitude of dramatic productions there are several discernible types. One of the favorite forms was the stage presentation of a plantation novel, the most distinguished example of this group being Augustus Thomas's version of Hopkinson Smith's *Colonel Carter of Cartersville* which delighted New York in the spring of 1892. The play retained the flavor of the original story, was interpreted by a strong

[106] Opened December, 1902; see *The theatre* for Jan., 1903.

[107] Opened in New York, November, 1902.

[108] Opened in New York, December, 1902.

[109] According to *Munsey's*, Feb., 1908, ran from Dec. 3, 1907 to May 16, 1908.

cast including E. M. Holland as Colonel Carter, Maurice Barrymore as Fitzpatrick, and Charles Harris, a real negro, as Chad, and increased its popular appeal by charming effects in the setting of Carter Hall.[110] Another type of plantation drama may be found in a small number of plays which depict the old life in works of so pronounced artistic excellence that they are differentiated by sheer superiority. There are few of these plays; perhaps the example that occurs first to the mind is another production of Mr. Thomas, *Alabama*.[111] The old traits, as they persist in a new era, are here elaborated with painstaking accuracy. The characters are indigenous to the plantation soil; customs and attitudes, from the fondness for the early morning cup of coffee to the proneness to duelling, are given recognition. The sweep of the play during the nineties made it a considerable factor in the development of the popular notion of plantation life.

Another class of plantation drama, not a very active one in these latter years, may be thought of as a continuation of the Stowe-Boucicault tradition. *The White Slave*, which had a run of twenty years, simply re-assembled such old materials as the distressed octoroon, the swaggering young Southerners, the innocent heroine — once played by Fanny Kemble — and a lovely old Southern matron.

More important numerically was the type which may be considered the spectacular plantation melodrama. The biggest money-getter of this group was C. P. Dazey's *In*

[110] See eulogy in *New York Dramatic Mirror*, April 2, 1892.

[111] The superiority here ascribed to such plays will be understood as relative, referring only to the class of plantation drama. Mr. Thomas has given us in this play one of the best dramatic representations of life in the old regime; the rank of this drama, however, in American stage-craft as a whole is another question. It may be doubted whether any of the productions here listed had much permanent literary or even dramatic merit.

Old Kentucky,[112] which, after a rather inconspicuous opening, moved out into a long, a really astonishing succes-
sion of triumphs, incorporating as it waxed wealthier more
and more minstrel elements. The racing, shooting, pickaninny bands, and the like, probably attracted the crowd,
but there was certainly much representation of Southern
character. E. C. Stedman called[113] Colonel Sandusky
"the best Southerner ever on the board." Almost as successful was J. K. Tillotson's *The Planter's Wife*, which
appeared in Chicago in January, 1883, reached New York
by the following April, and for more than a decade carried its impressive spectacle of the Graham mansion and
the social life centering therein to appreciative throngs.[114]
We might make yet another division of plantation drama
in the matter of pure spectacle, not minstrelsy and not
melodrama, of which class the Hippodrome exhibition,
Marching through Georgia, presented in the spring of 1911,
would be typical; in this production efforts toward realism
went so far as to exhibit actual cotton plants in supposed
fields.

If we turn for the moment from this attempt at classification or rough analysis of plantation drama to a chronological survey, we find that the presentation of Southern
figure and customs, more or less directly expressing plantation life, began fairly early in the romantic period. One
of the first actors to win favor in a study of this kind was
the famous minstrel, G. S. Buckley, who appeared in the

[112] This play opened, it seems, in 1882. For many years it was
a favorite vehicle of stock companies. In 1896 it was welcomed
back to the Grand Opera House, New York, as the "evergreen
success"; and in October it returned again to the Metropolitan.

[113] See *Mirror*, February 17, 1894. The present writer is not
prepared to guarantee the accuracy of commendations made by
Mr. Stedman, Colonel Ingersoll, or dramatic reviewers of the age.

[114] It was at Proctor's, New York, April, 1893 — never more
popular.

season of 1871–72 in a drama, *Zip*,[115] which blended many minstrel features into a pathetic story of an old slave's devotion to the child of his master. Better known as interpreters of character were John T. Raymond, who portrayed in Colonel Sellars of Mark Twain's burlesque the Missouri slave-holder, social, friendly, hospitable, at home in all circumstances,[116] and Frank S. Chanfrau in *Kit*,[117] the famous Arkansas play which had a large vogue during the early seventies. The following decade saw marked increase in the number of plantation plays and a considerable gain in directness of approach. Raymond continued in such a play as *In Paradise*,[118] in which he appeared as the ante-bellum gentleman " from Ole Virginny, by Gad, sah," the character speciality which had brought him fame. Belasco's *May Blossom*,[119] laid on the shores of the Chesapeake, contained many plantation elements, including a rather striking example of slave fidelity. In 1884, A. R. Cazauran's *The Fatal Letter*,[120] commended by critics for its " correct presentation of Southern character," portrayed life in a Carolina family which in continuation of the Thackeray story bore the name of Esmond. One of the most popular dramas of the whole decade was Harrigan's *Pete*,[121] resembling closely an earlier minstrel sketch, which

[115] See *And Yet Another, Mirror,* January 21, 1888, (p. 6).

[116] This is the suggestion of Mr. Howells in his review of the play, *Atlantic,* June, 1875. It must be borne in mind, however, that Sellars actually had more of the West than the South in him.

[117] In a review of *The White Slave* (*Mirror,* April 8, 1882), a writer asserts that *Kit* represented probably the fullest treatment of the picturesqueness and humor of Southern life that had appeared for many years. It was not, however, a strict plantation play.

[118] New York, January, 1883.

[119] Madison Square Theatre, New York, April, 1884.

[120] Union Square, New York, April, 1884.

[121] New Park, New York, November, 1887, with Harrigan as star and producer; exceedingly popular again in 1889.

built around the general theme of slave loyalty a large
body of pathos and comedy and touched the romantically
inclined public.

The crest of the flood came in the nineties. Another re-
arrangement of the Stowe-Boucicault materials appeared
in *The Beautiful Slave*,[122] which with its tragic heroine
of mixed blood, its devoted slave, its abundant comedy,
ministered to many tastes. Opie Reid's *The Kentucky
Colonel*,[123] with McKee Rankin in the title role and Mrs.
Sidney Drew in the heroine's role, had a fairly good run
in 1892. Greene and Grismer in *The New South* [124] exhibited much of the old South, particularly in the old-
time darkey, played by James A. Herne. In 1894 New
York witnessed three dramas containing various and sun-
dry plantation elements: *Blue-Grass*,[125] a spectacular melodrama exploiting Kentucky and its best known figure, the
colonel; Mark Twain's *Pudd'nhead Wilson;* [126] and the
popular *Coon Hollow*,[127] with vivid scenic effects and vivacious negro song and dance. The following spring William
Haworth's *On the Mississippi* [128] and W. R. Goodall's contrast of Vermont and Virginia gentlemen, *The Two Colo-
nels*,[129] contributed mildly to the further elaboration of
supposed Southern character. The Kentucky tradition,
particularly the horse, the flask, and the colonel, was utilized again in Franklin Fyles' *The Governor of Kentucky*,[130]
which opened in January, 1896. Later in the same year

[122] Niblo's, New York, April, 1891.

[123] Union Square, New York, Aug., 1892.

[124] Broadway, New York, January, 1893.

[125] People's, New York, Feb., 1894; had toured previously.

[126] Herald Square, New York, April, 1894; Frank Mayo in title
role.

[127] Fourteenth Street, New York, Aug., 1894.

[128] People's, New York, February, 1895.

[129] Washington, Dec., 1894; Palmer's, New York, April, 1895.

[130] Fifth Avenue, New York.

another plantation drama, which had an echo of the Pudd'nhead theme, *The Law of the Land*,[131] received "tremendous applause." In the fall of the same year, moreover, A. C. Gunter's fairy story, *A Florida Enchantment*,[132] introduced the old plantation darkey. Pudd'nhead reverberates again in such an imitation as David Higgins' popular *At Piney Ridge*,[133] with an old octoroon and a typically devoted slave in contrast. The negroes and the romance of Kentucky blended in another drama of 1897, Valentine and Ditrichstein's *A Southern Romance*,[134] with a somewhat interesting study of the romantically restless Southern girl. The next year saw E. W. Presbrey's *A Virginia Courtship*,[135] in which W. H. Crane glorified the old Virginia gentlemen of ante-bellum days; a post-war drama, *We Uns of Tennessee*,[136] with a devoted slave who confesses murder in an effort to save his young master; and another of the elaborately staged melodramas, *Down in Dixie*.[137]

The vogue of plantation drama persisted with considerable vigor in the first decade of the present century. The spectacular melodrama was continued in such a production as Lottie Blair Parker's *Under Southern Skies*,[138] which

[131] American, New York, April; W. H. Thompson appeared as an old slave.

[132] Hoyt's, New York, Oct., 1896.

[133] American, New York, Feb., 1897.

[134] Fifth Avenue, New York, Sept., 1897; adaptation of a popular novel.

[135] Knickerbocker, New York, Jan., 1898.

[136] American, New York, May, 1898.

[137] Appeared in New York late in 1898; returned for second engagement, Star, January, 1899.

[138] Enormously popular during the first five or six years of the century. In the 1901 appearance at the Republic, New York, Grace George played the principal role; three companies presented this play 1905–06.

utilized again the theme of the agony of racial consciousness. Many old favorites repeated former successes and
new plays came in abundance. Choosing a typical year,
say 1906, we find in New York alone the presentation of
Thomas Dixon's *The Clansman*,[139] a Reconstruction story,
but suggesting the plantation at least in characterization;
H. G. Donnelly's *Carolina*,[140] a regular plantation drama,
with the large mansion, the chivalric old colonel, the lovely
heroine, the devoted mammy; Travers Vale's *The Girl of
the Sunny South*,[141] which included, in addition to the element suggested by the title, much banjo manipulation; and
H. D. Cottrell's *A Southern Vendetta*,[142] with an ornate
picture of the South Carolina mansion and the home life
of its inmates. In these years the plantation in some
fashion or other appeared in plays which might have
moderate claims to distinction. Popularity alone would
lift to a position of eminence *The Gentleman from Mississippi*[143] which set in new environment Southern character and studied the reaction. Moody's *The Faith Healer*[144]
introduced with much congruity the mystic element in
negro religion compounded of faith and superstition.
Augustus Thomas drew largely upon Kentucky character
for his *The Witching Hour*.[145] Sheldon's *The Nigger*[146]
deals principally with the more modern race prejudice,
yet the tragedy is rooted in plantation sins, may be said
to begin with the selling of a girl " down the river," the

[139] Liberty, New York, January.

[140] American, New York, September.

[141] Third Avenue, New York, November.

[142] Philadelphia, August; New Star, New York, December.

[143] Came to Bijou, New York, Sept. 29, 1908, where it had a
run of over two years. Thomas A. Wise was the Southern gentleman, Douglas Fairbanks the enterprising young " Yankee."

[144] St. Louis, March, 1909.

[145] Hackett Theatre, New York, Nov., 1907.

[146] New York, Dec., 1909.

setting is the conventional Southern mansion, and the characters include the typical Southern heroine and the plantation mammy. Belonging to contemporary theatrical history are such works as Ridgely Torrence's cycle of plays dealing with manifestations of negro psychology,[147] some of them revealing penetrating insight, and Eugene O'Neil's *The Emperor Jones*, based on the innate superstition and vanity of the negro — large theme in plantation literature — and approaching the old system closely in the fifth scene when Jones has his vision of plantation society gathered around a slave sale. Booth Tarkington's *Magnolia*, which appeared in the summer of 1923, is laid in Mississippi in 1841 and includes many definite plantation elements. The number of moving pictures which employ the plantation resource is a matter of common knowledge.[148]

[147] *Granny Maumee*, for example, is full of echoes of the old race relationships and of traits of negro character conspicuous in the tradition; witness the old darkey's effort to conjure by means of an image.

[148] Some reference to the phase has been made in chapter 1.

CHAPTER VI

THE DEVELOPMENT OF THE CONCEPTION IN POPULAR SONG

THERE was yet another agency of great power in the development of the broad conception of plantation life. This was the melody or popular song. It penetrated where the drama seldom, if ever, reached; it recurred in haunting memories when the printed romance was forgotten; in inexhaustible cycles of variations, it has been sung and whistled almost everywhere. Best beloved of all the music of the masses, the plantation refrain has from its origin exhibited undiminished vitality; and it has mightily stimulated and colored that sentimentalizing which in the general public largely determines attitudes. Madame Gabrilowitsch's testimony[1] that her first recollections of music were of negro songs sung by her father, Mark Twain, is a suggestion, if not an epitome of national experience. The body of this melody with the images it conjures up is so familiar that it has entered into the subconscious existence along with the deep impressions of early childhood. One could hardly conceive the emotional poverty of Americans in the mass were they deprived of this resource. In no way has the heart of a whole people turned more spontaneously to the life of the old regime than in this hunger for the strains from, it is supposed, the soul of black folks and for the scenes amid which such songs took their rise.

[1] *Century*, Oct., 1922.

128

In centering attention exclusively on the popular influence, we necessarily eliminate many inviting considerations of plantation song. The origin of these melodies, for one thing, constitutes an interesting problem: how far they are actually folk-songs, rooted deep in the heart of a race, products of primitive African musical instincts; to what extent they include conditions of the American history of the negro; what proportion represents improvisations, enlarged from time to time in the never-ending repetition; how many are merely adaptations of the airs which floated from parlor windows to the slaves outside or are " rifacimenti of old English, Scotch, and Irish melodies." [2]   The reflection of racial temperament in these songs might be advantageously investigated; the lighter spirit of the fields, the harvest, or the dance, in which cases there was commonly strange harmony between the music and the bodily motion; the enigmatic sadness, reaching our own day in the *Blues*, echoing, it is asserted, the wailing sorrow-song of wretches on the slave-ship bidding their homeland a last farewell; the unique concreteness of the religious imagery which hears the roll of Jordan, the thunder of the gospel train, the blast of trumpet, the golden ringing bells, the everlasting harps, which sees visions of arks and chariots, the vale of tears, the icy rivers, the unending feasts and the shining sandals and robes of the blessed. Not least significant of the facts of negro melody is its influence on music in general, on such composers of high order as Dvorak, Gottschalk, Schoenfield, Chadwick, John Powell, on other popular forms, as sailor songs, many of which are reminiscences of the strains of colored dock hands. There is, it must be remembered, a considerable body of the purely literary song, the work of serious

[2] This assertion is made by Mackay, *Life and Liberty in America* (1859).

writers like Whittier or of plantation versifiers like the
great company of which Dunbar is probably most conspicuous; from time to time one of these compositions, set
adrift in a lilt, floated down the great current of popular
melodies.

In the development of the general conception of the
plantation, four types of song have been principally influential.   In the ante-bellum period, the minstrel song
was the all-powerful musical force.   There were other
forms; the abolitionists, for example, prepared labored
rhetorical appeals to heroic action, set them to church
tunes,[3] and thus accomplished inconceivably doleful effects.
Only one anti-slavery song ever succeeded, B. R. Hanby's
Darling Nelly Gray [4] of 1856; it surely gripped the heart
of the nation, even of the South; but its imitations, including the author's efforts to repeat, were of no consequence.   At the time of the Civil War there raged the
negro jubilee of freedom — not, of course, the negro's own
song — which may be regarded as the second song-mode
of importance.   A few years later there grew up tremendous interest in the negroes' native song, particularly in
the " spiritual," an interest caused partially by the contact of Northern soldiers with plantation life and figures,
but chiefly by the extraordinarily impressive tours of the
black Jubilee Singers.   In our present age we have the
continuing vogue of the vaudeville " coon song," lineal de-
scendant of the old material airs, altered occasionally by
such fads as rag-time and jazz.

[3] See, for example, *Songs of the Free,* and *Hymns of Christian
Freedom* (Boston, 1836), *Hymns and Songs for the Friends of Free-
dom* (Middletown, 1842), and W. W. Brown's *The Anti-Slavery
Harp* (Boston, 1849).

[4] Hanby's work is treated in an article by C. B. Galbreath in
The Ohio Archaeological and Historical Quarterly, April, 1905
(14:180–215).

The history of ante-bellum minstrel song may be divided roughly into two parts (1) before Foster and (2) Foster; for this composer is surely epoch-making. Such summary analysis must not, however, obscure the vogue of the minstrel ballad before the master of this form gave it most perfect utterance. It did not require his genius to popularize the type.

The minstrel song took firm hold of American imagination in the thirties, the decade notable as a period of the beginning of the plantation tradition. A singularly inclusive popular song-book of the late twenties contains nothing remotely resembling negro ballads. Dixon achieved in 1828 and 1829 some local reputation with his *Coal Black Rose*, but it remained for *Jim Crow* to captivate a nation's ears and set its feet to jigging. The success of this ditty was phenomenal. It went into every nook and corner of the country, indeed, of the British Isles; by 1850, for example, it, or some variation, had appeared in at least three song pamphlets of Glasgow, sometimes resting demurely in the very midst of native Scotch songs. Its happy melody was adopted for more serious efforts, as Morris' *A Southern Refrain*. Parodies, imitations, and adaptations fairly swarmed; one song book of 1847 includes a Jim Crow paraphrase of Hamlet's soliloquy with a refrain:

> Shuffle off this mortal coil,
>   Do just so,
> Wheel about, and turn about,
>   And jump Jim Crow.

Within a few years many other songs were swept into favor on the tide of enthusiasm; *Coal Black Rose, Old Zip Coon, Long-tailed Blue, Settin' on a Rail, Ole Virginny Never Tire*, and others, all followed by a company of

imitations.   The appearance of a really fresh song was
an event more important than can be imagined today;
tune and words flew from mouth to mouth.   By 1840
the musical directors of the political parties had prepared
campaign jingles for the beloved tunes and in 1844, when
the presidential campaign was marked by a peculiar
amount of singing, negro ballads were by all odds the
most popular.

The appearance of the regular minstrel companies in
the forties increased greatly the number of songs and, in
the main, the vogue of the songs.   At the first performance,
New York, 1843, *Dandy Jim of Caroline* made a decided
hit and it soon became one of the favorites.   To run
through the varied treatment given Dandy Jim or his
sweetheart Dinah, in multiplied variations of the Virginia
plantation melody, is to understand how easily the public
could be fed any musical morsel with minstrel flavor.
About the same time Emmet brought out *Old Dan Tucker*,[5]
greatest of the minstrel songs before the days of Foster.
It has been said that this melody was " sung more often,
perhaps, than any song ever written " — a claim, of course,
that cannot possibly be proved.   At any rate, its popularity was immediately as great as, and much more last-
ing than, that of *Jim Crow*.   In many ways, this sprightly
melody is the last of the class of songs that endeavored
with fidelity to reproduce the true negro character.   Sentimentalism, even super-sentimentalism, took the field.   The

---

[5] The question of the composition of the music of these early
songs is extremely difficult to solve.   Henry Russell, in *Cheer,
Boys, Cheer* (London, 1895), takes credit for *Old Dan Tucker*.   His
assertion is that he hit upon the tune by speeding up to jig time
the stately church measure *Old Hundred*.   Russell also claims *Coal
Black Rose;* but since he did not reach America until after Dixon
had been singing the song for several years, the statement must be
taken with reservations.

new spirit often expressed itself in ridiculous forms but it was at best a movement to soften the grotesque and clownish aspects of negro character, to convert the hearty, though somewhat derisive laughter, into sympathy. The finest exponent of this whole endeavor was Stephen Collins Foster.

Foster's two dozen plantation songs represent a small part of his production and an infinitesimal fraction of the number of minstrel songs, but they are the best of his work and of the whole musical output of the black-face world. No other American composer has been accorded a favor so wide-spread, so abiding; and if to melt a people's heart be a meritorious achievement, then he deserves his honors. It is quite true, as critics have repeatedly pointed out, that this writer who, while yet a youth in Pennsylvania brought out his ballad of Uncle Ned, who described the Southern cane brake before he ever saw one, did not in any sense interpret the plantation as it actually existed. But the fact cannot be gainsaid that however unreal the picture he called into public consciousness, he set it there with tremendous effectiveness. It should be remembered, moreover, that not all of Foster's songs can be charged with the wistful sentimentality associated with his name. His first song, *Louisiana Belle*,[6] written in 1845, is of a very different tone; *The Glendy Burk* (1860) is a famous steamboat song; *Don't Bet Your Money on de Shanghai* (1861) and *The Camptown Races* (1850) are rollicking reflections of the sporting life of the old regime; *My Brudder Gum* (1849) and *Ring de Banjo* (1851), devoid of any illusory emotionalism, are little more than farcical.

[6] Published, 1848. The dates of publication here recorded are from the *Catalogue of First Editions of Stephen C. Foster*, Library of Congress, 1915.

Foster's real work, however, is not in these lighter melodies. His peculiar genius lay in his ability to take a simple, universal emotion, as old as *Ecclesiastes* and as fresh in his day as the song in *The Princess*, the futile yearning for days that can come no more, and give to it a plantation setting. This, briefly, is the theme of *The Old Folks at Home* (1851), of *My Old Kentucky Home* (1853), of *Massa's in the Cold Ground* (1852), of *Old Black Joe* (1860). The music, of twin-birth with the words, was singularly appropriate. The conjunction of motive and melody with setting resulted in fixing with extraordinary vividness the plantation memory in the public affection. Whether an audience be listening to a prima donna in an unaffected encore, whether a casual group has gathered about a phonograph, whether the plain American endeavors to hum for himself a most familiar air, all are, for the moment,

> " Still longing for the old plantation
> And for the old folks at home."

Enriched by Foster's work, which ever afterward proved the leader, minstrel song swept on to new conquests of the popular imagination. The melodies not only delighted huge audiences who thronged the regular performances but were printed in manifold forms for wide dissemination. By the middle of the Civil War, the Christy organization had put out half a dozen volumes of their series of plantation melodies, White and Buckley had each sponsored four separate works, and at least a dozen more collections of minstrel songs were on the market. There was, of course, a liberal representation of these ballads in the miscellaneous song books, as in Beadle's fifteen volumes of the *Dime Song Book*. From various sources comes interesting evidence of the vogue of the airs. An indignant father writes a leading magazine that he regrets the purchase of a fine piano because his daughter will play nothing but these " modern melodies." Various authors [7] put minstrel ballads in the mouths of black characters, one of the writers noting apologetically that the minstrel song was really a typical American institution. The popularity of these melodies was seized upon by authors of other songs. A well known volume of Western ballads shows more than half of the verses set to minstrel airs.[8] At the approach of the Civil War, scores of patriotic hymns were devised for the popular tunes of minstrelsy; one particularly interesting specimen, *We'll Never Give up Dixie*, was an adaptation of Emmet's song, the Southern battle anthem.

A cursory examination of the content of the ante-bellum minstrel melodies reveals interesting variety in subject-matter. The most effective of all the songs were the sentimental types of Foster and his imitators. A few of these followed the lead of Hanby's *Darling Nelly Gray* in touching presentations of the grief of family separation. Romance was, of course, featured in a multitude of the ballads; some of these attempt a ridiculous loftiness of tone, as *She's Black but That's No Matter*, with its account of roses and woodbine twined by silvery flowing streams; others reveal equal absurdity in a straining for heightened pathos, as *Weep, Pompey, Weep*, laid " on a lone barren shore war de wild roaring billow " harmonizes with a spiritual desolation. Many are as foolishly ambitious in other respects; in *Tilda Horne* the love-lorn hero likens himself in restlessness to " Massa Shakespeare's Hamlet "

[7] G. P. R. James in *The Old Dominion* is guilty of a curious anachronism in having a negro about the time of Nat Turner's insurrection sing *Old Uncle Ned*.

[8] *Put's Original California Songster*, San Francisco, 1868.

and in *Jordan Is a Hard Road* the happy plantation blacks
sneer at the English ladies of anti-slavery leanings. Some
of the melodies are dance pieces; others celebrate plantation festivals, barbecues, coon hunts, and the like. The
parody is an unusually prominent form, sometimes on
other plantation melodies, as *Uncle Tim the Toper,* a burlesque of Foster's *Uncle Ned.* Many are broadly comic:
in *Rosa Lee,* for example, the heroine wears a shoe which
would make a cradle, and the lovely damsel of *Down by
the River* has " lips like luscious beefsteaks." A few of
the songs, remarkably few, are real narratives of plantation histories. It may be of interest to note in passing
that many of these early melodies have a strangely modern
note; *Oh, Silver Shining Moon* and *Take Me Back to
Tennessee* are not unlike the conventional song that may
be heard in almost any vaudeville house of today.

One of the most interesting of the popular musical reflections of plantation life is the darkey " jubilee " song,
immensely prevalent during and just after the Civil War.
This form is not to be confused with the " spiritual "
later sung by the troupes of emancipated slaves who were
known as " the jubilee singers." The hymn in its original
presentation was an artificial composition, the work of
writers who, sympathizing with the slave, endeavored to
enter imaginatively into his emotion at the approach of
freedom. But though it took its rise in the relatively
serious feeling of enthusiasts, the song soon became merely
a specialized minstrel melody, for it was incorporated in
the programs of burnt-cork entertainment and was reprinted in the numerous song books. Hanby, already famous for his *Darling Nelly Gray,* composed one of the
earliest of the jubilees, *Ole Shady* (1861); but the great
name in this connection is that of Henry C. Work [9] who

[9] Work is the composer of many other songs, including *Marching Through Georgia* and *Father, Come Home,* according to a

utilized for his musical efforts the acquaintance he had made with negro character while serving the Underground Railroad system. Work's fame was the result of his first great hit, *The Kingdom Coming,* which later called forth a eulogy from General Sherman, but the composer maintained his reputation with several other songs equally popular, such as *Babylon's Fallen* and *Wake, Nicodemus.* The imitations which inevitably follow a truly successful song came rapidly and before the struggle was half over, the jubilee was a well known and widespread song mode of the Union sympathizers. The general theme of all these melodies is fairly constant: the negroes' delight at the prospect of emancipation, the reversal of normal plantation procedure, and the frantic hullabaloo of celebration. Most of the songs have definite, though not unkind, references to the old order of plantation life and were therefore not without influence in elaborating as well as popularizing the conception. It is interesting, if not exactly pertinent in this connection, to note that these jubilee chorals represent somewhat crudely a song spirit that obtained on many of the estates, as the emboldened blacks with increasing candor revised their old psalms of eschatological hope to bear a more terrestrial significance.[10]

Shortly after the Civil War there sprang up unusual interest in the actual song of the negro on the plantation as opposed to the travesties rendered by minstrels. More

---

biography by B. G. Work in *The Songs of Henry Clay Work* (privately printed, New York, ca. 1920).

[10] In Elizabeth Johnson's *Christmas in Kentucky* (Wash., 1892) there is a striking account of the parade of slaves, singing in barbaric chant,

> "Ethiopie, Ethiopie, hole out yo' han'
> An' get yo' piece ob de promise' lan'."

One of the most vivid treatments of this slave psychology is in Grace King's *Bayou L'Ombre* (*Harper's,* July, 1887).

largely than may be suspected, this new passion for the genuine African melody resulted from the contact of intelligent Northern soldiers with darkies in their native haunts; for it must be remembered that since the corruption of minstrelsy, which had at best developed only the comic qualities of negro song, the North as a whole was entirely ignorant of the great volume of real plantation melody.   After their stay in the South, however, hosts of Northern warriors came home with charming memories of the singing blacks and some of the more intellectually minded set about recording and interpreting the extraordinary songs.   By 1867 Allen, Ware, and Garrison had brought out a carefully edited volume, *Slave Songs in the United States* (New York); the same year Higginson contributed a suggestive essay to the *Atlantic*,[11] and a few months later J. M. Brown published in *Lippincott's* [12] a general analysis of the kinds of song.   The practice thus inaugurated has continued,[13] enlarged after a season by the collections of Harris [14] and fellow writers of Southern birth.   Recent investigation in the characteristic folk elements of the negro ditties have not only proved fruitful for this kind of scholarship but have produced many delightful compilations of the songs, one of the most authentic being T. W. Talley's *Negro Folk Rhymes* [15] (New York, 1921).

Far more influential on the popular mind than these

[11] *Negro Spiritual,* June; see also *Army Life in a Black Regiment* (Boston, 1870).

[12] December, 1868: *Songs of the Slave.*

[13] See series by W. E. Barton, *New England Magazine,* 1898 and 1899.

[14] *Uncle Remus and His Friends* (Boston, 1892) has a specially interesting body of these songs.

[15] This volume includes a collection of exceedingly interesting pieces and is prefaced with an illuminating essay.

somewhat academic interpretations of negro song was the
power of the music itself as rendered by groups of colored
singers touring the North. The pioneers of this activity
were the Fisk University Jubilee Singers whose artistic
triumph, beginning with their first trip in 1871, was
astounding. Literally they came, they sang, they con-
quered. Greeted somewhat sneeringly at first, referred to
as " Beecher's negro minstrels " in New York, they converted cynics and scoffers into admirers and eulogists.
The very contrast in tone and sentiment with the jingles
of the burnt-cork performers heightened the effect. Great
audiences, one of which numbered 40,000 people, were en-
tranced. The North for the first time was hearing the
inimitable melodies, the weird, plaintive longings fraught
with spiritual symbolism, falling in the sad and sighing
cadence unique in a nation's musical experience. Cultured
critics testify that no sensation of their lives was quite
comparable to their emotional reaction to such memorable
numbers as *Nobody Knows the Trouble I See, Steal Away,
Swing Low, Sweet Chariot.* The vogue was established
and from that day to this real darkey singers have enjoyed favor.[16] The value of this type of song for the
tradition lay chiefly in the revelation of certain aspects
of negro temperament, the mystic religious quality, the
fondness for a story, the yearning [17] for freedom, the concreteness of imagery, the long-suffering patience, and other
distinctive racial traits.

The most pervasive musical influence of the last three
or four decades, so far as the conception of the plantation

[16] A performance in New York City, January 17, 1923, was
greatly appreciated.

[17] Undoubtedly many spirituals were not so obvious as they
may have seemed: such a song as *Go Down, Moses,* had in the
negro mind a temporal as well as a Biblical or religious significance.

is concerned, has been the popular vaudeville song, a heritage from the older minstrel form. While these crude melodies of the modern variety show may be easily identified as scions of the old songs famous in the days of the Christy singers and the Beadle song books, there have been, of course, new developments. The nineties saw the new vogue of " ragtime," of which *Oh, Didn't He Ramble* and *A Hot Time in the Old Town* may be cited as examples of extreme types; a few years later there was an artistic epidemic of the illustrated song when *Dear Old Dixie* and hosts of others were sung to the accompaniment of lantern slides; within recent years the many hued "Blues" have streamed out of Memphis, covering the nation in incredibly short time.[18] But the coon song remains essentially the same in at least the important aspects of amazing popularity and consummate unreality. The reach of this form into the affection of the non-aesthetic masses — indeed into no inconsiderable fraction of the " highbrows," if the truth could be known — is wellnigh immeasurable. It may be assumed that on this very day in this most enlightened year of grace there have been sung scores, nay hundreds, of these jingles in every important theatrical center of America; that every music store of any pretension has flaunted scores of the sheets, illustrated usually with highly colored scenes of plantation felicities; that the dispensers of phonograph records have diffused the canned melody in almost car-load lots; that myriad feet have yielded to the temptation of jazz. Even to guess what proportion of our citizenship has today reacted in some fashion to the appeal of these harmonies would be hazardous but it could not be an altogether wild estimate to reckon the number in millions.

[18] The preface of James W. Johnson's *The Book of American Negro Poetry* (New York, 1922) contains an interesting account of the rise of ragtime and jazz music.

The contrast of these songs, repetitions rather than variations of themes long threadbare, with the sincere and heart-felt folk ballads of the blacks' own composition is striking. Thirty years ago a critic suggested a formula for the composition of popular coon songs, recommending that they be incoherent, reminiscent if desired, distinctly commonplace, and "placed in a locality known only to the geographers or the police." [19] In large measure the directions have been scrupulously followed. The content of the majority of the musical effusions may be described as the utilization, or more accurately the tireless imitation, of stock elements both incoherent and commonplace. The more conspicuous of these elements are easily discernible: a romantic river, the survival, perhaps, of Foster's influence — for how impoverished would be our song literature without the inevitable Swanee; [20] happy levee scenes along the river shore; glorious moonlight that sleeps more sweetly on Southern banks than anywhere else; the gay girl of Dixie who may be white or black, tender or capricious, according to the mood of the composer, but who is ever incomparable and irresistible; the darkey frolic, specially the break-down; the arms of mammy and her crooning lullaby; a reminiscence of " Ole Massa " or of " Missy with her lovely silver hair "; the gustatory delights of chicken, 'possum, or watermelon; a cycle of songs on each of the Southern states; another cycle on the various causes

[19] See *Hints for Song Composers, New York Dramatic Mirror,* July 25, 1896. The reference to geographical location is given added point by the history of Foster's choice of the Swanee river; he knew nothing of the river, of course, but elected it because of the melody of the name; his first inclination was to use the Yazoo.

[20] For example, in the season of 1922–23, Eddie Cantor sang with great applause a song on this theme; another was featured largely in the popular negro comedy *Liza,* a characteristic levee scene of the Mississippi being placed along the banks of the river.

that can induce the " blues." Occasionally a new motive is introduced; in a shop window, for example, there repose side by side a song constructed around the somewhat familiar declaration of purpose, " I'm going to plant myself in my old plantation home," and a song with the novel — and deliciously irrelevent — application of a prominent literary theme of the hour, a tribute to " Lovin' Sam, the sheik of Alabam'."

It may seem to the thoughtful mind inconceivable that these melodies, reiterated through nearly a century and now more or less meaningless, could still make appealing contributions to popular imagination; but they all have what is accepted as the plantation flavor and " the flavor lasts," relished by successive generations of enthusiasts. In an age when fiction and drama have veered away from the romantic, popular song remains the agency which most universally, most persistently, suggests plantation types and customs, which perpetually re-creates, or at least maintains the vitality of, the plantation in the common conception.

CHAPTER VII

THE CONCEPTION COMPARED WITH THE ACTUAL

I. *Economic and Social*

A. *Introduction*

THE preceding chapters have dealt with the development of the tradition. We now turn in these final chapters to an analysis of that tradition for a study of its accuracy. The general plan will be to consider first the topics as they occur in the tradition, then as they actually obtained upon the plantation. The parallelism cannot be made exact in every particular. Exposition must necessarily be involved, sometimes obscure; but the method will be followed as consistently as possible.

As fundamental to this whole phase of the investigation, a general principle may be stated: the tradition omits much plantation truth and at the same time exaggerates freely certain attractive features of the old life. This somewhat sweeping indictment is made in no sense of sophisticated disdain for a theme dear to many hearts. Such distortions, resulting from the idealization of a given body of material, characterize the romantic mode in general; witness, for example, Scott's treatment of the past. If the judgment expressed here and in subsequent pages seems categorically harsh, it may be modified to the extent of an admission that the inaccuracies indicated are more largely quantitative than qualitative.

A brief emphasis of the last-named truth may be in order here. The student of actual plantation conditions discovers unmistakable evidence which points to the existence of an order of life in a few limited localities which approximates in real social charm the traditional social charm of the romances. In a few limited localities, be it remembered, this order existed; in tide-water Virginia, in the rice districts of South Carolina, in the lower Mississippi Valley, and, to a smaller extent, in certain Piedmont sections. The popular legend, however, ascribes this setting of splendor, this manner of cultured magnificence, to the whole South. There were, for example, fine mansions, but few Southern farms boasted a Westover House. There were beautiful girls, but Dixie was not over-populated with radiant damsels whose presence converted alike ante-bellum palace or post-bellum cottage into " a feasting presence full of light." There were devoted blacks, many of them, whose faith and faithfulness constitute a winsome chapter in the history of national character, but the makers of the tradition are hardly warranted in including upon the roll of dusky honor virtually every slave who ever nursed a baby, curried a horse, or swung a languid hoe in the cotton patch. The uniform portrayal of the very noblest, elements which may have existed in places, as the normal has resulted in idealization of the whole.

One of the most notable discrepancies, sufficient in itself to establish general inadequacy, is in the tacit assumption by the tradition that plantation society was feudalistically tri-partite: the lordly planter, the slaves, the " po' white trash." Such an estimate leaves out of consideration a fairly potent and a really large factor, the yeomanry of the South, comparable perhaps to the English farmers, but not to the English gentlemen. Bassett, careful student of the period, has drawn attention to this error.[1] " This class of men has received but little attention from those who have written of Southern society, and yet it

---

[1] *Slavery in the State of North Carolina,* chap. 3.

was the backbone of that society. There was little that was ideal about such men. They were humdrum, but they were honest, pious, and substantial, and they were numerous." These farmers, it is true, had many qualities ascribed by the tradition to the planters; they were not inhospitable, they sometimes shared the sectional point of view, and they were at times possessed of reasonable wealth. Most of them, however, made no pretence to spectacular living; they were not given to ancestor worship, though appreciation of blood in man or beast has ever marked the Southern temperament; they were not aristocratic in political view, being chiefly supporters of the Jeffersonian doctrines; they were not aristocratic even in religious preference, for most of them embraced the evangelical faiths as represented by the Baptists, the Methodists, or the Presbyterians. With moderate land-holdings and with few slaves, these small planters, not greatly unlike the substantial farming classes of other sections, offered little material for romanticists. Here, then, is a great element of society, its solidity if not its ornamentation, with which the glamorous plantation legend failed to make connection. Such an inaccuracy is not a casual one; it is not meaningless; it is basic and it is significant of the method in general.

The tradition seems to be wholly reliable in one important respect; it presents the plantation ideal, the great plantation ideal, as dominant in Southern life. It was the large planter, chiefly, who touched the outside world, in Congress, at summer resorts, in fiction. To be a great planter was the ambition of many. The large plantation was the *ne plus ultra* of society. The towns — strange contrast to the modern order — were, in effect, subsidiary to the country. Phillips [2] says of the rice section: " The

[2] *American Negro Slavery,* 97; see also Wallace, *Henry Laurens,*

towns were in sentiment and interest virtually a part of the plantation community. The merchants were plantation factors; the lawyers and doctors had country patrons; — and many prospering townsmen looked toward plantation retirement, carrying, as it did, in some degree, the badge of gentility, as the crown of their careers." Generally speaking, the statement is true of all the more highly developed areas of the plantation zone. The supremacy of the great estate in the thinking of the South cannot be successfully challenged, even though such estates were much fewer in number than has been supposed. The plantation was the ideal community of the South, " its laws and usages as dominant socially as its economic influence was dominant politically." [3]

B. *The Economic Basis*

The true economic basis of life is hardly suggested in the tradition of plantation splendor. It is not surprising, to be sure, that technical matters should find little representation in distinctly romantic themes; one does not expect in a cow-boy story a record of the economic evolution of ranching or a curve showing the fluctuation in the market at any given period. It is not just, moreover, to ask of writers of fiction more than, primarily, a good story appropriately placed. But however natural the omission, however justifiable, the fact remains that to this extent the tradition has fallen short of covering the whole life and is therefore misleading. The economic influences that played upon plantation development were of large significance.

124; Turner, *Social and Economic Forces in American History*, 227-8; Dodd, *The Cotton Kingdom*, 24, ff.

[3] Brown, *The Lower South in American History*, 46.

There is nowhere in the tradition, for example, any reference to the actual beginnings of the plantation system, the first century of rather primitive existence. The tradition assumes a finished product, sprung full formed from the English life. Certain fictional treatments, like Thackeray's *Virginians* or Miss Johnston's *Prisoners of Hope*, suggest some of the early anxieties over the problems of production and marketing and over the English laws of commerce. But most of the stories are laid late when the plantations had grown into a province of some social stability and political power. The indented servants composed a considerable factor in the colonial plantation life, but, valuable to the tradition neither as splendid ancestors nor devoted serfs, they are largely ignored. Miss Johnston elects one of this group as the hero of the novel to which reference has been made, but Landless differs from true plantation gentlemen only in political considerations. St. George Tucker introduces this group in *Hansford*, but largely for decorative effect; their very number enhances the glory of their lord. Now in English literature for many decades after Jamestown was settled, the American plantations were regarded largely as asylums for just this class; but our own native tradition is discreetly silent concerning this element.

There are other economic factors about which the tradition has little to say. The organization of labor is suggested, if at all, only in the persons of overseers and negro drivers, stock figures for villainy. Save in the most sympathetic reminiscences, there is hardly an example of a mild overseer; and the driver is not more generally favored, though Hildreth records one so merciful that he resigns and Simms [4] personifies loyalty in his Abram. In the

----

[4] In *Snake in the Cabin*. Contrast, however, Mingo, in *The Loves of the Driver*.

main, these figures have no significance for the routine of plantation management but are stage characters for the elaboration of some thesis. Systems of labor, task or gang, are not in the tradition. The problem of the relative value of slave and free labor, a question that has interested successive generations of thinkers, certainly is not illuminated by plantation romance — unless we may draw an inference from Ben of Mrs. Hale's *Liberia* who declined freedom because he knew it meant harder work. One of the most common misrepresentations is in the matter of the size of estates. Almost unfailingly the romancers assume a great realm bounded only "by blue horizon walls." There were, as a matter of fact, some large holdings; such properties as those of Byrd, Robert Carter, Washington, Henry Laurens, in colonial days, or of Houmas, Hairston, or Nathaniel Heywood in ante-bellum times, come to mind. But colossal estates were the exception, not the rule. Over certain zones, as most of North Carolina and Georgia, there were few big places. Page justly affirms [5] that the average Southern estate was small, that few Southerners owned negroes, that most of these possessed but a small number.

It would be futile in the present connection to linger over the great body of economic details, fundamental to any correct understanding of the plantation system, which finds no representation in the popular romance. The tradition is singularly deficient in definition of the plantation; it throws no light on the causes that underlay the origin of the system; it is vague concerning the subsequent development, the history and the influence of the various staples, the larger epochs of migration, the status of the several plantation zones at successive periods, the varia-

[5] *Scribner's Magazine,* November, 1904. This matter is further discussed in Edward Ingle, *Southern Side-Lights.*

tions of plantation economy in different states; it gives no idea of the organization of labor, the classification of slave service,[6] the task and gang systems, the proportion of skilled workmen; it illuminates dimly the mooted point of the relative efficiency of this labor; it refers only in horrible pictures of abolition fancy to the domestic slave traffic; it touches lightly, if ever, the monopolistic tendency of the system, the swallowing up of the small unit by the large with the consequent weakening as political factors of the yeomanry; it leaves no definite conception of the economic achievements of the system as a whole.

In only one serious matter is the tradition true to the actual economic life. This is in regard to the general precariousness of economic life, a condition arising from a certain thriftlessness, from the despoiling of fertility, from ignorance of scientific methods in agriculture, from ineffective and unreliable labor, and from other minor causes; a condition that culminated frequently in bankruptcy with the break-up of an estate and, sometimes, a westward migration. So strongly set is the tradition toward glorification, however, that the romantic tendency is to attribute the economic calamity to villainous overseers, grasping factors, or other causes not under the owner's control.[7] The fundamental wastefulness of the system, the persistent sense of threatened economic decay, these are confessed in many of the keenest portrayals from Tucker's *Valley of the Shenandoah* to Mrs. Harrison's *Crow's Nest* or Sidney Lanier's *Corn*. Bankruptcy, or at least great financial stringency, resulting in the dissolution of slave bonds, is a useful theme not only in the abolition indictments

[6] Some of these features occur, of course, in abolition works; but the abiding tradition is largely that one developed during the romantic period.

[7] These conditions, in fact, often were the cause.

but also in such stories of pathetic retrospect as Page's *Ole 'Stracted*. Migrations, prompted by actual failure or by the obvious need of larger economic opportunity, constitute a strong theme from the days of Carruthers and Paulding and are recorded in many of the reminiscences, like Mrs. Smedes'. In so far as it witnesses to a prevailing economic uncertainty, the tradition is true to fact. There were occasional good profits, of course, but the plantation was subject to such vicissitudes that one feels the chances were against it. The process of tillage rapidly wore out the soil, a fact realized not long after the founding of Jamestown, deplored by Washington, and fought by ante-bellum planters with never more than negligible success. Only a few plantations ever realized anything that approximated economic self-sufficiency. This dependence of the planters galled many Southerners. " From the rattle with which the nurse tickles the ear of the infant to the shroud that covers the cold form of the dead," declared an orator of 1855,[8] " everything comes to us from the North." There was never as wide-spread wealth in the South as has been thought. The illusion of sectional affluence was sometimes achieved by partisans [9] who resorted to the simple device of including slaves in the items of aggregate wealth and excluding them in the estimates of per capita wealth. Distress, even desolation, marked many of the older sections during the late periods. Planters were almost constantly making a kind of exodus from worn-out areas to newer fields. " The plantation regime was a broad billow moving irresistibly westward and leaving a trough behind." In the general consideration of presenting a fairly constant real or impending economic

[8] Quoted by Olmsted, *Seaboard Slave States*, II, 186..

[9] See articles by Henry A. Wise and Ellwood Fisher, *DeBow's Review*, July, 1857, and August, 1849, respectively.

depression, the tradition has approached fact more closely than at any other point in the range of economic life.

C. *The Structure of Society*

Though the legend is but dully luminous with economic light, it is aflame with social brilliance: the glamour of feudalistic splendor in the whole composition of society, of picturesque recreations, of charming manner, of cultivated personality, of rich life in mansions that stand as temples to the religion of hospitality. It is not all radiance, to be sure; sometimes there is a curious interplay of enigmatic half lights, sometimes there are deep shadows; but even these bear a certain distinction and are recognized as principally aristocratic shadings. On the social materials the romancers have loosed their imagination and have expended without stint their artistic energies. The result is that over-statement is as common in the social treatment as omission was in the economic consideration. The tradition, for example, manifests little interest in the number that composed a gang or the labor that made a task, cares nothing for the difference between a full and a three-quarters hand or for the amount of furlough granted pregnant women; instead, the romance seizes upon a bandanna glistening in the sun, upon a coon hunt, a break-down, a mammy's lullaby, and multiplies these things indefinitely.

The feudalistic structure of society is probably the foremost large fact reflected in the tradition. " Master and man — arch and pier — arch above, pier beneath," these dying words of Agricola Fusiler represent the creed of plantation civilization as interpreted by the romanticists. The literary tradition makes much out of this order. George Tucker and Kennedy recognized it; Cooke presented in the person of Squire Effingham a champion of this order and attempts in *Henry St. John* an analysis;

most of the post-bellum writers assumed it almost as axiomatic. The general conception of a great privileged class, living in little isolated kingdoms, served by hosts of subordinates, enjoying hereditary rights to a sort of social primacy, this idea is firmly fixed in all artistic portrayal of plantation life. Variations on the central theme occur; the struggle of the merely rich to enter the charmed circle forms one motive; the efforts of an uncommonly successful overseer to establish himself as a full-fledged planter is another; the persistence of ante-bellum lines of social distinction into post-bellum conditions — witness W. H. Page's *Nicholas Worth* — represents another derivation of the same idea; the mesalliance, occurring in even such stories of democratic Georgia as Harris' *Mingo* or Thompson's *The Balance of Power*, is one approach to the question of caste. A dramatic figure in the tradition, considered a by-product of this feudalistic structure, is the " po' white." In abolition stories he is frequently a mute indictment of the system, another " man with the hoe "; in some less violent tale, he may be a tool in the hands of his betters; in the apologetic treatment he is often made the scape-goat for many of the sins of slavery. Sometimes he merely broods over his wrongs, an ominous brooding, prophetic of later class struggle. Everywhere, though, he is recognized as the lowest of the castes, less blessed, usually, than the black slave. In many other distinctive fashions the tradition emphasizes the feudalistic nature of society: in pride of birth and love of place; in recreations, as, for example, the tournament modeled on the fashion of the days of Richard; in a reminiscent longing for the good old days when government was in the hands of competent aristocrats, when, as Unc' Edinburg says, "didn' nuttin' but gent'mens vote, an' dee took dee dram, and vote out loud."

In its various acknowledgments of feudalism, both in the spirit of the rural society and in certain institutional survivals, the tradition is close to the fact. The planters believed, to a certain extent, that their society approximated the social order of the chivalric period, that it was a personification of Carlyle's ideal. The similarity in general structure between the Southern plantation and historic English manor was noted by such travelers as Eddis, Lyell, and Van Buren, was pointed out by the negro, Douglass, was the boast of many Southerners of the period, and has been discussed by scholars since the Civil War. Further actual evidence of a sort of feudalism may be obtained from a study of the judicial and governmental qualifications; from the sports and recreations; from the literary fashions; from the conventions of home life; from religious and legal modes; from conversations; from the cleavage of social circles; from the autonomy, as far as consistent with state administration, of the individual estates; from the excessive chaperonage of woman; from the deep-rooted land-holding instincts; from certain conceptions of education; and from other public and private considerations. This attitude, controlling many social ideals, goes far toward explaining the peculiar status of plantation life.

The tradition, then, conforms roughly to the fact in registering the prevalence of feudalistic survivals; it departs sharply, however, in many inferences drawn. The pleasant romances suggest, for example, that since feudalism was relatively well established, there was a corresponding medieval splendor, a luxury of life for the leisure classes not unlike the reputed richness of the period of knightly magnificence. No point in the whole study deserves more careful investigation than the question of the amount of social brilliance. It seems reasonably certain that in some sections of the South, particularly those districts mentioned earlier in this chapter, there was a rather fine scale of life, the expression often of true taste, made possible by some affluence, expressing itself in appropriate home decorations.   Crevecoeur called the life around Charleston [10] " the gayest in America "; and even before his day an unknown visitor [11] had found Southern planters " more like gentlemen of fortune than any other settlers in America."   From that time on, most of the travelers in the South were impressed with the loveliness of home life in these sections.   Olmstead himself refers [12] to the rice planters as " having less vulgar display and more intrinsic elegance than in any distinct class among us." There was a rather notable appreciation of good furniture, of silverware, of many of the distinctive modes of interior decoration.   There was a stateliness, in certain districts, extending even to the elaborate epitaphs on monuments in cherished burying grounds; there was a social eagerness that encouraged the pageantry of entertainment.   Even in the less prosperous, less pretentious zones of the slavery society there were estates that maintained an impressive domestic life.   There was frequently, too, as a mark of society in general, an ease, a grace, a cordiality, hardly to be matched in any American society, equal to, in fact, the most cultured circles of old European countries.   But when all is said and done, the tradition of silver and shining glass, of illimitable luxury, as marking the South as a whole is freely overdrawn, is often fanciful.   The homes of real social culture existed, but they were not proportionately numerous.   One of the most accurate of

[10] *Letters,* letter 9.

[11] *American Husbandry,* quoted in Callendar's *Selections from Economic History.*

[12] *Seaboard Slave States,* II, 138.

Southern scholars, A. H. Stone, affirms: [13] " There is no more pathetically untrue picture than that of the typical ante-bellum planter rolling in wealth and living a life of luxurious idleness." Professor Turner's [14] judgment may be taken as summing up this matter: " It had never been a luxurious society."

Among the specific by-products of this feudalistic richness, none has been more dramatically emphasized than the culture of the plantation gentry. Abolition onslaught has vied with native apologetics in elaborating the intellectual content, the scintillating artistic finish of the old regime. More ambitious romancers have claimed for this social order the philosophic tone of Greece, the dominant political energy of Rome, and the beauty of chivalry softened by the spiritual quality of Christianity. Mrs. Holmes' New England heroine is amazed by the culture on a Georgia plantation, surpassing everything in the vicinity of the stern and rock-bound coast; Mrs. Southworth's knights of Dixie astonish Europe with their social polish; in one romance a breakfast-table conversation runs playfully through several languages; in many novels Mr. Pope and Dr. Johnson, to say nothing of the ever-present Lord Byron, are quoted with the unconcern of a modern citizen's reference to his morning newspaper. Every form of the tradition accentuates this ease of perfect culture. When we investigate this condition to find how much of it actually prevailed on the plantation, we face again the quantitative exaggeration. There were many highly educated planters, from the days of William Byrd on, and most of these men manifested extraordinary felicity in the social utilization of such culture as they possessed. The

[13] *The Negro and Agricultural Development, Annals American Academy,* Jan., 1910.

[14] *Social and Economic Forces in American History,* 238.

effect of education on the Southern temperament was not
to produce the "Dryasdust" but the cultivated gentleman.
Certain plantations were justly famed for high intellectual
interests; many mansions could show creditable libraries;
an appreciable number of planters sent their boys to college, frequently to Northern schools, and employed tutors
for their daughters. Society in the more conspicuous expressions of forum, pulpit, or printed page, yes, even conversation in certain circles, was remarkable for a mastery
of parts of classical literature; no people could make larger
use of such a resource. Much of the power of personality
which marked Southern leadership was based on the confidence that comes from wide, if not profound, knowledge
and the readiness with which that knowledge could be
made available. In simple justice, let it be recorded that
the plantation zone could point to not altogether rare
examples of erudite men and to many examples of su-
perbly balanced development. Having made all possible
allowance for individual excellence, we face the stubborn
fact that the plantation system, thought of in terms of the
whole, operated powerfully against anything like wide-
spread culture. Isolation was detrimental alike to schools
and to common resorts for intellectual concourse. Emphasis on caste, to which reference has been made, served to
weaken the great middle class, always the moving force
in popular education.[15] A small element of the leading
group never enthusiastically supported public education.[16]
Illiteracy was distressingly great.[17] The whole plantation
system was lamentably unproductive of achievement in
the ways of arts and letters; many explanations, some

[15] See summary of the influence of the plantations on education
in Knight, *Public Education in the South* (Boston, 1922).

[16] See *The State's Duties* in *DeBow's Review*, Feb., 1856.

[17] Olmsted, *Seaboard Slave States*, II, 176.

sound and adequate ones, have been offered, but the fact cannot be gainsaid. Talented as were many planters, the system as a whole was by no means as rich in cultural value as is the plantation of romance.

A resultant of the feudalism of society was provincialism, which looms as large in fact as in fancy. The interpretation of the tradition may, however, be questioned. In plantation legends, this quality is associated with a "splendid isolation" resulting in conservatism of delightfully archaic flavor, in the flaming love of liberty which Burke emphasized, an emphasis, by the way, which the planters themselves hugely enjoyed. As a matter of cold fact, this condition of life is responsible for a stubborn pride which sometimes took the form of self-praise, a characteristic satirized by Mr. Dooley [18] — though it is doubtful whether there was as much boastfulness in the old South as has been reported by unfriendly critics — and is responsible for an excessive individualism which effectually prevented much co-operation or mutual helpfulness. "Of all descriptions of men," despairingly said Colonel Allston,[19] who ought to know what he was talking about, "planters are the least given to acting together in combination."

One of the large, one of the largest, facts in the actual structure of society receives in the tradition, except for abolition broadsides, scant attention: the influence of slavery upon white character. The white South, as it has been said, sat in the shadow of the Ethiopian. It is not

[18] " He did not boast iv his section iv the counthry. A thrue Southerner niver does. It wud ill become him to suggest that th' South is annything thin th' fairest spot of Gawd's footstool, inhabited by th' bravest men, and th' loveliest and most varchous women, th' most toothsome booze, and th' fastes' ponies in th' wurruld."— *Dissertations by Mr. Dooley* (New York, 1906).

[19] See address published in *DeBow's Review*, June, 1854.

conceivable that this shadow could have failed to tinge, to a certain extent, not only customs but also character. Anti-slavery writers made much of this influence; it is, in truth, the text of a considerable body of preaching, of which *Dred* is the best known example; but the romantic tradition of glorification falls strangely silent or contents itself at best with delicately veiled hints. The student of the facts of plantation life is conscious of many questions which the tradition makes no effort to answer. What effect did slavery have upon the purity of life, upon the unrevealed thought as well as the deed? [20] How far did it go toward brutalizing feeling,[21] toward creating indifference to lower classes, toward so petrifying sensibilities that, even in a society marked by real sympathy and sweet charity, justice was often not understood? Was slavery productive of indolence upon the part of white character, of disapprobation of hand labor, of the lack of discipline gained by the accomplishment of a task? Did the presence of an inferior race, held in bondage, stimulate violence, born of despotic individualism and of irresponsible mastery? Did slavery encourage intellectual intolerance and repression of free speech? How much of domestic chaos and of the prodigality of great estates can be attributed to the enforced labor on the part of a reluctant class? How far did black superstition reach into white life? Did slavery dull artistic faculties and make futile whatever artistic impulse may have existed? Such questions [22] are

---

[20] Unchastity will be considered in more detail under race relations.

[21] This influence, perhaps the gravamen of abolition writing, has been noted by Southern writers; see Sherwood Bonner's *Colton's Lesson*, one of the stories in her *Dialect Tales*.

[22] These topics are of prime importance in a full presentation of plantation society; in the present connection, however, they cannot be given adequate treatment because they are not prominent enough in the popular conception to justify the space.

barely suggested in the tradition of uniform joy; they confront squarely the student of fact.

Of all the probable effects of slavery upon the whites, only the violence of life, a resultant in some degree of uncontrolled power, receives liberal representation in the later tradition. Immorality, which bulked large in the abolition chronicles, is diverted in the post-bellum treatment to the tragedy of tainted blood, a sensational theme of loveliness that beats frail wings of hope against the bars of convention and finds only an ending of despair. Violence of temper, in itself both an effect of slavery and a minor expression of feudalism, continued as an inviting subject. In the tradition this quality is chiefly presented as a fine imperiousness or, at worst, unreasoning hot-headedness. Even the most sympathetic writer, as Page, admits freely the irascible temper, the swift fits of ungovernable passion. Sometimes this mood crystallizes in the duel,[23] a popular motive from the days of Carruthers. Occasionally it takes more permanent form in the fashion of a feud.[24] In certain retrospective pieces, the duel, grim reality of olden times, is turned to purpose of comedy. In this use of violence, the tradition has adopted a fact of real importance on the plantation as it actually existed. The duel, for example, impressed a number of visitors, as Miss Martineau, Frederika Bremer, Bayard, and Fanny Kemble; unprejudiced Southern writers, like Paul H. Hayne, Mrs. Gilman, Mrs. Meade, and others, bore somewhat regretful witness to its vogue. Southern states passed laws against it, but it had taken deep hold.[25] There is no

[23] One of the best fictional treatments of the duel is in W. G. Brown's *A Gentleman of the South.*

[24] See DeForrest, *Kate Beaumont;* Underwood, *Lord of Himself;* Eggleston, *The Master of Warlock;* Dunbar, *A Family Feud.*

[25] See article in *Russell's,* May, 1857, defending the practice, an argument similar in spirit to the modern reasoning in behalf of war.

real evidence that feuds were more common, save perhaps in border regions, than in other sections; but violence was more prevalent than it is pleasant to contemplate.

The tradition colors with romantic hues certain of the vices of the feudal lords of society. Drinking is an example. Whiskey holds in plantation romance almost as important a place as does wine in the quatrains of Omar. The popular conception is rich with images of side-boards, decanters, and dignified servants, who offer at not too rare intervals refreshments of liquid nature. No meal could be complete, the legend runs, without a warning drink about an hour before the feast, a cocktail as appetizer, and abundant wine during and after the repast. Every mansion must have its cellar and, if in Virginia or Kentucky, its mint bed close by. The mint julep is the most honored of all the fluid institutions. It was more than a drink; it was a symbol; a symbol of hospitality, offered sometimes, as told by Ingraham, James, and others, to the guest before he got out of bed; a symbol of reconciliation, solemnly taken as if in the performance of an ordinance by erstwhile enemies who would seal a perpetual friendship. Come what will, the popular imagination will cling to the dram, the toddy, the julep as indicating the flavor of plantation life. In sober reality, drinking was more than a social grace; it was often a great vice. There were some who controlled at all times the appetite for drink, but many planters suffered greatly because of this weakness. The legislature of Virginia early grappled with this evil,[26] but the cavaliers of old were continuingly noted for a " noble thirst." [27] Russell [28] stood aghast before the

[26] See chapter on amusements in Bruce, *Economic History of Virginia*.

[27] Jno. R. Thompson, *Colonial Life* in *Southern Literary Mess.*, June, 1854.

capacity of some South Carolina planters; and even a friendly student, James Lane Allen,[29] takes cognizance of the frightful prevalence of drinking in the blue-grass country.

Gambling was another vice all too common among the sporting gentry of the plantations. The frequency of this theme in plantation writings, even of such men as Harris, is well known. The tragic figure of Eckhardt, in Simms' *The Last Wager*, who has gambled away three plantations, is characteristic of a large class. Slaves and plantations often changed hands during a night. Murder, or at least a serious quarrel, was a not uncommon concomitant of the gaming table. Such a custom has a dramatic possibility of which the tradition has made full use. Chiefly, however, in the romances of plantation life these practices are presented as genial little vices, the redeeming vices, as it were, of an order of feudal lords. Actually in the real plantation society they were personal, even social, iniquities of distressing magnitude.

D. *The Social Institutions*

Among the social institutions which the tradition has employed with great generosity, one of the most conspicuous is the manifold recreational life, indoor and out-door sport, festivity for whites and for blacks alike. This element is found not only in the fiction and poetry, but also in dramatic presentations, in songs, in reminiscence, in virtually every form of plantation record. One of the foremost factors in the history of sport is the horse, with his connotations of racing and hunting. The passion of the gentry for the noble, highly bred animal is firmly fixed in the whole tradition; the young Kentuckian of Elizabeth

[28] *My Diary*, 127.
[29] *Blue-Grass Region of Kentucky*.

Bellamy's *Hannah Calline's Jim* who, having resolved upon suicide, first kills his favorite horse, is fairly typical in attitude of the plantation gentlemen. Kentucky, it may be noted in passing, is specially favored as the home of fine horses, though the equine legend is rich in Virginia settings. Skill in riding, on the part of girls not less than boys, is a proverbial quality. The race, or the " mad dash," is a large motive; races to the aid of a dear one in distress, particularly in war time, races on the outcome of which depends the realization of love's young dream, races for all conceivable objectives, have their part in the thrilling stories of the old regime. The horse, as demonstrated by the racing melodramas, has been popular on the stage, as well as in fiction. Many of the estates are presented with private racing courses; men of wealth are shown devoting their energies to the development of blooded strains; duels are fought with race horses as weapons; county or state races are used as points of concentration for the gathering of society. The significance of the great races, as a matter of fact, to which throng the plantation gentry in great state, and at which other equine amusements, as the tournament, are supplied, has been the theme of a lavish tradition. Hunting is hardly less important. From the days when, according to *The Cavaliers of Virginia*, William Berkeley led the chase, down to the very end of the regime, as portrayed in Harris' *How Whalebone Caused a Wedding*, men and women, masters and slaves, entered with enthusiasm upon the pursuit of game. The mention of Harris' story calls to mind the fact that the dog is no small factor in the sporting life; and both narratives mentioned bear witness to the participation by negroes in this form of amusement, though it must be remembered that the darkies had their own distinctive fashion of trailing " de 'possum and de coon."

The tradition evolves an interesting calendar of festive occasions, in spite of the fact that apparently little excuse was needed for rounding up a frolic at any time. Supreme among the feast days of plantation life stands Christmas. It is a great theme for the romancers, friends and foes alike. Two such utterly diverse spirits as Simms and Mrs. Victor each produced a work centering largely in the plantation ·Yuletide. Harris, Page, Miss Glasgow, Mrs. Stuart, virtually all Southern writers have embodied the holiday spirit in large fictional treatment, while even Tourgee almost glows over the season, as in the opening chapters of *Toinette*. Russell, Boner, Dunbar, and a host of other singers, have voiced in poetry the joy of the Christmastide. Now Christmas is, to be sure, a fairly constant theme of social ecstasy the world over; Irving contributed some happy pictures of English Christmas even before the plantation romance was established; but these makers of the native legend insist that on the old estates there was happiness not easily paralleled. There were other of the seasonal festivities. The plantation tradition, strikingly unlike the Puritan records, has almost established Sunday in the group. The planters made dignified pilgrimages to church, usually in the great coaches, and dozed piously through sermons — they were nothing if not orthodox; but the large import of the day was social rather than ecclesiastical. Among the blacks, such plantation operations as harvesting, corn-shucking, rice-beating, tobacco-curing, hog-killing, and the like, were observed as gala occasions; some of these have been the subject of comic operettas of frivolous toil. Weddings served in both races as sufficient provocation for an extended celebration, often covering several days, transferred from house to house; such observances were elaborate among the whites and grotesque among the blacks, but enjoyed by all. To the darkies the camp meeting was a sort of ecstatic jubilee. Even a negro funeral could be made to serve purposes of social fellowship.

In the traditional treatment of recreational life, we find exemplified the method of taking a real, a potent condition of plantation life and heightening it for dramatic effect and multiplying the number and the scope of individual instances. Beyond the shadow of a doubt, the frolic was an important part of the ante-bellum plantation life. It may be affirmed that no class in our history has been characterized by greater eagerness for festivity, for gaiety. The makers of the tradition could probably cite actual occurrences that substantiated, roughly, the fictional record. But in the aggregate there is the exaggeration that marks romance. It is curious to note, with regard to this particular element, how almost all workers in the tradition, whatever the motive of their work, have collaborated to enlarge the effect of frivolity. The abolition writers relieved severe tragedies with the antics of the blacks or intensified the portrayals of white heartlessness by giving a detailed picture of a brilliant party in the mansion while in the cabin there was deep misery; minstrel performances have in endless repetition presented almost exclusively the clownish capers of frolicking coons; post-bellum story-tellers have drawn freely upon this delightful theme; reminiscent authors, seeking the distinctive, have presented as a peculiar quality of the old regime its well-nigh unalloyed mirth. The cumulative force of all these representations has been to suggest that plantation life was an unbroken mardi gras; and such a conception is, of course, extravagant.[30]

[30] It should be clearly understood, though, that sports and recreations did have uncommon prominence in the aspirations and the activities of all classes. The private race-course and the herd

There remains for consideration a large social institution, the plantation mansion with the home life it compre-
hended and the hospitality it expressed. The supremacy
of the plantation seat has already been suggested; it is
central in the feudalistic love of place, it is the stage of
much social pageantry. But the mansion is in the tradition more importantly than in mere relation to other
themes. It is itself the subject of sentimental idealization.
Hallowed, usually, by age — the historic quality of the
plantation home is emphasized in such diverse works as

---

of thoroughbreds could actually have been found on many Virginia and Kentucky estates, though it must be remembered that
a stock farm was not necessarily a plantation. Fithian records
(*Journal and Letters,* 58) that every "gentleman of condition"
in Virginia of pre-Revolutionary days had his coach and six or four.
As early as 1724, Jones (*Present State of Virginia,* 49) noted an
almost universal fondness for the horse. Eddis (*Letters,* Nov. 2,
1771) was impressed with the jockey clubs of Maryland and Virginia, while Mrs. Gilman in *Recollections,* Hall in *Travels,* and
others speak with enthusiasm of the Carolina races, racing balls,
and the racing society in general. Van Buren (*Jottings,* 232)
refers to the frequency of the riding whip and the spur in the
best Mississippi society. Mrs. Pringle (*Chronicles of Chicora
Wood,* 119) verifies, so far as the Allston family is concerned, the
skill of Southern girls on horseback. Averitt (*The Old Plantation,*
102) declares that he can not remember when he learned to ride.
Sufficient corroboration of the colonial love of the hunt may be
found all the way from Beverley to Bruce. The varied seasons of
mirth were appreciated. Virginia seized upon the church calendar
for festivals; an interesting document of early days is a program
for St. Andrew's Day, 1737 (*Colonial Life,* in *So. Lit. Mess.,* June,
1854). Virtually all of the autobiographies of Southerners testify
to the reality of Christmas joy. Periods of relaxation were frequently turned to mirth (See *Cotton on the Plantation,* in Turner's
magazine, *The Plantation,* March, 1860). All seasons of co-opera-
tive labor yielded their due measure of frivolity, a fact which
impressed Bryant (*A Tour of the Old South,* 31, 32). Negro weddings on the larger estates were occasions for greatest merriment

Swallow Barn, Dred, and *Dorothy South* — it is a store-house of memories, a conservatory of spiritual heritage. No tradition is ever quite complete without it, for it gives an ultimate tone.

In any decorative effect, the mansion is generally central, the focal point of the whole plantation pattern. In regard to definite details, the romances are vague. *In certain of the novels of domestic sentiment, there is merely the implication of grandeur, the assurance that the house is a fitting edifice to serve as "the capitol of a small republic." There is no consistency of architectural effect but the element of significance is never lacking. Kennedy, Tucker, Miss Johnston, in her colonial stories, present frame houses; Kentucky developed a characteristic type; Louisiana and the lower South are credited with a large house lifted on pillars, or on a little-used basement, above the "malarial soil." In the main, however, certainly in stories laid in late ante-bellum times, the mansion is conventional. Commonly the house is a large, two-story, rectangular edifice, of either brick or frame, with an impressive width of porch and great white columns, usually Doric, though the entablature varies. Often a small platform above the main entrance gives the effect of a minia-

---

(see Holcomb, *Plantation Life,* in *Knickerbocker,* June, 1861). House-parties were frequent, sometimes on a large scale; Dr. J. L. M. Curry attended one which included 70 guests (*The South in Olden Times, So. Hist. Ass'n.,* Jan., 1901). Many other elements of the tradition might be given reasonable confirmation: tournaments, cock-fights, the social value of the old-fashioned court day, the fairs, the political assemblages. Many of the planters sought urban pleasure, not only in such Southern centers as Richmond, Charleston, and New Orleans, but also in the North. Olmsted was disgusted with the "swell-head aristocrats" of the Natchez district who spent a large part of their earnings in excursions to Northern resorts.

ture piazza on the second story. Many of the mansions of colonial romance are constructed of imported brick with prodigious thickness of walls. Sometimes the central mansion is flanked with wings, one story in height, which may be joined to the central portion by arbor-like passages. The tradition employs liberally the beauty of landscape-garden; the distant approach through the two avenues of trees, the shrubbery of the lawn, the gardens for flowers, the walks, not infrequently the fountains, the terraces, the offices and out-buildings in picturesque design, the gabled end of barn seen through a vista of branches, negro huts in quaint arrangement, a host of details varying from the stone wall that faced the James to the honeysuckled summer house of the Mississippi delta, — all these are fairly common materials for the tradition.

The tradition is impressively pictorial and often conveniently vague concerning the interior. Doors are ever invitingly spacious and halls are wide — one is described as sixty feet long and thirty feet broad. A great stairway rising easily to the second floor enhances the effect of amplitude. Each of the several rooms has its own distinction but the dining room is most habitable and most used, with furniture, as G. P. R. James noted, closely resembling that of English mansions; indeed, according to the tradition, it was often English furniture. Occasional emphasis, as in *The Virginia Comedians,* is laid upon the family portraits, accorded honored positions on the walls. Kennedy was not impressed with this array of ancestral likenesses, but the body of the tradition credits these departed spirits with even potency in family council. Nothing of the domestic life is more inviting than the kitchen, sometimes separate from the main house. The bustle of great preparations is emphasized in numerous romances;

the thriftless mode of operation is a fairly common theme; rich profusion of kitchen comedy is found in the rivalry of competing cooks, in the yarns spun by plantation blacks, to whom the kitchen is a sort of social center, in the preference of these hands for the delicacies of the kitchen rather than the rations of the field hand, in their adroit thievery. Out of these kitchens there come the most amazing meals in all the chronicles of sumptuous victuals. Kennedy's record of the abundance at Swallow Barn where even a tiny bald spot on the table was accounted a disgrace, Hungerford's loving memories of a mere breakfast which was in effect a banquet, Marion Harland's menu for Westover meals — vouched for by that authority in the art of cookery — Miss Johnston's bill of fare for some colonial dinner, — these may strike experts in dietetics dumb with wonder, but they have mightily made the collective popular mouth to water.

When we attempt to check this legend of grandeur against the actual facts, we are again face to face with what we have called the quantitative exaggeration. The South was no more thick-set with elegant mansions than Elizabethan England was crowded with Kenilworth castles. There were, of course, in reasonably large number, houses of comfort, and there were a few homes of great beauty. No Southern planter would, as has been said of farmers of other sections, build his barn first and then construct his house of what was left over. Any history of American architecture will probably contain reference to plantation manors of dignity.[31] Advertisements in colonial papers indicate a measurable frequency of substantial farm houses. There was among the wealthier classes a fairly well defined architectural ideal,[32] approximated, if not

[31] See, for example, Glenn, *Some Colonial Mansions.*

[32] Metcalf, *Architecture in the South* in *The South in the Building of the Nation,* vol. 10.

realized, on many estates. Columns were greatly favored,
" giving even second-rate or tumble-down places a grandeur ";[33] and over the plantation zone as a whole there
was a passion for shade, for flowers, for attractive grounds.
But the inaccuracy is in the suggested prevalence of a
somewhat ideal type. A thousand stories, stage " sets,"
or motion pictures, all assuming a Mount Vernon or a
Montpelier, lead eventually to the conclusion that there
must be tens of thousands of such mansions, placed conveniently a few miles apart on every public road. Visitors entering the South gaze wildly around for a flock of
colonial mansions. But Rosewells or Naomi Halls do not
come in flocks. As a matter of fact, the fine house, when
it came at all, came late and never in great abundance.
There was hardly a home of beauty in Virginia during
the seventeenth century.[34] Wealth increased and some
" genteel homes " were erected, but they were not common.
Warner's claim that in all Virginia there were not more
" than two or three magnificent houses " is a rhetorical
over-statement, but it was always possible for the traveler
to cover great stretches without seeing any pretentious
mansions, as Olmsted records. Fanny Kemble scoffed at
the reputed splendor of the rice planters' homes. Olmsted
found many log houses in Alabama, not alone in the pioneer
sections, and confirmed Ingraham's report that, in spite
of notable exceptions, the homes of even wealthy planters
in the lower Mississippi Valley resembled neat cottages.
In general we may conclude [35] that while plantation
architecture varied from the double log house to the colon-
naded mansion, the usual residence was commodious in a

[33] Dodd, *The Cotton Kingdom*, 71.
[34] See chapter on houses in Bruce, *Economic History of Virginia in the Seventeenth Century*.
[35] This conclusion is from Phillips, *American Negro Slavery*, 309.

rambling fashion but had no great distinction without, no
great luxury within.[36]

Home life was as important in fact as it was in the
tradition but with a different, a much worthier, significance. In reality the home was not the place of dances,
of a pseudo-epicurean plenty, though the better class of
Southerners probably enjoyed more delicious food than
any other American class.[37] The home was, in a peculiar
fashion, supreme. This supremacy was due to the fact of
isolation. Home had no competition from theatres, clubs,
and other institutions of urban life.[38] Interest was concentrated in extraordinary degree upon the family circle;
and family life had a power, a persistence of influence,
almost a sacredness, not often suggested by the tradition
of groaning tables and shuffling feet. The home " meant
intensely." There were, of course, contradictory tendencies.
The very presence of another, a less refined race, not only
servile but too commonly unchaste, had at least the possibility of an effect too obvious to need elaboration. Yet
the home life was in essential respects almost unparalleled;
nowhere else in this Republic was it fraught with more
softening influence or with a richer charm of reciprocal
affection. This quality is not in the frivolous tradition.
It is the quality that is found in *The Cotter's Saturday
Night* or in *Snow-Bound* on a somewhat less ambitious
scale; but its real depth has not been sounded by the
plantation romances.

[36] The tradition of furniture and of rather beautiful home
equipment is probably truer than the legend of the big house.
Materials for building mansions were not easy to transport; the
finer tastes were gratified, therefore, by these smaller luxuries.

[37] Professor Hart smacks his lips over the thought of Southern
cooking, but properly calls attention to the fact that this art was
limited to the better classes (*Slavery and Abolition*, 100).

[38] See Calhoun, *A Social History of the American Family*, II,
334.

The famous tradition of hospitality seems to have a singularly substantial basis of fact. This quality of the ancient regime is in Beverley's history and in Hanby's *Memphis Blues*, in Kennedy and in Mrs. Stowe, in virtually every record of plantation life. If the average American has any conception whatever of the old order, it is sure to include this feature. The actual existence of a relatively universal hospitality cannot be denied. The cold-blooded investigator, whose delight is in iconoclasm, may suggest that the spirit has been often presented in a kind of glittering dramatization — how many hotels have ever been operated on the system described in Page's *The Old Planter's?* It may be further noted that the tradition is not always explicit as to the causes that underlay this hospitality; it did not spring altogether from all-compelling disinterestedness, though he would be bold who would seek to discredit a certain genuine self-forgetfulness which marked plantation entertainment; isolation, lack of contact with life in the large, anxiety for a break in monotony, these features sharpened the edge of the planter's delight in " company." Nor does the tradition elaborate the almost foolish wastefulness, going far beyond the most liberally interpreted necessities of courtesy, so that "the gods of household liberality were doubtless delighted but the gods of thrift and household peace hid their faces and groaned." [39] An ante-bellum chronicler [40] actually records the existence in Virginia society of the " professional visitationists," gormandizers and epicures.

Without going afield in the way of attempted philosophical analysis, we may simply say that the reality of plantation hospitality is practically unchallenged. There seemed to be no appreciable class distinction in the enter-

[39] W. P. Trent, *William Gilmore Simms*, 34.
[40] *Social Classifications*, in *Southern Literary Messenger*, March, 1841.

tainment, no limit to the generosity. Hungerford tells us
that even the Yankee peddler was cordially entertained,
a statement verified sixty years later in Oscar Straus'
recollections of his boyhood in Georgia. No fact of Southern life more deeply impressed the visitors. Lyell was
warned that Southern courtesy would even interfere with
his scientific studies, but that courtesy was delicate as
well as abundant and the scientist was not disturbed.
There seems to be every reason to believe that the tradition, whatever incidental variations may exist, was close
to the large truth. Such a truth must be given consideration in any final estimate of plantation civilization; generosity is ever a redemptive quality, operating with the
magic of bounty "enhancing the charm of many features
and making attractive others, that under white, cold light
might mar the whole." [41]

[41] Ingle, *Southern Sidelights*, 46.

CHAPTER VIII

THE CONCEPTION COMPARED WITH THE ACTUAL

II. *Plantation Characters*

CHARACTERIZATION is a major effort of the plantation romanticists. It may be reckoned most successful if we concede triumph to an art of portraiture that results in a few distinct and relatively simple types. The tradition of the plantation has achieved larger conquest of this kind, perhaps, than any other of our legends of personality. To refer to a man as " a Southern gentleman " is to pass sufficient, if not always lucid, eulogy; to allude casually to a Dixie girl is to conjure up visions of loveliness; to introduce a comic anecdote with reference to a Southern darkey is to invoke a spirit of expectancy that argues well for the attempt at humor. No other of our national ideas of " folks and places " is more immediately responsive.

It is not unlikely that these conceptions of plantation character have rooted deeply and flowered generously because they are conveniently few in number, not too many to crowd the limited soil area of popular fancy. There are, in the large, but three types: the old planter, the belle, the negro. Other figures are in the pattern only in less conspicuous perspective. The belle, for example, is submerged by matrimony into the less colorful type of the mistress. The young gallant sometimes divides the stage with his more picturesque sire. On the fringe of the scene may stand the sinister figure of the overseer. The stock negro may appear in any one of many guises. But the three dominant types are fairly constant.

The plantation belle, placed with fulsomeness of praise in the popular tradition, does not lend herself to psychological analysis. Miss Glasgow in *The Battle-Ground* distinguishes with some care between the fragile loveliness of Virginia and the tom-boyish vigor, the vivacious magnetism, of Betty. The true heroine of plantation romance, however, is both of these figures rolled into one; a crystallization of all legends of fair women, perfect and peerless, " created out of every creature's best." The " surpassing loveliness " of Carruthers' Virginia Fairfax, the " dewy freshness " of Cooke's heroines, the " bloom " of Miss Woolson's Bettina Ward, the " rose-order of Southern women," alluded to by Allen, to say nothing of the celestial radiance of the stars of sentimental romances, these qualities are as frequent in the romances as are the darling buds in May.

Obviously the tradition of the plantation, like romantic portrayals of all ages and countries, emphasizes primarily a beauty which is as impalpable a thing as the fragrance of the lilies, though it may include many tangible things from a gentle voice to a dainty foot. Certain factors to enhance the illusion are employed with fair consistency. The belle is usually credited with lavish costumes; thus she concentrates in herself much of the tradition of social splendor, for the sheen of wealth in a social order is often most glittering in the attire of its womanhood. Extreme youthfulness is another device used in giving to plantation heroines a distinction. The Southern clime developed a tendency, it seems, for the " rose-order " to bloom more prematurely than her sisters of more frigid zones. The " teen " age is the favored time for these romances. Many of the heroines can boast of only the tender years of Juliet. Others, as Zemira in Mrs. Hale's *Northwood,* have reached fifteen. The ravishing charm of sixteen, as found in

Cooke's *Last of the Foresters*, Miss Woolson's *East Angels*,
or Cable's *Gideon's Band*, is favored by many writers.
At all events, the young lady must be "standing with
reluctant feet" at the point of migration from earliest
girlhood. Youth is eager, hungering, as has been said,
not for the bread of life but for the sweetmeats. There is
a hint of deeper psychological charm in the heroine of
this fascinating age, a hint that expresses itself in even
the contradictions. This bundle of complexes is excitingly
inconsistent; she is both impulsive and reserved; frivolous,
even inconsiderate, but charitable; frank, yet coquettish
— no trait of character is more frequently employed;
heartless as the lady of chivalry, tender as Cordelia.

Though the emphasis is on this dazzling youthful temperament, the plantation maid is endowed with a singular
group of accomplishments. High intellectual power of
either native capacity or of extended mental training is
not in the tradition. More candid writers, like Porte
Crayon and Thompson, confess its absence; others merely
imply that there was neither occasion to acquire it nor
need to use it. The education of woman is referred to
chiefly in connection with the tutorial system; sometimes,
as in Mrs. Southworth's *Shannondale,* or even as early as
Greene's *A Yankee among the Nullifiers,* this condition
is used as the basis of a love affair, usually a mesalliance.
The social attainments of the young ladies were, however,
considerable. Poise of manner, resourcefulness and ease
of conversation, sparkling vivacity, refinement of judgment, to say nothing of graceful supervision of entertainment, these faculties seemed instinctive. Skill in dancing
and some development in musical culture were early
acquired. It must not be supposed, however, that the
heroine is presented merely as a hot-house flower; she is
a hardy plant, much at home in the out-door world. From

the days of Spotswood's daughters, as described by Carruthers, true plantation belles have been mistresses of
horse and hound; even the girl in Mrs. Victor's Louisiana
story, an arrogant, languid young lady, proves a surpris-
ingly good shot. A more serious accomplishment, probably too unromantic to enter largely into the tradition,
is proficiency in domestic management.

The tradition has developed a heroine who is more than
" the embodiment of pure beauty," as Cooke described
Rosebud Summers, who is more than a fascinating co-
quette of social cleverness. There are in the presentation of the Southern girl many spiritual qualities, certain
hints of idealism which are not suggested in the characterization of the masculine world. The chastity of Southern womanhood is almost axiomatic, a spotlessness of
thought and act, striking in these days when on the pages
of much of our literature " the Magdalen has eclipsed the
Madonna "; and even as we remember that this quality
is common to most women of pure romance, we recognize
in the present connection an accentuated whiteness of
soul by very reason of the contrast with the deeply
colored civilization in which these women lived. More
important for the tradition is the innate heroism, the
staunchness, the fibre of steel in these gentlest of creatures.
This quality has been developed very largely, particularly
against the unique historical background. The existence
of the slave system offered opportunity for the exemplifi-
cation of this spirit, whether an epidemic swept the quarters or an insurrection was threatened. The caste structure of society was admirably adapted to serve as a frame-
work for a story that centers in feminine self-immolation
in the cause of true love. The horror of a great war
fought at their very doors challenged a Spartan fortitude
on the part of plantation women, as evidenced in Miss

Woolson's *In the Cotton Country* or Mrs. Harrison's *Crow's Nest*. For final demonstration of this spirit, we need consider only the great body of work which portrayed many a Southern girlish heart following, after the Civil War, the leadings of love toward some Northern soldier, and resisting the claim of sectional allegiance, in-bred attitude, even family.

Less conspicuous in the tradition is the plantation mistress. Her character is developed throughout with measurable uniformity. Occasional exceptions, like Mrs. St. Clare of *Uncle Tom's Cabin*, may be noted, but Mrs. Stowe would have called Mrs. Shelby a more typical mistress. The general picture of this figure is that of a busy and unselfish woman; "mother of a romping brood of her own and over-mother of the pickaninny throng"; arbitrator of petty difficulties, teacher of ignorant blacks, executive of the complicated system of plantation domestic economy, visiting nurse to the cabins, director of plantation charities; "mistress of distant realms — the house and the cabin — and guardian of the bonds between the two." The immense routine of duties which fell to her lot is suggested in many stories. The dependence of the blacks upon her forms another large theme; the old negro who in Mrs. Preston's *Aunt Dorothy's Funeral* prayed for a dying mistress because she was needed more on the plantation than in heaven voiced many sentiments. The bravery of her struggle against the vicissitudes of her existence, as in Miss King's *Bonne Maman*, and her fortitude during the war have been frequently portrayed. Hints of tragedy, it is true may be found; they are but hints, however, for the romances concentrate on her domestic efficiency and her inexhaustible generosity.

When we seek to verify in the actual plantation life this feminine tradition, we can do no other than find a

reasonably strong case for the women of the plantation
society. It goes without saying that the legend, after the
fashion of the romance eternal, multiplies freely the number of lovely maids, makes

> " Every goose a swan, lad,
> And every lass a queen."

But it cannot be denied that the higher circles of Southern
society had as large proportion of gracious and interesting women as any class in America ever boasted; perhaps,
the South, in this respect, has not been equaled. It is
not going too far to affirm that this plantation society
appears to best advantage in the character of its women.
The very structure of this social order at once safeguarded
the girl and threw her into high and noble relief. There
is little evidence to the contrary. A few visitors [1] thought
they observed a languor in Southern women, a judgment
confirmed by Fanny Kemble [2] who also commented upon
"the negro mode of talking that characterized" Southern
women. These are unimportant fragments. In the main,
travelers who could find little or nothing else of good to
say paid tribute to these women. Eddis,[3] Van Buren,[4]
and others substantiate the statement of Olmsted [5] that
Southern womanhood was "unexcelled for every quality
which commands respect, admiration, and love." Certain
minor elements in the tradition appear approximately true.
There was, for example, almost universally an early debut
and a correspondingly early marriage; [6] and between the

[1] See *South Carolina*, in *Southern Literary Messenger*, March,
1845.

[2] *Journal of a Residence*, 211.

[3] *Letters from America*, letter of Dec. 24, 1771.

[4] Scattered through *Jottings of a Year's Sojourn*.

[5] *Seaboard Slave States*, II, 146.

[6] Ursula Byrd, wife of Robert Beverley, died a mother before

two events there was often a social career of great popularity. Interest in dress was wide-spread, a characteristic of belles everywhere, perhaps, but true of plantation society in surprising degree, considering that it was a rural life. Elaborate wardrobes were in the colonies not long after Jamestown; as the plantations became more stabilized and more affluent, dress was more and more a passion; edicts of fashion were studied, discussed, and followed with an eagerness not excelled in many foreign countries.

The tradition of the mistress has not passed unchallenged but there is no reasonable doubt that it was fairly true to facts. Fanny Kemble commented on the untidiness of the plantation lady and Frederika Bremer [7] recorded an instance of cruelty; but the bulk of the evidence is favorable. Miss Martineau [8] was amazed at the industry of the mistress; Bayard,[9] praising stingily, was enthusiastic over the character of the planter's wife; Lyell [10] was impressed by both the energy and the kindliness; modern scholars [11] not disposed to undue sympathy have reached substantially the same conclusion. Phillips, who has made extensive investigations in this field, is satisfied [12] that plantation mistresses were, almost without exception, industrious and charitable. It may be noted, finally, that few foreigners have ever dreamed how many

---

she was 17. Mrs. Clayton's sisters married at 16, she herself at 17. Other examples, numerous ones, might be cited.

[7] *Homes of the New World,* II, 189.

[8] *Society in America,* II, 103–104.

[9] See *Sewanee Review,* Jan., 1904.

[10] Various references in *Second Visit to the United States.*

[11] For example, Hart, *Slavery and Abolition,* 148, and Calhoun, *A Social History of the American Family,* II, 317.

[12] *American Negro Slavery,* 323.

Southern women were actually relieved when the system of slavery no longer existed.

The tradition of womanhood, for all that, is not wholly adequate, not entirely fair. The indictment against it is based not so much on a charge of exaggeration as on a charge of omission. The tradition did not so much unreasonably glorify the plantation woman as remain strangely silent about certain important, exceedingly important, phases of her existence. To apprehend dimly the vast unsaid, one need only imagine what a strictly realistic attitude might have made of the material. The tradition does not suggest, as a matter of fact, the status of women under the slavery regime. Honored with a real, a peculiar reverence, the boast and the idol of masculine society, she was, nevertheless, the pathetic victim of that society. The pleasant legend does not develop the excessive chaperonage which hedged her in, the denial of development which we recognize as hers by right, the utter economic dependence of these high-spirited women. Particularly notable is the failure of the tradition to hint at a certain orientalism which operated from the moment when the belle, abdicating her throne of social dominion, yielded herself to the program of the plantation lord. This " till death do us part " theory had under the conditions of the old regime, a tremendous literalness, fraught with terrible possibilities. In all the romance there is a conspicuous absence of the psychology of lovely girls who married young sports and found that matrimony locked a door and threw away the key, locked a door so thick that not even the cry of pain could ever penetrate to the outer world. DeForrest was coming close to this matter in his study of Nellie Armitage who " married to her hurt and kept it hid," but he is remote from the main current of the tradition. Nor does the plantation idyl take cognizance of those waters of deep agony through which passed many a spotless Southern woman as she became slowly and unwillingly aware of the loose morals of her men. Miss Tiernan in *Homoselle* makes probably the closest approach to this field; the women of the family knew that the handsome quadroon was really the daughter of the head of the house; but the fact is merely stated and we never learn what stirred in their hearts. The whole generalization of woman's character is glittering but it is thin; behind it are the shadows of deep grief that give cause for wonder.

The character of the plantation lord is one of the large themes. A fairly wide-spread conception of this figure,[13] in fact, appears to have been in the public consciousness even before the plantation tradition took definite shape. In general, the old planter is thoroughly conventional. Certain of the more careful writers, as Baker in *Inside*, DeForrest in *Kate Beaumont*, and Miss Glasgow in *The Battle-Ground*, suggest certain differentiations in the shadings of character; Bagby in *The Old Virginia Gentleman* describes five distinct types of plantation gentleman. But the public at large has not been altogether patient with these subtleties of temperament. A great range of qualities, from those of the volcanic fire-eater to those of a cultured aristocrat, have been rolled into one bundle and dubbed the Southern gentleman. The tradition is nowhere more insistent than upon the *sui generis* characteristic of the manhood of plantation life. There is almost no form of plantation chronicle which does not confess, even if it does not elaborate, a landed gentry quite incompatible

---

[13] References to this conception will be found in chapter 2. Note also Bickley's *The Aristocrat* (1833) which apparently reflects a general opinion that the average planter was a fox-hunter, a gambler, a drinker, a duellist.

with any other idea of men. The result of this unanamity and confidence of portrayal has been to place the plantation master in public consciousness as a unique social type, set apart in picturesque singularity.

The substance of this tradition is that the old planter was really a knight of old, or more strictly, a cavalier of romance, as that type is generally understood. This is the basic conception. The lord of the plantation is really a nobleman, subject only to such modifications as superficially conform to the Declaration of Independence. He accepts titles, democratic appelations, to be sure, but conveying principally a social distinction. He is punctilious in dress. He believes devoutly in his own aristocracy, a heritage of nobility from an ancestry of which he is proud and he acts on the conviction. The duty of perpetuating the social customs of distinguished forbears is recognized as a pleasant obligation; Colonel Buckingham of Robert Criswell's novel sought to maintain on his Carolina barony something of the manner of George Villiers. Loyalty to the province is pronounced in the temperament of the old gentlemen; witness Beverley Tucker's men, Miss Seawell's Colonel Beverley who regarded Virginia as the center of the planetary system, or Miss Glasgow's Major Lightfoot who affectionately referred to his state as " the school for gentlemen." This sectional pride is the expression of a confidence that the blue blood of creation coagulated, as it were, in the plantation zone.

The graces of the rural gentlemen, as set forth in the tradition, are but the chivalric modes of a feudalistic nobility. Courtesy of manner extended from delicate deference shown to equals down to a patronizing kindness manifested to inferiors; courtliness of address toward women included even very young girls and was so inwrought with the character that humorous innuendo or slanderous re-

mark concerning individual women was notably absent
from a conversation not characterized by great pudency.
The extraordinarily sensitive honor is suggested in multitudinous ways, even in such small details as closing the
gates on public highways, which, according to Eggleston,
every Southerner did by instinct.   This honor is perhaps
the aristocrat's consciousness of the *noblesse oblige* of his
caste.   All of these traits belong to the nobleman's code
of etiquette, to conform to which satisfied his sense of the
dignity inhering in becoming conduct.

The traditional vices of the planters are largely the
peccancy of a patrician class.   Immorality, for example,
which tinges in romances many high-born cavaliers, may
be regarded as partly a result of slavery but partly a
consequence of uncontrolled individualism, the feudalistic
attitude that private morals are not public concerns.   Ab-
solutism of temperament appears in the choler, the ungovernable rages, common even in most sympathetic portrayals.   The cavalier custom of good round swearing,
frequently an innocuous emphasis in conversation and
nothing more, of drinking, of gambling, which however
desperate must be conducted according to inviolable conventions, of duelling that was easy for those whose " hot
blood was on fire with constant cocktails," these qualities,
of which the whole tradition is full, are forgiven, are even
vicariously enjoyed, because they are part of a romantic
profligacy to which we allow a license.

The tradition, then, is focalized on an aristocrat, one
" bawn a gentleman and can't get over it."   This assertion does not mean that there is everywhere developed a
perfectly symmetrical characterization along the lines suggested.   There may be no more than a magniloquent gesture, a " By Gad, Sah "; but the general conception from
so slender a thread reconstructs the whole design.   There

are, moreover, certain geographical variations. The Virginia gentleman is the type, but he fades in purely aristocratic coloring as he gets farther from the tide-water. Kentucky developed a colonel all her own, though pride in Virginia ancestry is one of his traits. This type, which has been brought forcibly to public attention by racing melodramas, is in the tradition as early as Postl who observed in the blue-grass gentleman exaggerated fierceness of temper, weakness for drink, and love for horses. Other local differentiations have been suggested. The Carolina planter is often regarded as most opulent; the Louisiana type is credited probably with the greatest number of violations of the moral law. But the tradition as a whole is one of well defined type which may include all general.

The young gallant, chiefly an unseasoned chip of the old block, is not so prominent as the elder cavalier; this condition may be due to the influence of the Civil War romance which usually pictured a youthful Southerner as standing in the path of the progress of inter-sectional love. As far as he enters the tradition, he comes in more of a fire-eater than his father; witness Fairfax Cary in Miss Johnston's *Lewis Rand* and the brace of spit-fires in Cable's *Gideon's Band*. Cooke immortalized the plantation fop in Champ Effingham, but commonly the heir of the estate is vigorous and assertive. His consciousness of caste is emphasized by his refusal to fight duels with inferiors, a theme utilized from *The Knights of the Horseshoe* to *The Battle-Ground*. The second generation goes beyond the first in lawlessness, as in abolition stories like *Dred* or retrospective narratives like Harris' *A Run of Luck.*. In the main, however, the plantation youths are, as represented by Page, for example, with a slightly accentuated impetuosity of temperament, fresher copies of their sires.

To test the validity of the tradition of plantation manhood involves as great difficulty as any investigation connected with the whole of that epoch. There are two distinct obstacles in the way. The first problem is concerned with the nature of material. Data that aid in adequate estimates of personality are not abundant and are rarely satisfying. The romance has penetrated deeply even what we may term unscientific history. Northern writers have been more than willing, certainly in these latter years, to concede a vague manly excellence and a social peculiarity to the planters; and Southern essayists have too frequently looked upon the men of the old regime as demi-gods. When the student finds in a historical publication the assertion that " The chivalrous, courtly, courageous Southern gentleman of the ante-bellum period was the grandest embodiment of the most superb manhood that ever graced a forum or died upon a battle-field," [14] he may admire the loyalty represented but he does not feel that light has been thrown upon the subject. The ultimate result is that conclusions must be drawn from a slender body of evidence; even the reminiscent writers, be it remembered, present figures that cannot, as a rule, be accepted as typical.

In connection with these writers of gracious recollections, in fact, we may think of the second difficulty that confronts us in an effort to appraise the actual manhood of the plantation. This fact is that there were really two types of Southern manhood; let us denominate them, for lack of better phraseology, the real and the ideal, types actually existent. The task is, therefore, a two-fold one: to determine whether the tradition is true of the real manhood, whether it is true of that limited group that approximated the ideal cavalier.

By way of clearing the ground, we may call attention

[14] See *Plantation Life in Mississippi before the War, Miss. Hist. Soc.*, II, 87.

to one fact which can hardly be disputed. The plantation system tended to develop male personality to a degree and in a direction quite without parallel in American history. One can find no analogy in our modern civilization, certainly not in the industrial order and not even in contemporary agricultural districts, for the peculiar encouragement given to the largest possible unfolding of life. The dominance of the plantation, resulting in a ruralized, not an urbanized society; the isolation of the plantation, as remote from the currents of life in some respects as were the medieval castles of Germany, which took the individual out of the set mold of convention; the structure of the plantation which gave the white master uncommon power and subjected him to uncommon influences; these factors obviously tended to develop a unique character.

Another truth which seems well substantiated is that over the plantation zone as a whole, and most especially in certain favored sections, the manhood of rural life was characterized by a real grace of manner, varying in external polish, but so consistent in numerous external manifestations that it appears innate. It must be borne in mind, of course, that there were districts which were largely " home-spun " and that even in the more prosperous areas there were always the newly rich and the " professional Southerner," [15] boor and bore, respectively. For most of the planters, " Courtesy set upon them like a well-fitting garment." [16] English visitors,[17] sensitive to such qualities, were impressed by this condition. Northerners, as Bryant, found widespread urbanity; Fanny

[15] See, *e.g.*, Harris Dickson, *Gentlemen of the South*, *Everybody's*, Aug., 1910.

[16] W. P. Trent, *William Gilmore Simms*, 35.

[17] Mackay, *Life and Liberty in America*, I, 371; Hamilton, *Men and Manners in America*, II, 283–4.

Kemble, who saw little to win her commendation,[18] admitted that Southern men had a " grace and spirit that seldom belongs to the deportment of a Northern people." Melville recalled in *White-Jacket* that Southern officers were more likely to prove gentlemen; Olmsted [19] conceded a superiority " in the qualities for which a man is honored in society, for refinement of manner, and the power of being agreeable. . . ."

The final conclusion is that the tradition is one of great inaccuracy. We reach this verdict not by shredding [20] the romance and following painfully the several fibres to some real or fancied connection with life. It is when we look at the legend steadily and see it whole that we recognize in it a dramatization of the lurid, the volatile, the sensational, of plantation life. The tradition is false of both classes of Southern men which have been suggested in this chapter.

The tradition — let us call it, to consider it most favorably, the Colonel Carter of Cartersville tradition — is notably untrue of the great mass of small planters and farmers who made up the bulk of Southern society. Sober, industrious, democratic, men who fought the Revolution and championed what they considered the principles on which that contest was waged, what have these to do with that class of gay birds of aristocratic plumage, that " generous, fox-hunting, wine-drinking, duelling, and reckless race " of Carruthers and all his myth-makers?

[18] *Journal,* 305.

[19] *Seaboard Slave States,* II, 137.

[20] It would not be difficult to point out minor inaccuracies. The tradition of specific vices is over-drawn; it is, perhaps, a generalization of individual instances, fairly numerous, but not universal. On the other hand, there was in the temperament of the best Southerner, for example, almost a puritanical strain which is not at all reflected in the romances; study, for example, the spiritual life of Lee.

The tradition does not apply to the higher circles; there were traits of character, there were virtues, for which the tradition cares nothing. Harriet Martineau, whose eyes, lit with crusading zeal, saw as little beautiful in the old South as any that ever swept it, records " nowhere can more touching exercise of mercy be seen than here "; and again she notes that in patience the slave-owners " probably surpass the whole Christian world." [21] If there are two qualities that do not fit into the legend, they are these of Miss Martineau's affidavit. The abolition zealot, the managing director of a variety show, the romance-intoxicated expert in plantation social registers and plantation heraldry, — what cares one of these for mercy or patience?

We may visualize plantation manhood, it may be repeated, in one of two types. There was the average, a small planter, living in a modest home, tilling a hundred or so acres of soil, earning by the sweat of his brow and a very little Ethiopian perspiration a none too luxurious living, courteous, hospitable, withal simple, frolicking in mild fashion on rare occasions, voting for Jefferson and those he felt the followers in spirit of the great democrat, genuinely but not painfully pious, after a Methodist, Baptist, or Presbyterian fashion, raising — not rearing — a family of children, and sleeping at last with his fathers. There was also the type we have called ideal. We may visualize this group, not in Colonel Carter of Cartersville, but in R. F. W. Allston, in Thomas Dabney, in Robert E. Lee. Beside either of these varieties, the gentleman of the tradition is a rather tawdry figure.

No consideration of white character could be complete without at least passing reference to the overseer. In a sense he belongs to the economic tradition — Mrs. Pier-

[21] *Society in America*, II, 107 and 109.

son in *Cousin Franck's Household* attributes to him the economic desolation in Virginia about 1840; in another sense he is one of the factors in race relationship; but most importantly he is in the tradition as a social figure. He is usually the uncondoned villain of the plantation cast, a merciless task-master, a grafter by instinct, a moral contamination. The conception was in abolition literature, as in Hildreth's *Archy Moore*, long before Mrs. Stowe molded the arch-fiend, Legree. Reid darkened the pages of his *Quadroon* with the licentious Bully Bill, carried over by Boucicault as M'Closky of the well known drama. All of these rascals, it is interesting to note, were New Englanders. Civil War romance and retrospective studies have elaborated the theme. In Brown's *A Gentleman of the South*, Henry Selden loses his temper, for the only time in his life, in connection with an overseer; in Thorpe's *The Master's House* the overseers organize a kind of union for the protection of villainy; in Harris' *Daddy Jake the Runaway* the most devoted slave leaves home because of the overseer's cruelty; in Richard Malcolm Johnston's *Mr. Neelus Peeler's Condition* an overseer is presented as so lazy that he enters the ministry. After the war, the tradition runs, many overseers, as in Page's *Red Rock* or Harris' *The Bishop and the Boogerman*, enjoyed ill-gotten wealth which increased their power for evil.

The facts of plantation history record in large measure the accounts of cruelty and irresponsibility. Washington was almost continually complaining of trouble with his overseers. Henry Laurens dismissed several for viciousness, one having whipped a pregnant woman till serious results followed. Olmsted cites numerous cases. Intelligent negroes, like Frederick Douglass or R. R. Moton, recall with special bitterness the overseer. In defence of this rather unattractive factor, two truths may be stated.

There was, in the first place, wide variation in the calibre of overseers; some were ambitious but poor young men, struggling to work up in the world; some were small farmers temporarily connected with large estates; some, of course, were purposeless opportunists. Another fact of importance in this connection is that the system itself encouraged much evil doing on the part of the overseer. In colonial days his salary was usually a part of the crop; this plan was productive of such notorious abuses that a fixed wage was substituted, but it seems to have been permanently true that the overseer who made the largest crop got the best position; and no overseer had the master's economic motive for kindness. It seems hardly necessary to add, in conclusion, that there is no evidence to show as large a proportion of New England's citizens serving in this capacity in the plantation of fact as appear on the pages of romance.

As white character has been employed by the tradition for an impressive pageantry of plantation life, so the negro has been utilized widely for a kind of emotional relief. It may be true that the varied contribution of negro temperament has had a wider sweep than all the motives of social magnificence or the romantic exaltations of white character; the vogue of minstrelsy, to choose only one example, argues for this fact. In the analysis of the tradition of black character, to which we now turn, we shall see that emphasis is laid, on the one hand, upon certain stock negro functionaries of the plantation, but, also on the other hand, upon the more conspicuous traits of negro psychology, as popularly conceived; it should be remembered, in this connection, that some of the largest qualities of darkey nature, happiness and loyalty, for example, will be considered under the general study of race relations.

The tradition in fullest development presents a rather elaborate retinue of household servants, each with well defined characteristics and responsibilities. The whole corps is detailed in Page's essays, in Hungerford, in Ingraham, and in fictional treatment like Mrs. Southworth's *Shannondale*. One of the most interesting troupes is in Miss Glasgow's *The Battle-Ground,* including, among others, the cook who in pride of her handiwork avows " ain' gwine be no better dinner on Jedgment Day, nurr, I don' cyar who gwine cook hit," and the driver who soothes his master's wrath over the impending Yankee invasion with the promise, " We'll des loose de dawgs on 'em, dat's w'at we'll do."

Prominent among all these dusky personages is the mammy. Related usually to her whites in the capacity of nurse, she is the most affectionately regarded. She is, in fact, the subject of many rich metaphors. Her devotion surely passes all description; it " seeketh not its own " and " it never faileth "; it burns with undimmed luster in the dark period of the war-time; it acknowledges no emancipation; it defies the flight of time and claims as baby even the adults far removed from the epoch of the slumber-song. This fulness of love is usually only implicit in the tradition; it is suggested by the mammy's loving tyranny, by her gently scornful disapprobation which is the very frenzy of love's vocabulary. The mammy who esteems her master's children above her own is in the tradition as early as Isabel Drysdale's *Scenes from Georgia* of 1827. The affection that runs through the mature years without diminution is in Simms' *The Sword and the Distaff,* in Mary J. Holmes' *Tempest and Sunshine,* and in numberless other works. The autocracy of mammy in matters of juvenile conduct is shown in *Red Rock* when Blair Cary appeals from mother to mammy.

The old nurse out-Herods Herod in her resentment of the
coming of the uninvited Yankee warriors, as in Peck's
The McDonalds or Palmer's *The Vagabond.* The steadfastness of her devotion in the strain of post-bellum conditions is the theme of a large body of writing. The
greatest group of cradle-songs in our literature is credited
to her lips.

Various other domestic officials enter into the picture.
There is the butler. Old Essex of Carruthers' *Knights of
the Horseshoe,* amazingly diplomatic in manifesting to
each guest precisely the proper deference, and Bob of Miss
Seawell's *Children of Destiny,* who regarded the Duke of
Wellington as " po' white trash," are representative of the
dignity and the poise which marked these functionaries.
Such positions, as in Mrs. Harrison's *Penelope's Swains*
and Mrs. Preston's *Aunt Dorothy's Funeral,* are often regarded as matters of hereditary descent. The driver is
hardly second in importance to the butler; one of the
most interesting of these studies is Frank Stockton's *The
Cloverfield's Carriage.* The cook is of greatest significance; stable-boys crowd the spacious barn lots; body-
servants, maids, master-musicians, cooks' helpers, and a
host of less sharply defined figures, are common in the
romances.

One other figure, a most important one, is the plantation story-teller. Harris popularized, though he did not
originate, the type in Uncle Remus. Page gave added
momentum to the practice, though he centered in reminiscences by darkies rather than fables told by the slaves.
The vogue has been considerable. As early as 1855, *Anti-
Fanaticism* contained an old patriarch who delighted the
children of the family with his yarns. The custom continued through such modern representations as the stories
of Chesnutt and through A. C. Gordon's delightful recital

of the effort of old Jonas to wean his young master from feminine influence by telling to him irresistible tales. In many plantation narratives, as Miss Woodville's *Mammy*, Miss Bonner's best tales, or Mrs. Boyle's *Devil Tales* and *Brockenburne*, it is a mammy who recites. Whether an auntie or an uncle tells the stories, however, whether the story itself be pure fable, as in Wilkinson's *Plantation Tales of Louisiana*, or a sketch like Dunbar's *A Cabin Tale*, whether primary interest be concentrated upon Brer Rabbit or upon some condition that existed in the good old days, the aggregate effect has been to set the story-teller powerfully in public consciousness as one of the most winsome figures of the ante-bellum regime.

Compared to the actual plantation, these traditional figures illustrate again the tendency of the romantic interpretation to dramatize, to make universal. Take, for example, the mammy. It does not require profound insight into the philosophy of civilization to appreciate the importance of the nurse, or a wide knowledge of history to understand that in any servile class many slaves would seek, would value, and would discharge creditably positions of intimacy in the family circle. As a matter of fact, the plantation nurse was a fairly constant factor and in some homes was almost an institution. One does not need to go to written records to demonstrate the truth of this statement; many mature Southerners of today recall numerous instances. There can be no doubt that with the peculiar African capacity for devotion, the old mammy dearly loved her charges, that she often, under the condescending tolerance of her owners, exercised real sway over these children. But it is obvious, nevertheless, that the tradition, finding this figure particularly attractive, has standardized her. It has, in many cases, simply put a black mask on a character of romance that was already

centuries old, the honored and dependable female retainer.
It is dangerous to insist upon subterranean continuities
but this type is apparently as old as history. It was prominent, for example, in the Italian drama of the Renaissance
and it was carried over into English in such examples as
Romeo and Juliet. Consequently a writer of the tradition
could come never farther south than Bangor and still draw
a mammy wholly acceptable to the popular conception.
It is an old role in the pageantry of sentiment, played
by an actor whose complexion and head-dress are new;
but the role is one.

The plantation story-teller is an interesting example of
this conventionalizing process. Undoubtedly many of the
old patriarchs and many of the nurses told stories to eager
childish ears. Page,[22] Professor Winston,[23] Mrs. Pringle,[24]
perhaps the majority of Southerners even in the present
generation,[25] heard in their youth stories like those recorded in literature. Moton tells that his mother often
entertained the children of her whites in this fashion. Here
was, undoubtedly, a real practice; but the general custom
has been dramatized into one spectacular figure who tells
yarns known in every literature of any volume. Harris,
for example, gathered his material from manifold sources
but expressed it in some conventional mode. In the plantation of fact there is a real basis for the story-teller but
in the plantation of fancy he serves as a kind of phonograph record.

The plantation darkey is in the tradition more amply in
the form of generally accepted African traits, generic,

[22] *The Old-Time Negro, Scribner's,* Nov., 1904.
[23] *Relations of the Whites to the Negroes, Annals Amer. Acad.,*
July, 1910.
[24] *Chronicles of Chicora Wood,* 19..
[25] Even today old Southern darkies will tell little children
stories which could not possibly have been learned from books.

though not entirely disembodied. Not infrequently, as a matter of fact, these qualities are represented in a particular type; negro religion, for example, may be personified in the dusky divine. Generally, however, these large attributes of character cannot easily be crowded into one person.

This brand of religion is one of the conspicuous elements of negro psychology as the popular conception knew it. It is in the tradition in somewhat contradictory manner; it is sentimentally real and ludicrously unreal; it is pathetically fervent and grotesquely humorous; it is mystically weird and emotionally orgiastic; it is the mournful rites of captives who sorrow in a strange land and an ecclesiastical [26] break-down; it is the Book of Revelations and a manual for minstrelsy. For a tribute to a sincerity which redeems negro worship from absurdity, one need turn only to *Dred* or to Simeon in Baker's *Inside;* for a tribute to the effectual ministry of negro zealots in influencing even their masters, to Marion Harland's *Alone* or Miss Seawell's *Hale Weston;* for the potency of negro prayer, to Mark Twain's *The Gilded Age* or Bret Harte's *Colonel Starbottle.* The tradition in the main, however, utilizes the spectacular and the comic rather than the genuine. A favorite device is the use of queer exegesis; in Annie Hobson's *In Old Alabama* a darkey places the story of Daniel and the lions in a sweet potato patch; in Stockton's *A Story of Seven Devils* a colored divine generalizes that since the devils were cast out of only one woman they must still be in all others; in Dunbar's *Trial Sermons on Bull Skin* a minister explains that the prepared table for the psalmist was really a 'possum dinner; in Russell's well

[26] A recent New York musical comedy presented a stage full of negroes passing insensibly from worship to a general shuffle, all in the same bodily rhythm, as it were.

known poem, the negro gives a biblical origin for the banjo. The symbolism of darkey faith is emphasized; the old mammy of Mrs. Hentz's *The Planter's Northern Bride*, dying, sees visions of shining streets and a big house; other negroes see white doves, pieces of paper with new names written thereon, hear bells, and experience all forms of symbolic excitement. The demonstrativeness of negro pietism is another theme; the turbulent joys of saints is in Stockton's *The Late Mrs. Null*, with its almost baccha-nalian gambols, and the convulsive frenzies of sinners lend interest to Edwards' *How Sal Came Through*. One of the most widely established conventions concerning the darkey's religion is its total severance from moral conduct, the easy dissociation, let us say, of faith and works. The funda-mental dogma seems to be a continuing in sin that grace may abound. From the divine in *Miss Ravenel's Conver-sion*, who offended easily the seventh commandment in a test of the permanence of heavenly pardon, to the eccle-siastic of *The Leopard's Spots* who devoutly stole chickens in order that the everlasting mercy might have large op-portunity to exercise itself, the record of negro religion is chiefly a burlesque.

When James Whitcomb Riley speaks in *North and South* of negro eyes

" Lit with the old superstition
Death itself cannot disguise "

he hints at one of the great characteristics of the planta-tion black. It is not easy even to suggest the ramifications of this theme. Worship, for example, shades off into baldest superstition; Page's *The Trick Doctor* presents rival preachers competing by witchcraft for congregational favor, and Mrs. Boyle's *De Hant er de Buzzard's Nest* tells of a prayer-meeting held by plantation slaves frightened at the small number of buzzards hatched. The great body of folk-lore is interpenetrated with racial superstitions; Uncle Remus attributes the prestige of the rabbit's foot to the respect of the darkey for the rabbit himself. In the present connection only a few major motives may be untangled from the mass. Prominent in the whole tradition is the "hoodoo" or "conjur." Fear of a spell paralyzes economic activity, as in Miss Woodville's *How Ham Was Cured;* individual negroes withering under an imaginary curse are legion, from the time of Simms' *The Lazy Crow;* Bras-Coupe's sorcery in *The Grandissimes* blasts a whole estate, whites, blacks, growing crops. Sometimes this peculiarly dark art is turned to purposes of good; it may heal; it may win reluctant love; it may, as in Chesnutt's *The Goophered Grapevine,* protect the white man's property. Another theme of popular superstitions is connected with the cemetery and the "hant"; few American citizens have not laughed heartily at this quality in some manifestation. Less conspicuous, but equally real, are minor beliefs; the theory of the jack-o'-lantern, for example, conforming closely to the idea held by Caliban, occurs in several places; even the neutralizing method of turning the pockets inside out is found in such stories as Harris' *Spirits Seen and Unseen* and Dunbar's *Anner Lizer.* A catalogue of signs and wonder would be extensive. One might take a certain belief, say the superstitions concerning new-born babies, and trace out interesting illustrations and variations; one might take, on the other hand, a particular story, say *Huckleberry Finn,* and follow the suggestions of negro magic found in its pages. One of the themes of special interest to the student of literature is the African interpretation of the Faust legend, as found in Mrs. Boyle's *Devil Tales* or John Bennet's *Madame Margot.* The point of consequence here is not a detailed investigation of all the details of superstition but the fact that the tradition has accepted it as fundamental in African temperament, has presented it in diversified form, and has thereby given to the public many laughs and not a few thrills.

Hardly less significant in the popular romances is the inherent musical genius of the black. This quality, we have suggested, proved influential upon the song content of our history and was one of the fruitful inspirations of minstrelsy. The power of this characteristic in negro psychology is sometimes illustrated by weird out-workings; there is, for example, a group of reversion to type stories, like the anonymous *Toward the Gulf*, Mrs. Atherton's *Senator North*, or Hergesheimer's *Ju Ju*, in which the result is produced by an instinctive response to the call of melody. Usually, however, the trait is entertaining rather than motivating. Banjo playing and singing are resonant in the whole tradition, the stories as well as the multitudinous stage presentations. Music in every detail of romantic imagery, from crude contests in the quarters to stately performances of negro orchestras in the mansions, is conspicuous in this romance.

Dearest of all negro traits in the popular conception is humor, a broad comedy of dialogue, of conduct, of character. This quality is all pervasive; religion, superstition, music, are frequently turned to ultimate ludicrous effects; animal fables are narrated in droll style and usually reach a laughable climax; all processes of thought, including the proverbial wisdom, are marked by whimsicality; even negro sins are more ridiculous than reprehensible. The tradition insists that the plantation black is intrinsically a clown. Not all the pathos of abolition revelation, not all the tenderness of reminiscent treatment, can weaken this, the strongest of our convictions. The comedy of costume may be cited as illustrative; whether on the stage or in a story, the negro's attire must be mirth-provoking; whether garbed as a scarecrow or arrayed in fantastic splendor, the darkey must be presented as essentially absurd. Postl enjoys this merriment in his account of the antiquated haberdashery of plantation blacks; Simms elaborated the toilette of Mingo, in *The Loves of the Driver,* who would a-wooing go; Cooke, in *Henry St. John,* achieves one of his most popular treatments in the description of a slave dressed in a military uniform; Porte Crayon smiles at the parade of Little Mice, " all dolled up "; Allen makes Peter, one of his *Two Gentlemen of Kentucky,* almost pathetically amusing; Tarkington pauses in *The Two Vanrevels* to suggest the vanity of Mamie; the list might be indefinitely prolonged. A smaller image of comedy, but rooted, we may say, over the entire plantation zone, is the watermelon — indeed, it wanders as far from the South as the Whilomville of Stephen Crane's stories. The weakness of the " coon " for melon follows him all through his pilgrim journey. Harris and John Charles McNeil break into song on this theme; a colored poet, D. W. Davis, in paradisiacal vision, substitutes the melon for the promised milk and honey. What shall we say of the mule, favorite theme from the days of Russell's *Nebuchadnezzar?* There is, moreover, the 'possum. Dunbar has a savory story of *Mt. Pisgah's Christmas Possum,* Elizabeth Bellamy gives in verse the old coachman interpretation of the family motto, *possum,* — hundreds of references may be found. The fondness for orders, as in Cobb's *Hark from the Tomb,* the bombastic chivalry of negro courtship, the extravagance of diction, various comic customs from dice rolling to baptism, — these are phases of a great tradition which has touched in extraordinary fashion the risibilities of a people.

Axiomatic in the plantation legend is a large and genial irresponsibility of negro temperament. The darkey of romance is lazy, takes no thought for the morrow, lies, steals. Sometimes a philosophical explanation is offered, as the fatalism reflected in Dunbar's *Viney, Put the Kettle on;* sometimes the psychology of the rascal is skilfully elaborated, as in Russell's *Business in Mississippi;* usually, however, the tradition is satisfied with a simple chronicle of thievery or general dishonesty. This theme is a very large one, in literature as well as in the popular anecdote. It is as frankly in Hildreth the abolitionist as in Edwards' *The Two Runaways;* Postl in his *Life in the New World* presents roguery as universal, and St. Clare of Mrs. Stowe's chief work scoffs at the very possibility of negro honesty. Chesnutt, the colored author, weaves the theme into a tragedy, *Dave's Necklace,* the ornament suggested being a ham. There is hardly a better known comic song than the ditty, " Some folks say a nigger won't steal." Vaudeville and minstrel stages have developed thousands of sketches of negro peculation. Even in so serious a modern novel as Stribling's *Birthright* the dusky heroine falls into the villain's power because she is too " light-fingered." Unrestrained lying is equally common in the tradition, as manifested by the hero of Miss Seawell's *Unc' Ananias* who boasts among his acquaintances Washington, the vicar of Wakefield, and Aladdin. Certainly there is no more appealing thread of the story, to the popular mind, than the darkey's invincible laziness, elaborated in such folk-lore as Harris' *Death and the Negro Man,* and in such studies of real life as Harris Dickson's *Old Reliable,* the title having been bestowed in irony. The improvidence of the black, comic in a thousand stories, is pathetic in Miss King's *The Pleasant Ways of St. Medard* and tragic in Miss Woolson's *King David.* Various other themes, such as ignorance and

unchastity, have re-enforced the popular conviction that
the old-time negro is cheerfully but irredeemably outside
the pale of moral accountability.

In anything like exhaustive analysis, many other traits,
firmly fixed in the tradition, would call for attention. One
of the most interesting is negro pride in several curious
manifestations; the darkey's vanity over the standing of
his family, whether during the slavery regime, as exemplified by Tiff of *Dred,* or in fearful post-bellum struggle,
as manifested in Johnston's *Travis and Major Jonathan
Wilby,* is one expression of this feeling; another device in
the tradition is to emphasize the slave's exultation in having commanded a good price. There is, furthermore, a
hint of caste, even among the darkeys; thus in Peacock's
Creole Orphans the social gradations are outlined as they
obtained on a Louisiana estate, Virginia negroes rating
highest, Carolina imports second, and the native stock,
"gray owls," lowest. There is, moreover, the large body
of aphoristic wisdom which, in the tradition, the slave
utters. A historical treatment would have taken account
of the glorification common in early abolition treatments,
as Mrs. Stowe's "image of God in ebony" or Whitman's
"You dim-descended, black, divine-souled African"; a
study of the popular conception can ignore such attitudes,
for they never influenced in permanent fashion the public
imagination.

In attempting to test this large, this solid tradition of
negro temperament, one must proceed carefully. It is, on
the one hand, earnestly believed by many people; thus
when an American citizen speaks of " knowing a nigger
like a book," he usually has in mind such traits as are
here suggested. A small but positive minority, on the
other hand, rejects the conception *in toto,* a position voiced
by an indignant leader of the race, who, he says, finds him-

self " set forth in every phase of ridicule and derided in
every mood and tense of contempt." A wholly dispassionate study leads to the conclusion that the darkey of the
tradition is not in any general sense the darkey of the plantation but is rather a stage figure constructed of the most
spectacular traits, which though not altogether rare, are
not invariable and are not in themselves the complete
psychology of the true negro. If we think in terms of the
millions of slaves, we are forced to the conclusion that
neither Tom nor Remus nor Topsy nor Sambo, end man
of the minstrel line, nor a composite of all these, delineates
the actual black of the old regime.

So far as these generic traits of character are concerned,
the tradition exercises what may be termed a vulgar
eclectism. It chooses what makes " good copy "; it dis-
torts as far as desirable; it omits at pleasure. In the
case of the negro's religion, for example, the tradition
presents unquestionably one side of the picture; the worship of the blacks was chiefly cataclysmic emotionalism;
it lacks clear-cut dogma, ethical implication, even the
faintest moral compulsion. All negroes, apparently, were
religious but this universal pietism was singularly remote
from a program of character building. The mass of evidence supports this fact, though the ostentation of cere-
mony deceived Dr. Adams,[27] and Miss Bremer thought
she saw in certain mystic rites " a beautiful transfiguration." [28] The religion was rhapsodic and little more; it was
a cherished theme for, and mode of, conversation — no
people ever enjoyed more fully the phraseology of eccle-
siasticism; but, as Olmsted recognized, the average
theology carried no more moral significance than did an
Indian war-dance. After we have admitted these facts,

[27] *South-Side View*, 53.
[28] *Homes of the New World*, II, 165.

we must acknowledge that there is something left out of the tradition. In view of the conditions from which the slave came, in view of the brevity of the civilizing period, in view of the peculiar conditions in which the negroes lived during that period, was not their religion about as good as could have been expected? Is not the testimony of the tradition itself, subsequently to be recorded, concerning loyalty and other sterling qualities an argument for the fact that this religion was not wholly barren of the fruits of the spirit? [29]

With regard to superstition, exaggeration seems impossible. Writers representing varying points of view have concurred in affirming that its influence was wide-spread, was almost immeasurable. Fanny Kemble Butler and other abolitionists noted this fact; Warner and his class of postbellum visitors from the North recorded numerous examples; Mrs. Gilman and almost every subsequent writer of reminiscence have elaborated the strange credulity.[30] There was, perhaps, hardly a black of the old regime who was not susceptible; and the total effect upon thought and behavior was considerable. To grasp the whole truth, however, it is necessary to recall that all primitive people are given to superstition — and many who are not primitive, as, for example, numerous masters of these plantation blacks — and that fewer of these practices than we usually think are purely African survivals. Thomas, in a study of Kentucky superstitions, concludes that the only original contribution of the blacks was the " voodoo " sign.[31]

The musical temperament of the slaves, as indubitable

[29] See later in this chapter the discussion of irresponsibility.

[30] See Handy, *Negro Superstitions, in Lipincott's,* Dec., 1891, and "S. M. P.," *Voodooism in Tennessee, Atlantic,* Sept., 1889.

[31] *Kentucky Superstitions,* 4–5.

in fact as in fancy, affords an illustration of the traditional method of accentuating elements that charm the romantic vagaries. The banjo, for example, is suggested as the universal mode of negro music, the inevitable instrument of this unique genius. No less an authority than Harris [32] affirms, however, that the banjo is not the favorite instrument of the negro, a judgment corroborated in part at least by Cable and Allen. Now the banjo was certainly employed; Jefferson [33] noted it in Virginia, Bryant [34] in South Carolina, Dr. Wyeth [35] in Alabama. The fact remains, however, that this instrument was not so common as the tradition pretends. No one has ever seen, as Harris points out, anything resembling the minstrel tambourine in the hands of a real plantation negro. It is certainly true that the super-sentimentality of much " negro song " — Foster's, for example — is not to be found in actual plantation melodies, though the religious song of the slave had sometimes a particularly plaintive note, a sort of cry for release. It is likewise true that the number of native African airs is smaller than has been supposed. Details need not be multiplied. The important fact is that the tradition has employed the genuine negro musical temperament as license for presenting under an Ethiopian guise conventional modes of entertainment. It is a far cry from the negro who in a rhythmic chant swings his hoe to the minstrel dandy who sings of his fairy fay; from the old fiddler before the cabin door to these days of the high collars and tortoise-rimmed glasses that mark the metropolitan cabaret orchestra.

[32] Harris' Article, and several others, *pro et con*, in vol. 3 of *The Critic:* Cable, *The Dance in Place Congo, Century,* Feb., 1885; Allen, *The Blue-Grass Region of Kentucky*, title essay.

[33] *Writings*, III, 246, footnote.

[34] *A Tour of the Old South*, 30.

[35] *With Sabre and Scalpel*, 61.

The tradition of negro comedy may be easily recognized as spectacular symbolism. The negro is endowed with humor. His utter abandon in enjoying his mirth, his eagerness in the pursuit of merriment, his unfailing jocularity, these are proverbial; John Kendrick Bangs defends the thesis that the negro is the long-sought natural humorist.[36] The tradition, however, selects certain tokens of this quality and from them develops unusual effects. The love of finery illustrates the point here. On the actual plantation there was often an effort at impressive display, sometimes ludicrous. From the Virginia body-servant who affected the frock coat of Lord Botetourt's wardrobe to the field hand of the lower South, resplendent in his provincial costume, as Postl saw it, of a nankeen frock coat and red striped calico trousers, there were some effects that were rich and laughable. But one can take half a dozen inventories of slave clothing and be convinced that the conventional stage costume, if it existed at all, was ultra-occasional. The plantation mule is another symbol. This beast was a large economic factor of the old regime; he is in himself a droll figure, capable of surprises; and the darkey would naturally be thrown much in company with the mule. The negro, moreover, loved his watermelon — so did his master. All of these things, primordial expressiveness in dress, mule, melon, all of these are transmuted in the tradition into elaborate symbols of comedy. The negro of the romance is funny in conventional fashion, usually accompanied by set devices. It is interesting to note, by way of parenthesis, that the conventional comic coon must be black; who ever heard of a funny yellow negro? Yet there were numbers of yellow negroes on the estates. Thus we have allegorized negro comedy; and the symbolism, much of it

[36] *Echoes of Hampton*, in *Harper's*, Dec., 1888.

based on actual traits, has developed far from the simple original who went his easy and amiable way upon the plantation.

The general principle of dramatization operates so universally in the tradition that probably one additional illustration will suffice. Irresponsibility, as typified chiefly in a stock figure, lazy, lying, thieving, improvident, is a kind of theatricality. As to its truth, it represents at best a compromise. Actually, the ethical range of the negro was wider than suggested by uniform, genial roguery. The negro was both better and worse than he has been pictured, whatever apologists or scoffers may say to the contrary. The qualities intimated in the wholesale characterization existed, often in considerable abundance, but they were usually tempered by other elements. The slave, for example, was given to stealing. Every chronicle of the olden times bears witness to this fact; modern students, like Odum,[37] recognize it as a proverbial vice; such champions as Douglass have tried to distinguish between "taking" and stealing, but no one has ever denied the consummate ease with which the black could appropriate that which was not his own, suffering therefrom no disquiet of conscience. The negro also lied — Olmsted [38] says, in his "very prayers to God." But there is more to be said in this connection than the tradition indicates. It is patent, for example, that under such a system of bondage only characters of extraordinary fibre would not yield to occasional temptations of this kind. It must always be remembered, moreover, that there were shining exceptions. John Dabney continued to pay for his freedom long after emancipation; [39] Bob [40] was called by his

[37] *Social and Mental Traits of the Negro*, 164.

[38] *Seaboard Slave States*, I, 128.

[39] Page, *The Old-Time Negro, Scribner's*, Nov., 1904.

[40] Fleming, *Jefferson Davis, the Negro and the Negro Problem, Sewanee Review*, Oct., 1908.

owner, Jefferson Davis, "as truthful a man as I ever knew"; Grandaddy Cairn of the Avirett [41] plantation was never caught in a theft or a falsehood; old Ben of a great Red River estate never told a lie and was infallibly honest; [42] these are but a few of that really large company who desired a better country and who sternly kept faith. The negro, again, was lazy, almost constitutionally so; he pitted invincible indolence, as Bryant suggests, and his skill in shirking against his master's power, and won many concessions. But he was far more industrious than he has been painted. At least five percent, Hart estimates, [43] were proficient in some skilled trade; and the civilizing force of plantation life, recognized by every student, including Booker Washington, would have been impossible had the negro been totally devoid of the power of application. But if the tradition damns the negro for certain mild derelictions, it also covers up many graver faults. Inter-racial unchastity, for example, has somewhat overshadowed the negro's own licentiousness which, Madison [44] said, "only stops short of the destruction of the race." The case for promiscuity, as hinted at by Calhoun, with its suggestions not only of a lack of standards but of venereal disease and all sordid concomitants of unrestrained vice — such terrible shadows are not in the bland tradition. Phillips [45] reveals a surprising amount of slave crime, including what has been denied by much of the tradition, rape. In general the plantation black was but

[41] Avirett, *The Old Plantation*, 49.

[42] *DeBow's Review*, July, 1860.

[43] *Slavery and Abolition*, 93

[44] Quoted by Miss Martineau, *Retrospect of Western Travel*, I, 191.

[45] Calhoun's work is in the chapter on negro family life in his *Social History of the American Family*. Phillips has recorded the results of his investigation in the chapter on slave crime in his *American Negro Slavery*.

a human being, naïve but still a human being, comprehending in his collective character all shadings of human
conduct, the white and the dark. The negro who shuffles
his grinning way through the tradition is a creature of
distinctly theatrical hues.

CHAPTER IX

THE CONCEPTION COMPARED WITH THE ACTUAL

III. *Race Relations*

THE juxtaposition of two races on the plantation constitutes the distinctive feature of the system, alike in tradition and in fact. It is primarily in this respect that the ante-bellum Southern estate is unique, unique as a resource for imaginative effort, unique as an economic and social unit. The importance of this racial duality cannot be over-stated; it is everywhere in the romances of the period, enhancing picturesqueness of setting, tempering characterization, motivating action; it penetrated other forms of literature than the merely fanciful, journalism, essays, political orations, religious homilies; it was the issue that made the occasion for a great war. Widest possible application may be given the statement of Phillips [1] that "after the close of the seventeenth century, the plantation problem was mainly the negro problem."

Although in the realm of fact the difficulty of the study of race relations is commensurate with its importance, such is not the case with the tradition. Nothing could be simpler than the connection as ordinarily interpreted by the romancers. The chroniclers of the legendary plantation life, save a few abolitionists, focus attention on an idealized relation of feudalism, benign supervision and happy dependence. Even the anti-slavery writers, in deference to popular taste, include many episodes of idyllic

[1] *Plantation and Frontier Documents,* I, 94

nature. Abolition literature, it must be remembered, is not the norm of plantation narrative. From the rise of retrospective writings in the last third of the nineteenth century, a beautiful felicity of racial contact has been presented, not as occasional but as constant; an imperious kindness on the part of the whites, matched by obsequious devotion on the part of the blacks. The volume of work emphasizing this point of view is immense. Such a conception is the crowning charm of the whole romance. The shadow of unchastity disturbs at times the universal sunshine; but it is only a grey shadow, not black. The net result is a mere sensationalism that gives piquancy to the romance.

When the investigator seeks to know the actual facts of race relationship, he faces one of the most stubborn facts in American history. A part of the difficulty inheres in definition. In the tradition, a plantation was uniformly the same, whether one of Richard Malcolm Johnston's small Georgia farms, one of the more spacious estates of Page's fancy, or one of the great agricultural provinces of the lower South. In sober fact, the personal note in race relations varied largely, according to the kind of plantation. An even greater difficulty lies in the fact that, certainly since opinion began to be divided, say as early as the thirties, material has been collected and presented chiefly from partisan points of view. A mighty mass of evidence was gathered by agencies professedly hostile to the whole system; such evidence could point in only one direction. It must be borne in mind that such documents as the reports of the Anti-Slavery Society, still employed as sources by writers [2] of unquestionable power, were designed for propaganda; and that such men as Olmsted,

[2] For example, by Calhoun in his *History of the American Family*.

honest as they were, never saw a certain type of plantation life. It must also be remembered that the Southern apologist sometimes writes out of the fulness of loyalty to a cause which, if not regretted, is remembered with immeasurable affection.   John S. Wise has stated this point: [3] " It is made doubly difficult to judge her (the Old South) by the character of the writings concerning her. On the one hand we have the extravagant eulogisms and fond laments of those who laud the old-time history and people, and admit no defects in them; on the other, the always unfair and often ignorant denunciations of the anti-slavery folk who are unwilling to admit, even at this late day, that any good could come out of the Nazareth of slavery." No other American question has become so curiously and fearfully tangled with the passions of even our professed publicists.

The whole matter of race relations, then, appears to be thrown into a distorted perspective: in the tradition the spectacle of patronage and adulation, in the serious writings, merciless stricture or indignant justification. For the sake of emphasis, we may state at the outset what seems to be the largest single fact connected with the status; a fact rarely emphasized because it contributes nothing to the theatrical romances or to the argumentative violence. This fundamental quality of race relations was naturalness; it was the absence, in the large, of any definite interracial mood. Born to the situation, whites and blacks alike accepted it without rationalization or self-pity. The one fact that seems most certain is that over the slavery zone as a whole the relation was not one of sentimentality. On smaller farms or more patriarchal estates, children of both races frolicked together in the fashion of immemorial juvenile democracy; as the years of maturity approached

[3] *The End of an Era,* 61.

there was a natural cleavage into the positions of masters and servants. Customarily there was no attitudinizing on either side. The master provided at least a modicum of comfort, exercised the general care dictated by business prudence, public opinion and his own sense of justice, and demanded in return labor; the slave accepted the provisions, yielded with no great enthusiasm some work, proved docile, was content. The whole epoch, governed by earlier standards than ours, was not critical, certainly not introspective, as masters and slaves in the twentieth century would probably be. The law of habit operated in admirable conformity to Professor James' description of that force as the balance wheel of society. Custom largely prescribed the master's duty, custom with the added motive of jealousy for his own interests; custom made the slave acquiescent, unthinkingly satisfied. This custom may even have led the black into a sense of locality, a consciousness of and feeling for his social group, a dim affection, perhaps, for the social establishment of which he was a part, a vicarious enjoyment of his master's glory. The negroes of abolition fancy do not represent the plantation blacks but shadow forth what their authors would have felt had they been slaves; neither do the cringing, self-immolating retainers of the romantic tradition precisely interpret the average worker. Both races accepted the situation as they found it, did not analyze, balanced in their behavior the somewhat contrary motives of getting the most for self and of manifesting ordinary human interest in those with whom destiny had closely associated them.

Now this naturalness of race relations is nowhere in the tradition. Uncle Tom, Old Black Joe, Uncle Remus, and all their kinds, interesting as they may be, are sentimental perversions. Mrs. Stowe's book was written to excite opposition to a system, Mr. Page's stories excited sympathy for that system after it had ceased to function. They are inaccurate simply because there was, on the whole, nothing exciting in the situation. This statement does not imply that such bright glimpses of inter-racial fraternity as found in Allen's *Two Gentlemen of Kentucky*, Thompson's *Ben and Judas*, and Edwards' *The Two Runaways*, are to be accepted as typical. The two races made as good masters and as good slaves, respectively, as could have been expected, but the result was not obtained by a perpetual pose. There was a natural division between responsibility and labor, a natural joint participation in many of the activities of life, but there was no racial, or inter-racial, consciousness.[4]

Considerations of space and immediate pertinency must be offered as excuse for the omission of many matters properly belonging to more extensive study. The whole theory of slavery, including the shift of Southern opinion from the time of Washington, Henry, and Jefferson, to the days of Dew, Bledsoe, and Fitzhugh, can hardly be traced here.[5] This philosophical controversy may safely be ignored here for the whole tradition is not one of ratiocination[6] but one of mood. Similarly we may pass over the laws relating to slave life, though such an omission would appear inconceivable to the author of *A Key to Uncle Tom's Cabin*. Legal considerations enter in no important fashion the tradition; the slave code is attacked in Adams' *Manuel Pereira*, defended in Mrs. Schoolcraft's

[4] Olmsted, traveling late in the period, notes this; *Seaboard*, I, 19–20.

[5] Good summary in Dodd's *The Cotton Kingdom*, chapter 3.

[6] This statement is not altogether true of the period of forensic writings; many abolition stories were written to defend a thesis and the pro-slavery novels incorporated " bodaciously " the arguments of the later leaders of Southern thought.

The Black Gauntlet, suggested sometimes in Cable;[7] but it is of small moment in the large tradition.

It seems best in the present study to consider first the relations in the tradition and then the race relations of fact; for while the whole problem may be simplified into the two questions of how the white treated the black and how the black reacted, the details involved in exposition are intricate. The parallelism cannot be made exact. In the tradition, by all odds the largest theme is slave devotion, before, during, and after the war; but in the realm of fact, the largest issue has been concerned with the other half of the inter-racial partnership, the master's attitude toward the slave. There are, also, certain qualitative differences, some of them exceedingly important. The question of slave marriage and home life in the tradition has been toned down, certainly in these recent decades, into themes of grotesque courtship, ridiculous examples of the imponderable nature of the negro's domestic ties, or, at worst, into gentle narratives of severance, as Page's *Ole 'Stracted* and Mrs. Stuart's *A Golden Wedding.* In the world of reality, however, the impossibility of stabilized family life constitutes one of the momentous and, on the whole, unanswerable arguments against the system.

A. *Race Relations of the Tradition*

If we were considering primarily the historical development of the tradition rather than the form in which that tradition finally crystallized, it would be necessary to comment on the chronological variation in the presentation of race relations. It is at least worthy of passing mention to note that while setting and characterization have

[7] See *The White Slave* in *Strange True Tales of Louisiana;* of some interest in this connection is *The Lost Fortune* in *The Flower of the Chapdelaines.*

been fairly constant, the traditional portrayal of race relations has been subject to change. One might gather from abolition writings, even from such later literature as Harris' *Free Joe,* a body of material which would cast doubt upon the widely accepted idea of slave happiness. But as the tradition permanently took shape, these historical denials or minority reports have largely given way before an attitude that yields the richest sentimental value; and the ultimate verdict is practically unanimous.

One of the most obvious things about the tradition of race relations is that we enter the field, the romantic field, through the negro's psychology. In the matter of social life, the mansion is probably more important than the cabin; in the case of plantation characters, the whites at least share the stage with their slaves; but in the relationship of the two races, the negro is emphatically in the leading role, even the kindness of the master being reflected chiefly by the happiness of the black.

Foremost among the themes of plantation life is slave loyalty. This trait is often inseparable from slave contentment; the oft-repeated motive of the slave's refusal of freedom, in the tradition as early as Paulding's *Westward Ho!* or Simms' *Yemassee* shadows forth at once loyalty to the master and solid satisfaction with the station in life. The general topic of the servant's allegiance has been manipulated by the romancers with marked fertility of invention; in the large, however, there are three cycles of stories, one concerned with the conduct of the blacks during the ante-bellum era, one dealing with the behavior of the negroes in war time, a third, most dramatic of all, presenting undiminished fidelity in the devastated years after the war.

The faithfulness of the Africans during the undisturbed existence of slavery is usually suggested by either the

thrilling episode in which the black reaches the heights
of self-sacrifice or the quiet exposition of long and persistent integrity of affection. To the former class belongs
the common device of the declining of proffered freedom.
The capacity of the slave for self-immolation is recorded
as early as Defoe's *Colonel Jacque,* in which Mouchate
wants to die in his master's place. Further developments
represent the black as actually giving his life for a beloved white, as in Page's *Ashcake* or Gordon's *Kree.*
Other expressions of this feeling are found in the stories
of negroes who venture capture in behalf of some white,
as in *Huck Finn* or Harris' *Blue Dave;* of negroes who
give their hard-earned savings — usually designed for the
purchase of freedom — to serve a master's need, Harry
Gordon of *Dred* being a famous instance; of negroes who
are bold enough to endanger their lives by disobeying their
master for his own good, a situation found in Gilmore's
Among the Pines. The noble behavior of blacks during
an insurrection is in James' *The Old Dominion,* Mrs.
Hale's *Liberia,* Miss Tirenan's *Homoselle,* Mrs. Child's
Black Saxons, and many other stories. The greater number of portrayals of devotion do not, however, rely upon
one tense moment but deal with the affection that en-
dures and is patient. The story of faithfulness in days
of evil report, for example, may be found in the account
of Tiff in *Dred,* in Balaam of Harris' narrative by the
same name, in Mortimer of Mrs. Chopin's *In Sabine,* in
the mute of Cable's *Jean-Ah-Poquelin,* in even the unhappy servants who are at the auction block, a situation
of Boucicault's *Octoroon.* Other manifestations of this
spirit may be seen in the slave's solicitude for some sick
member of his white family, as in Edwards' *Ole Miss and
Sweetheart,* and in the slave's pride in his master's family,
a sentiment as old as Tucker's *Valley of the Shenandoah.*

In all narratives touching the war itself, slave devotion, a heroic quality, is featured. Herein the tradition found a rare opportunity. The very existence of a great war, even one, as the Revolution, in which the blacks had no great concern over the outcome, might well encourage disorganization if not servile insurrection. But when the purpose of the war was emancipation, when the liberating armies were sometimes at the plantation gates, the steadfastness of the bondmen is most impressive. This is the situation which the romancers have liberally used. The large fidelity may be presented either on the field of action or on the estate; in Miss Glasgow's *The Battle-Ground*, one slave goes with his master to the front, rescuing him when wounded, while another assumes supervision of the plantation during the absence of the white men. The body-guard, following because of sheer love his master into danger, ministering to his suffering lord, solacing his dying hours, perhaps carrying home the final message, is in Page's *Marse Chan*, in Gordon's *Maje*, in Dixon's *Leopard's Spots*, in even so unexpected a place as Harrigan's drama, *Pete*. The equally loyal retainer who serves at home is given a place in a considerable cycle of writings, including Page's *Meh Lady*, Marion Harland's *Sunnybrooke*, Dunbar's *The Strength of Gideon*, and Miss King's *Bayou l'Ombre*.

A great part of the tradition is dedicated to depicting the persistence of this stubborn loyalty into the postbellum period; the devotion which, recognizing no freedom, grew stronger as family fortunes waned and, reversing the ante-bellum order, stood as a kind of local providence for the bewildered whites. All things considered, this is, with the exception of negro comedy, the largest single motive; the clan of Hopkinson Smith's Chad is second only to the tribe of Jim Crow. Certain conventional methods for presenting this glad voluntary servitude are employed with marked frequency. The favorite formula calls for a desperate poverty on the part of the whites, under which circumstances the black acts as a genius of the lamp. He may share meager earnings, or, as in Harris' *Aunt Fountain's Prisoner*, may even divide the rations issued by the Freedman's Bureau; he may steal for the suffering dear ones, as in Miss Woodville's *Uncle Pompey's Christmas;* he may fight for his former owners, with either a grasping overseer, as in Octave Thanet's *Half-a-Curse*, or an insulting Yankee, as in Dixon's *Clansman*. A variation of this motive is found in the slave's transferring his affection to successive generations, as in Harris' *The Baby's Christmas*. One of the most pathetic effects is secured by the chronicle of the old slave's effort to maintain the pristine dignity of the dilapidated establishment, a motive of Mrs. Boyle's *Brockenburne* and Miss Baylor's *Claudia Hyde;* Dunbar achieves novel poignancy along the same general line with *The Colonel's Awakening*. The black who has his fling at the new freedom and then returns to a condition approximating his old happy bondage, as portrayed in Edwards' *A Fence-Corner Oration* or Harris' *Mom Bi*, is a fairly common figure. Aunt Martha of Baker's *Mose Evans* who refuses to entertain any notion of freedom because the idea is incompatible with her religious principles is typical of a small group. It is interesting to note, in this connection, that this phase of the tradition has made a special appeal to Northern writers, including Miss Woolson, Stockton, Octave Thanet, Miss Jewett, Miss Spofford, and others.

The question of slave happiness is closely allied to that of devotion; we may accept this loyalty, in fact, as expressing invincible contentment. The popular conception of this satisfaction the slave manifested with his lot in

life is the product of many strong forces: every minstrel
show, every familiar song interpreting the darkey at work
or play, many anecdotes, a host of stories and theatrical
performances, all argue for the gaiety, as well as the comfort, of the ante-bellum slave. With the sole exception
of certain scenes in abolition literature, and a not very
intelligible wail in the negro spiritual, every part of the
tradition has asserted the joy of negro existence. Even
anti-slavery writings revealed a certain felicity in the
slave's condition. Uncle Tom was happy most of the time,
Boucicault's negroes manifested resilience of temperament,
Hildreth's oppressed bondmen staged a great party in a
warehouse. The retrospective writers have accepted a state
of cheerfulness and good humor as the natural frame of
mind for the slave and have clustered about this theme
a large treatment, running all the way from Mrs. Boyle's
A Kingdom for Micajah, in which a slave returns to his
old life after a month's experiment with freedom, to Edwards' *Coming from the Fields,* a little operetta of negro
merriment even in their toil.

Now a suggestion of the master's attitude toward 1 .·
slaves, as interpreted by the tradition, may be obtained
from this representation of negro happiness. " Naturally,"
assumes the collective popular mind, " the black would
not have been so happy if he had not been kindly handled."
There was, in the days of the great controversy over
slavery, pronounced diversity of opinion concerning this
point; abolitionists accumulated examples of horrible cruelty, apologists retorted with illustrations of almost divine
commiseration — Colonel Buckingham of Criswell's novel,
discovering a negro sleeping in a field he should have been
hoeing, places his own handkerchief over the ebon counte-
nance. But when the tradition passed into the hands of
the retrospective writers, the dispute was virtually over.

The plantation lord was endowed with the spirit of beneficence; he would not only, as the elder Carter in Smith's
novel, purchase some Henny for the delectation of his
Chad, but would even, as in some of Page's stories, risk
his own life for one of his dependents. Illimitably, if
condescendingly, generous; barking much but never biting;
visible providence, and no bad one at that; such, in rough
outline, is the master as the tradition knows him.

This matter of the master's treatment of slaves is an
example of the ease with which the tradition can hurdle
difficulties. The question under consideration was the
crux of the whole slavery discussion. For a season the
disputation was as fierce in the realm of art, if we may
call it that, as elsewhere. But as the conception through
the works of the romantic period became more favorable,
the principal items in the indictment of the abolitionists
were palliated or ignored. As representative of the con-
solidated view, we may cite two novels by Northern authors, both appearing in the eighties: Bache's *Under the
Palmetto* showed slave quarters as attractive as those of
Swallow Barn, and other care correspondingly generous;
Elizabeth Meriwether's *Black and White* represented a
young master as taking a course in a medical college,
solely that he might provide for the health of his servants.
Excessive punishments, a common arraignment of the
earlier days, are found but rarely in the later treatments,
while the matter of slave breeding, bitterly denounced by
Whittier, Lowell, and others, has almost entirely disap-
peared. The smashing of family life is turned to purposes
of mild sentiment. In most stories of this nature, as Chesnutt's *The Wife of His Youth* or Mrs. Stuart's *A Golden
Wedding* or Mrs. Boyle's *How Jerry Bought Malindy*, the
essential tragedy is relieved by a happy ending. The
runaway woke profound sympathy among the anti-slavery

crusaders, but the final tradition has made the destiny of the fugitive far more tolerable. Sporadic recurrences of this theme may be found in its original form, as Cable's *The Clock in the Sky*, but the preferred form is different. Daddy Jake of Harris' story " flies the coop " but only for a most harmless adventure; Shadrach of the same author's *The Colonel's Nigger Dog*, while absent without leave, continues not only to come and go at will but even to manage the plantation; Old Isam of Edwards' *The Two Runaways*, far from being pursued by bloodhounds, is joined by his master for an experience of the simple life. Surely we have progressed far from Eliza on the ice. Such insurrections as are in the contemporary tradition are not occasioned by the master's unkindness. In short, the popular conception exonerates him of every charge save one; and that one leads us to the final large topic of race relations as found in the tradition.

Unchastity is the sole shadow across the bright picture of plantation race relations, a shadow of considerable dimensions. This theme is usually one of two motives, or a fusion of both: the personal licentious conduct of the master, or the tragic status of the slave of mixed blood; a course of behavior, on the one hand, a condition of being on the other. For practical purposes the two elements are completely interlaced. The near-white slave is a product of unlawful lust and, if a girl, is in danger of the same thing. Thus Honore Grandissime, a colored man, is denied the privileges of the society to which he feels he belongs, and Zoe of Boucicault's drama is the helpless victim of a white man's unworthy passion; both situations are, however, the out-croppings of a deep-seated unchastity. This theme, it may be noted, was prominent in abolition writing — some of the writers were fairly obsessed with the idea. It is in Hildreth, Mrs. Stowe, Reid, Trowbridge, in virtually every anti-slavery writer of consequence. It is significant that many of the more sympathetic portrayals, even of the early period, utilized at least the dramatic possibilities of this motive; Ingraham made it central in his *Quadroone*, Mrs. Southworth secured additional sensationalism, as in *Retribution*, with this motive; even a proslavery novel like Peacocke's *The Creole Orphans* bears witness to the prevalence of this sin. In post-bellum attacks, the topic is mighty still, as in Tourgee's *Toinette* or Miss Porter's *Told by an Octoroon*.

This theme has persisted even into the romantic treatment as a motive of absorbing interest, the only one of the abolition charges to outlive the great controversy. The tendency of the recent romance [8] is to minimize bestial lust and concentrate upon the agony of characters whose blood is mixed. The idea is incidental in a fairly large group, Mark Twain's *Pudd'nhead Wilson*, Miss Woolson's *Jeannette*, DeForrest's *A Gentleman of the Old School*, and others; the theme is the very heart of a much larger body of material. To call the roll would be tedious, but reference may be made to some of the varieties of treatment. In two popular novels of the eighties, *Subdued Southern Nobility* and *Toward the Gulf*, rich young planters have unwittingly married wives with the fatal taint. In Matt Crim's *Was It an Exceptional Case*, the heroine finds an involuntary shrinking on the part of her Northern lover when he knows the truth, a situation not unlike the principal scene in Mrs. Deland's *The Black Drop*. In Sherwood Bonner's *A Volcanic Interlude*, one of three devoted sisters proves to be tainted; in Jones' *Beatrice of Bayou Teche*, the almost white heroine conceives a hopeless passion for her young master; in Harben's *White Marie* a

[8] See group of modern treatments suggested in the final section of Chapter 4.

pure Caucasian girl is ruined by the very suspicion; in Harris' *Where's Duncan* a revenge is achieved by an outraged slave-mother. Cable, of course, employed the theme frequently and usually with effect. If from all such stories, one must be selected as worthy of special mention, the distinction would belong to Mrs. Chopin's *Desiree's Baby*.

Although the later tradition shows a continuing interest in the tragedy of the taint, in the moral laxity of the master class and in the misfortunes of those homeless between two social worlds, we must not overestimate the importance of this interest in its effect upon the popular conception. Makers of the tradition may still tinker with this problem of social maladjustment, champions of the negro may still denounce the masters for their treatment of female slaves — an attitude phrased with cogency in DuBois' *Darkwater*. But the public mind is, in the large, satisfied that race relations on the old plantation were reciprocally cordial and productive of common happiness.

B. *Race Relations on the Actual Plantation*

The actual facts of race relationship under the plantation regime are more complex, more difficult of approach, than the pleasant tradition indicates. The romance is commonly in high relief; there is an emphasis on a few conspicuous features. One needs familiarity with only a few of a given type, minstrel man, plantation song, literary treatment, to be able to predict the general salience of the type as a whole; the true conditions, however, involve great detail, a perfect tangle of detail. We must remember, too, the shift of approach; in the tradition, the negro, fairly simple and invariable, is at the center, but in the realm of fact the master is the crux, not at all simple, comprehending, in fact, many types. In order to parallel the present section with the division just concluded, we shall begin, nevertheless, with the negro as a factor in the inter-racial situation.

Categorical statements are nowhere more perilous than in the present connection, but it seems entirely probable that the average black on the Southern estate was, in moderate degree, happy and loyal. The very genius of African temperament offers a certain initial argument for the truth of this statement. The negro is instinctively kind and affectionate, contented in unambitious fashion, quick to respond to the stimulus of joy, quick to forget his grief. He entered upon his plantation status, be it remembered, not from a civilization such as we know to-day but from his African background. It is probable that his peaceful frame of mind was not greatly disturbed by the mere condition of slavery; only when that condition subjected him to actual suffering did he feel any spirit of protest. This suffering was not unknown, it is true, but the fact remains that the burden of proof is on those who assert the misery of exceptional cases as the rule. Keenest students of plantation life have concurred that the negro's lot was reasonably tolerable to him.

— That the slave accepted this lot with complacency, that he did yield a sort of unconscious allegiance, may be inferred from several facts. For one thing, the behavior of the blacks during the war period, if not so glitteringly heroic as in the tradition, is unquestionably corroborative of this truth. The loyalty of the black in the Revolution, as portrayed by Cooper or Simms, has a basis of solid fact.[9] The war of 1812 did not come close to the plantation zone as a whole, but the conduct of the Louisiana slaves was most creditable.[10] Most conspicuous, however,

[9] Mrs. Gilman tells of the devoted body-guard who brought home her grandfather's body; other examples are on record.

[10] *DeBow's Review*, Jan., 1861.

was the action of the blacks in the Civil War, a theme
that challenged Grady's eloquence.   However skeptical
may be the investigator, he can draw no other conclusion
than that the slave of the war period generally kept faith.
There were hundreds, probably thousands, of body-guards
who served on the line of action with patience and courage; Major Moton's father was one, refusing a proffered
freedom that he might fulfil his obligation.[11] Back on
the plantation, there may have been occasional electric
thrills at the approach of freedom, but there was extraordinarily little of the disorder and rebellion which might
easily have occurred, and there was often real nobility.
"In order to defend the women and children who were
left on the plantation when the white males went to war,
the slaves would have laid down their lives." [12]   This re-
mark was made not by Mr. Page but by Booker Washington.   There are few more dramatic episodes than the approach of Federal troops to the Davis estate and their
indignation at the stubborn loyalty of the slaves.[13]   Instances not wholly dissimilar have been noted of many
plantations. Slave insurrections are regarded generally as
symptomatic of seething discontent; actually they reveal
a fine devotion on the part of the majority of the slaves;
it was this fact that explained, largely, the failure of the
Nat Turner uprising.[14] The general conclusion here stated
is substantiated by most of the travelers. DeTocqueville,
to whose soul the very idea of slavery was abhorrent,[15]
confesses with amazement the negro's stolid indifference
to his "calamitous situation" and his affection for "his

[11] *Finding a Way Out*, 12.
[12] *Up from Slavery*, 13.
[13] Fleming, *Jefferson Davis, the Negro and the Negro Problem,*
Sewanee Review, Oct., 1908.
[14] See Drewry, *The Southampton Insurrection.*
[15] *Democracy in America*, I, 428.

tyrants." Frederika Bremer, Sir Charles Lyell,[16] Olmsted,[17] and others cite many individual instances. The life stories of Southerners who reflect at its best the old regime are full of allusions: the tearful love of the slaves for Henry Laurens, the deep affection of Bishop Polk's negroes, the universal veneration felt for their master by Thomas Dabney's servants. The autobiographers tell the same story; Bradley [18] of the Louisiana estates, Mrs. Clayton [19] of her Alabama home, Mrs. Pringle [20] of South Carolina, Dr. Avirett [21] of North Carolina, Page [22] and Mrs. Pleasants [23] of Virginia. There are on record, as a matter of fact, cases in which slaves having tasted freedom petitioned for re-enslavement. While there is in existence [24] no inconsiderable evidence pointing to some suffering of extreme nature, the preponderance of testimony indicates a measurable contentment and a measurable devotion on the part of those who were slaves.

In a great many cases this fidelity did extend into the post-bellum period. Bruce [25] reports that negroes on the tobacco plantations usually wanted to stay in their old home. Toombs and Stephens retained virtually all of their slaves.[26] A servant of Jefferson Davis accepted his

[16] See the account of the feeling of Richard Henry Wilde's slaves, in *Second Visit*, II, 105.

[17] See *Seaboard*, II, 77, for account of slave conduct during epidemic.

[18] *Some Plantation Memories, Blackwood's*, March, 1897.

[19] *White and Black under the Old Regime*, chap. 5.

[20] *Chronicles of Chicora Wood*, 54.

[21] *The Old Plantation, e.g.*, 15.

[22] Many writings, *e.g., The Old-Time Negro, Scribner's*, Nov., 1904.

[23] *Old Virginia Days and Ways, e.g.*, 120.

[24] For example, slave autobiographies in Bibliographical Notes.

[25] *A Tobacco Plantation, Lippincott's*, Dec., 1885.

[26] See R. B. Elder's travel articles in *Lippincott's*, March, 1878.

freedom as license to knock down a low-bred Northerner who spoke insultingly of the Confederate chief, a situation of fact not unlike an incident in Dixon's *Clansman*. There is no need to go to written records for the larger proof. In virtually every old community of the South there are today families of negroes who have lived on virtually uninterruptedly under the patronage of, and with clan feeling for, their erstwhile owners.

We may accept, as dominant in slave life a mood of forbearance, of patient acceptance, of even rough affection. This statement cannot be taken as quite validating the tradition of a frequent, if not a perpetual, self-renunciation. The average black does not fit the conception of a hero of disinterestedness, an inevitable burnt-cork offering upon the altar of devotion. He did not go around seeking for opportunities for self-immolation. At the best this childish race had a strong sense of dependence and returned a respectful devotion. Certain of the house servants, the higher type, would have sacrificed themselves; but for these, and certainly for the great body of field hands, condemned to hopeless drudgery, we can assume no more than that they were contented, blissfully ignorant of their " calamitous situation "; and that they were commonly appreciative of kindness. To picture the entire slave population of the old regime as finished and sycophantic courtiers, addressing themselves to the whims of aristocratic masters, or to paint the average plantation " coon " as a joyous martyr — the idea is clearly fantastic.

The master's attitude toward, and treatment of, the slave has been the subject of endless disputation. One might begin with, for example, Beverley's spirited defense in his *History of Virginia* and construct a plausible essay to prove kindliness the rule; one might as easily begin with, say, Crevecoeur's famous letter and draw up a brief

for the existence of much cruelty. Either of such proce-
dures would be alien to the purpose of the present study.
This whole matter may be here reduced to three general
conclusions which seem reasonably well authenticated.

In the first place, the opinion of post-bellum scholars
who have gone with care and conscience into the ramifications of the subject tends more and more to give a favorable interpretation to the master's conduct. Bishop
Bratton, representative of the Southern position, affirms: [27]
" (The master was) the shepherd of the plantation flock.
He had his motives, of course, but his motives did not
destroy the fact of his persistent and devoted care which
developed the relations between himself and his people
into one of love and confidence." The whole school of
historical study, North and South, might not go as far as
the metaphor implies; but the great body of scholarship
would subscribe to Fiske's statement: [28] " It is generally
admitted that the treatment of slaves by their masters
was kind and humane." Professor Hart, who writes himself into the record as the son of an abolitionist, generalizes that [29] " on good plantations there was indeed little
suffering and much enjoyment." Daniels [30] concludes that
the master usually felt his great responsibility. Bassett,
in his analysis of North Carolina slavery,[31] defines the
central idea as a determination to perpetuate the system
" and at the same time a disposition to make it as gentle
as possible for the slave. . . ." Phillips is unequivocal: [32]

[27] *The Christian South and Negro Education, Sewanee Review,*
April, 1908.

[28] *Old Virginia and Her Neighbours,* II, 195. It is the present
writer, not Fiske, who applies the thought to the South as a
whole.

[29] *Slavery and Abolition,* 144.

[30] *The Slave Plantation in Retrospect, Atlantic,* March, 1911.

[31] *Slavery in the State of North Carolina,* 47.

[32] *American Negro Slavery,* 307.

" There was clearly no general prevalence of severity and strain in the regime." It is worth noting, as Phillips further points out, that there was " little of the curse of impersonality and indifference which too commonly prevails in the factories of the present-day world where power-driven machinery sets the pace, where the employers have no relations with the employed outside of work hours. . . ."

The second general truth is that the theory [33] of the slave-holder's conduct, as that ideal was held by planters themselves, was uniformly benign, even if occasionally severe. It is true that most of the formal phrasing comes late, after sharp criticism by the enemies of slavery. But many masters of the earlier regime, as Washington and Henry Laurens, had specific rules for the treatment of

[33] Those interested in this phase will find helpful reference as follows:

a. The best single treatment is in Phillips, *American Negro Slavery,* Chap. 14.

b. Plantation and Frontier Documents, vol. I, edited by the same scholar, contains extracts from the instructions of several planters.

c. Full individual documents are Hammond's *Plantation Manual,* in the Library of Congress; Allston's *Management of a Southern Rice Island, DeBow's,* April, 1859; Collins' *Management of Slaves, DeBow's,* Oct., 1854 (quoted in part by Olmsted, *Seaboard,* II, 353); J. W. Turner, *Plantation Book,* Richmond, 1860.

d. Briefer discussions: " A Planter," *Management of Slaves, So. Lit. Mess.,* Nov., 1841; " A Citizen," *The Negro, DeBow's,* May, 1847; anon., *Management of Negroes, DeBow's,* March, 1851; " Mississippi Planter," *Management of Negroes, DeBow's,* June, 1851; John Perkins, *Relation of Master and Slave, DeBow's,* Sept., 1853; " Affleck," *Duties of an Overseer, DeBow's,* March, 1855; " Agricola," *Management of Negroes, DeBow's,* Sept., 1855; J. S. Wilson, *Management of Negroes, DeBow's,* July, 1860; DeBow, *Plantation Life, DeBow's,* Sept., 1860.

e. Religious treatises covering many phases: Jones, C. C., *The Religious Instruction of Negroes,* Savannah, 1842; McTeire, Sturgis, and Holmes, *Duties of Masters and Servants,* Charleston, 1851; Thornwell and Smith, sermons in *DeBow's,* April, 1851.

slaves. In general, these principles represent the code of
best public opinion, and they are sufficient to convince that
the professed intention of the master was not unkind.

The third and last of these conclusions is that these
professions of the ruling class were carried out, on a somewhat lowered scale, as well as could have been expected;
carried out after the standards of an earlier age than ours;
carried out, in part at least, more because of rough convention than conscious philanthropy. Such essays and
manuals as have come down to us, it is true, represent [34]
" rather the aspirations of the high-class planter than the
actuality on the average plantation "; but there was honest
effort along the line of the aspiration. The illustrations
of great consideration must not, of course, be taken as
typical: Washington's effort to facilitate the return of
the wife of one of his distressed slaves, though, as he says,
" I never wished to see her more "; Henry Laurens' generosity in endangering the food supply on his own estate
to avert a threatened famine among the slaves of a neigh-
boring plantation; Thomas Dabney's uniform justice;
Bishop Polk's heroism at the time of an epidemic; the
unusual condition, approximating slave self-government, on
the plantation of Jefferson Davis. Southern mistresses did
not always, as Dr. Adams [35] thought, take the same pride
in the appearance of the slaves that Northern mothers
took in their own children. There was not always perfect
harmony between the ideal and the real. But there was
assuredly a high average of kindness which expressed itself in the forms most helpful to the blacks. We may not
feel that Ingraham's account of negro cabins completely
equipped even to mosquito bars is typical; but we cannot
discount the evidence of visitors, many of them hearty

[34] *Plantation and Frontier Documents,* preface, I, 99.
[35] *South-Side View of Slavery,* 32.

foes of the system. Lyell testifies to the prevalence of consideration; Mackay hated the institution but reported [36] that the slaves were " better clad, better fed and cared for than the agricultural laborers of Europe "; Mrs. Trollope, in *Domestic Manners of the Americans*, admitted that slaves, particularly in the Northern states of the plantation zone, were tolerably well clothed, fed, and cared for; Mrs. Stowe deplores the irresponsible power of the slave-holder, but adds [37] " probably that power was never exercised more leniently than in many cases of the Southern States." Olmsted, in spite of his conviction that slavery was bad for both races,[38] sets down honestly many examples of kindness; and he bases his opposition to the system on grounds other than any mis-treatment of slaves.

The truth seems to be that while there were some exceptionally kind masters and a few notoriously cruel masters, the great majority followed the code prescribed by custom and public opinion; and this code, though an imperfect one and a sadly flexible one, represented a crude approximation of the attitude of the best of Southern spirits. In the large, the negro who did his share of the work received a modest sufficiency of life's necessities and was not often subjected to any form of physical torture, either of punishment or of over-work.[39]

[36] *Life and Liberty in America,* I, 311.

[37] *Key to Uncle Tom's Cabin,* 35.

[38] *Seaboard,* II, 16, 119, 314, *et seq.; Back Country,* 6, 47, 73, 83, and others.

[39] The master's relation to his slaves was chiefly expressed in matters of detail which in the tradition, certainly after the polemic spirit yielded to the romantic, became stereotyped features. Full treatment of these concrete problems is not feasible here, but they may be suggested, with a word or two concerning the traditional attitude, and the barest hint of the condition that probably obtained on the plantation.

a. Houses, Food, Clothing: The traditional conception of negro

To make out a case for the prevalence of a certain natural consideration for slaves, tempered by ethical standards of another age, is not, surely, to vindicate the tradition of regal patronage and of feudal beneficence. Normally just

_____

homes is the squalor of abolitionist portrayal or a comfortable, even gay, cabin of the later romances. Olmsted and Ingraham found attractive huts, even in the lower South, noted as the worst place for negroes, and most of reminiscent writers describe fairly satisfactory quarters. It is likely, however, that if the negro had a hut which did not allow real suffering, he was as well off as the average; living conditions of modern rural negroes are significant of old conditions. On better estates, the slave had gardens, pigs, or chickens; often the cabin had the advantage of shade. But over the zone as a whole, houses were bare of any great comfort.

Food in the tradition is the feast for the darkies on the surplus of the mansion kitchen. Many, notably house servants, profited from the prodigality of the big house. Some slaves enjoyed their own produce from garden or pen. The game which negroes caught was no small item; and special plantation seasons, like hog-killing, brought supplement. The actual allowance was none too abundant and was simple; 3 to 5 pounds of bacon, a quart of molasses, a peck of meal or sweet potatoes, made up an average weekly ration for a full hand. No master, though, as Hart says, " would keep his slaves down to the point where they could not do full work."

Clothing in the tradition, like food, is supplied by the excess of the mansion's needs. Nothing is farther from the truth. The clothing was an improvement on African modes, doubtless, but was little more than enough for bare decency by summer and bare comfort by winter. This was not cruelty; the slave did not suffer as much as did abolitionists of tender sensibilities.

b. Amount of Work: Abolition writers emphasized this charge; the practice of killing off blacks by toil, counting their labor worth more than their lives, was charged frequently. There were, of course, seasons of severe strain; there were overseers who tried to make a record by merciless driving. The charge cannot be substantiated for the system as a whole. Olmsted's argument against slavery was, in part, that the negro worked much less than

in the matters of physical care; humane in caring for those who needed special attention; rational in the administration of punishment; [40] willing for his slaves to advance themselves in technical skill; all these things the planter

---

the free laborer. Marryat found the negro doing little and doing that badly. If the working day was long, there was usually rest at noon and then long seasons of inactivity.

c. Absenteeism: The master was most unkind, frequently, when he removed himself from the direct supervision of his slaves. This evil is not particularly prominent in the tradition; but so far as it existed, and it did exist in those sections of large estates, it was productive of great unhappiness. See Phillips, *Plantation and Frontier,* I, 81.

d. Sickness: The care of the sick was a point of sharp issue in the days of debate. Fanny Kemble is bitterest at this point; her assault cannot be entirely dismissed; but economic consideration, if no other, dictated moderate provision. Larger estates had regular physicians, and often some sanitary regulations. The better type of master was anxious for the health of his dependents; he often had difficulty, however, in telling whether the slave was sick or was merely playing off.

e. Family Life: A real problem arises here; there is no way to avoid the conclusion that the slavery situation in this respect was fraught with evil; a small rift in the dark cloud may be observed in the disposition of good masters to minimize the tendency to instability of home life. But even the leaders of Southern thought, as Jones and McTeire, felt that there was peril in this phase of the situation. A common defence is the plea that the negro's love for his own family was shallow compared to his affection for his master; see Hammond's *Letter to Clarkson* or Page's *Old-Time Negro.* The argument is not convincing. Permanency of home ties, legitimacy of offspring, proper rearing of children, — all were out of the question. The separation of loved ones was too often a reality; there is no way for traditional sentimentalizing to soften the horror of such facts. This is a notable evasion of the later

---

[40] The tradition takes little account of the service of the plantation as a civilizing force; see article under this heading in *Sewanee Review,* July, 1904 (Phillips).

was, but spectacularly and melodramatically kind — he is this only in the tradition. Fundamentally we are near the truth when we repeat that the relation was one of naturalness.

The motive of unchastity is in the tradition with such prominence that reference to it must be made here. It

tradition but it is one of the tragedies of the actual plantation life.

f. Breeding: Abolitionists believed in the custom of breeding slaves for the market; even modern Northern scholars, like Rhodes and Calhoun, seem to accept the practice as fairly common. Olmsted had his suspicions but did not commit himself. The declaration of a Mississippian, H. S. Foote, that if the internal slave trade were stopped, Virginia and Maryland must emancipate shows contemporary opinion (*DeBow's*, Aug., 1859). Mumford's *Virginia's Attitude* vigorously refutes the assertion, and Phillips finds no evidence for the general practice. Callendar suggests that the older states profited from the internal slave trade though they did not necessarily go into breeding as a business.

g. Slave Sales: Boucicault's vivid scene is representative of thousands of utilizations of this theme. Even the figures were conventional — brutal auctioneer, cowering slave, bigoted prospective purchasers. This element woke echoes in England as early as Macaulay's speech on the sugar duties; and it received full exposition in anti-slavery literature. Evidently the whole proceeding was a repugnant one — witness the Southern dislike for all who engaged in any form of slave trafficking. The usual defence is the claim that feelings of slaves were callous — Olmsted presents a group of negro children playing "auction" — or that surface manifestations were misleading, a thesis supported by Adams. But the coffle, the slave-dealer, the auction-block, these remain unpleasant features, though the sales were not, of course, as universally productive of misery as the abolitionists pretended.

h. Punishments: For this type of problem statistics are necessarily lacking; judgment must be partially inferential, partially based on individual cases. This theme was powerful in abolition writings, even in some sympathetic portrayals. Some of the facts are ominous; irresponsible power is dangerous, specially if delegated to overseers or drivers; even the fairest masters approved

should be said that the South produced many men of notable personal purity, a purity all the stronger because of peculiar temptation. Yet, having put this statement on record, we can do no other than admit that immorality of a particular type existed on a deplorably large scale.

---

punishment; in some cases very trivial offenses called for dreadful retribution; occasionally the motive of revenge entered; sometimes ingenious and horrible modes were devised. There are to-day in Southern communities traditions of exceptionally cruel masters. Such were not the rule; there are few traditions of kind masters, simply because the kind master was the normal one. Thousands never punished, other thousands never punished brutally. Even the treatment of runaways, most powerful single theme in crystallizing Northern sentiment, has been exaggerated, greatly so; there is no doubt, however, that this was a serious offence and that punishment was meted out with a view of deterring the culprit or his fellows.

i. Mental and Moral Training: The denial of educational opportunity to blacks was denounced from DeTocqueville to Fanny Kemble. The fact cannot be denied. Harper defended such laws and Toombs laid blame for them on abolitionists. The common defence advanced by apologists for slavery is that the law was virtually a dead letter. It is certainly true that in many instances the slave received rudiments of education, law or no law. Nat Turner was taught to read by his master, Major Moton's mother conducted a school for slave children, Miss Bremer visited a similar institution in Louisiana. Instances might be multiplied. The conclusion is that there were many masters who were kinder than the slave code. These stories are true, however, not because of, but in spite of, slavery. Plantation life was not favorable for training the blacks.

There was a fairly general effort to promote religious training. It is likely that every master who was devoutly pious wanted his slaves to receive the benefit; and it is certain that many more worldly-minded masters offered religious training for its good effect on slave order. Hedged in by many regulations as it was, the plantation religious life was better provided for than has been supposed.

The abolitionists made rather frantic charges, freely over-drawn. But that this condition existed is demonstrated by the admissions of the leaders of Southern thought; Harper,[41] Hammond,[42] Grayson,[43] and Simms[44] recognized what the latter termed " the illicit and foul conduct of many among us who make their slaves the victims, and the instruments alike, of the most licentious passions." The growth in the number of mulattoes has significance; but little evidence is really needed to establish a fact that has been sorrowfully conceded by even the fondest admirers of that old regime. The extent of this unchastity is one thing; the import of it is another, perhaps even more important. The negro was not the only sufferer, was not, under the existing organization of society, the chief sufferer. Tragic as was the destiny of offspring, at least occasionally, this was not the direst consequence. One of the severest penalties was the demoralization of social ideals of the dominant class, a condition that has harmed the South up to the present; another tragedy was in the agony of Southern white women.

[41] *Memoir on Negro Slavery,* in DeBow's *Industrial Resources,* II, 219.

[42] *Letter to Thomas Clarkson, ibid.,* II, 245.

[43] *The Dual Form of Labor, Russell's,* Oct., 1859.

[44] Review of *Society in America, So. Lit. Mess.,* Nov., 1837.

BIBLIOGRAPHICAL NOTES

Since the number of individual works mentioned in the text is large, an effort has been made to give sufficient bibliographical identification with the reference. Works listed here are those of more general significance.

Chapters 2, 3, and 4

Some guidance into the literature of the plantation may be obtained from the following works: Johnson, J. G., *Southern Fiction Prior to 1861, An Attempt at a First-Hand Bibliography* (University of Virginia, 1909); Hubbell, J. B., *Virginia Life in Fiction* (Columbia University Press, N. Y., 1922); Davidson, J. W., *Living Writers of the South* (Carleton, N. Y., 1869); anon., *Living Female Writers of the South* (Claxton, Remsen, Phila., 1872); *The Library of Southern Literature* (Martin and Hoyt, Atlanta, 1907); Trent, W. P., *Southern Writers* (Macmillan, N. Y., 1905); Moses, M. J., *Literature of the South* (Crowell, N. Y., 1910); and Mims, E., *History of Southern Fiction* in *The South in the Building of the Nation,* vol. VIII (So. Pub. Society, Richmond, 1909) Brief discussions of the major figures in fiction will be found in Pattee, F. L., *A History of American Literature since 1870* (Century, N. Y., 1915); in Carl Van Doren's *The American Novel* (Macmillan, N. Y., 1921); and in chapter 1 of the same author's *Contemporary American Novelists* (Macmillan, N. Y., 1922). Suggestive magazine articles are: Page, T. N., *Authorship in the South before the War* (*Lippincott,* July, 1889, also in *The Old South,* Scribner, N. Y., 1892) and the same author's *Literature in the South since the War* (*Lippincott,* Dec., 1891); Rollins, H. E., *The Negro in the Southern Short Story* (*Sewanee,* Jan., 1916); and Tandy, Jeannette, R., *Pro-Slavery Propaganda in American Fiction of the Fifties* (*So. Atlantic,* Jan., 1922).

Chapter 5

There is no standard history of negro minstrelsy. Interesting brief discussions may be found in: Matthews, B., *Banjo and Bones* (London *Saturday Review,* June 7, 1884) and *The Rise and Fall of Negro Minstrelsy* (*Scribner's,* June, 1915); Hutton, Laurence, *The Negro on the Stage* (*Harper's,* June, 1889, also in his *Curiosities of the American Stage* (Harper, N. Y., 1891); Nevin, R. P., *Stephen C. Foster and Negro Minstrelsy* (*Atlantic,* Nov., 1867); Keller, Ralph, *Three Years as a Negro Minstrel* (*Atlantic,* July, 1869); Turx, J. J., *Negro Minstrelsy Ancient and Modern* (*Putnam's,* January, 1855); Greenwood, I. J., *The Circus* (Dunlop Soc., N. Y., 1898). Less reliable are Rice, E. L., *Monarchs of Minstrelsy* (Kenny, N. Y., 1911) and Jennings, J. J., *Theatrical and Circus Life* (Laird and Lee, Chicago, 1893). Any study of native drama must rely largely on Ireland, J. N., *Records of the New York Stage* (Morrell, N. Y., 1866) and Brown, T. A., *History of the New York Stage* (Dodd, Mead, N. Y., 1903) as well as on similar records of other cities (see text); but for the present purpose the files of a theatrical journal, preferably the New York *Mirror,* are indispensable.

Chapter 6

References to the sources will be found in foot-notes.

Chapters 7, 8, and 9

The bibliography of the slavery question is extensive. Certain works which treat specifically the organization of plantation life, as distinguished from other phases of the larger subject, are indicated here.

I. General: Ballagh, J. C., *A History of Slavery in Virginia* (Johns Hopkins Univ. Studies, extra vol. 24, Balto., 1902); Bassett, J. S., *Slavery in the State of North Carolina* (*Johns Hopkins Univ. Studies*, vol. 17, Balto., 1890); Brown, W. G., *The Lower South in American History* (Macmillan, N. Y., 1902); Bruce, P. A., *Economic History of Virginia in the Seventeenth Century* (2 vols., Macmillan, N. Y., 1895) and *Social Life of Virginia in the Seventeenth Century* (Whittet and Shepardson, Richmond, 1907); Calhoun, A. W., *A Social History of the American Family* (2 vols., Clarke, Cleveland, 1918); Callender, G. S., ed., *Selections from the Economic History of the United States* (Ginn, Boston, 1909); Dodd, W. E., *The Cotton Kingdom* (Yale Univ. Press, 1919); Dodd, W. E., *Social Philosophy of the Old South* (*Amc. Journal Sociology*, May, 1918); Drewry, W. S., *Slave Insurrections in Virginia, 1830–1865* (Neale, Washington, 1900); Fiske, John, *Old Virginia and Her Neighbours* (Houghton Mifflin, Boston, 1897); Fleming, W. L., *Jefferson Davis, the Negro and the Negro Problem* (*Sewanee*, Oct., 1908); Hamill, H. M., *The Old South* (Smith and Lamar, Nashville, 1904); Hart, A. B., *Slavery and Abolition* (Harper, N. Y., 1906); Hart, A. B., ed., *Social and Economic Forces in American History* (Harper, N. Y., 1913); Holcomb, W. H., *Sketches of Plantation Life* (*Knickerbocker*, June, 1861); Hundley, D. R., *Social Relations in the Southern States* (Price, N. Y., 1860); Ingle, ed., *Southern Sidelights* (Crowell, N. Y., 1896); James, G. P. R., *Life in Virginia* (*Knickerbocker*,

Sept., 1858); Looney, Louisa, P., *The Southern Planter of the Fifties* (So. History Ass'n. Pub., July, 1900); Mallard, R. Q., *Plantation Life before Emancipation* (Whittet and Shepardson, Richmond, 1892); Mumford, B. B., *Virginia's Attitude toward Slavery and Secession* (Longmans, Green, N. Y., 1909); Odum, H. W., *Social and Mental Traits of the Negro* (vol. 37, Col. Univ. studies in history, economics, and public law, N. Y., 1910); Phillips, U. B., *American Negro Slavery* (Appleton, N. Y., 1918), *Plantation and Frontier Documents* (2 vols., Clarke, Cleveland, 1909), *The Plantation as a Civilizing Factor* (*Sewanee*, Oct., 1908), and *The Decadence of the Plantation System* (*Annals Amer. Academy*, Jan., 1910); Wertenbaker, T. J., *Patrician and Plebeian in Virginia; or the Origin and Development of the Social Classes* (University of Virginia, 1912). The files of Southern magazines of the period yield much interesting material, notably *DeBow's Review*, vols. 1–30 (January, 1846 through April, 1861).

II. Travel: A list of the more important works of travelers, together with some of the digests of foreign opinion, may be found in the bibliography of *The Cambridge History of American Literature*, Book II, chap. 1 (Putnam, N. Y., 1917). Of these digests the earliest significant one is Tuckerman, H. T., *America and Her Commentators* (Scribner, N. Y., 1864). Professor Hart in the bibliography of *Slavery and Abolition* provides a special list of those visitors who were particularly interested in slavery. The small list appended here is composed of those whose observations concerned the plantation; it is unnecessary to add that many are the product of a rather fixed point of view: Adams, N., *A South-Side View of Slavery* (Marvin, Boston, 1854); Bremer, Frederika, *Homes of the New World* (2 vols., Harper, N. Y., 1853); Bryant, W. C., *A Tour of the Old South* (N. Y., 1843, in *Prose Works*, vol. 2, ed., Parke Godwin, Appleton, N. Y., 1901); Buckingham, J. S., *The Slave States of America* (2 vols., London, 1842); Crevecoeur, M. G. St. J., *Letters from an American Farmer* (London, 1782, pub. with preface by Trent, W. P. and introduction by Lewisohn, L., Putnam, N. Y., 1904); De Tocqueville, A., *Democracy in America* (2 vols., Paris, 1835, 1840); Eddis, Wm., *Letters from America* (London, 1792); Faux, Wm., *Memorable Days in America* (London, 1832, in *Early Western Travel*, Clarke, Cleveland, 1905); Featherstonhaugh, G. W., *Excursion through the Slave States* (2 vols., London, 1844); Hall, Basil, *Travels in North America* (Edin. and London, 1829, 3 vols.); Hamilton, T., *Men and Manners in America* (Edin. and London, 1833); Kemble, Frances Anne, *Journal of a Residence on a Georgian Plantation in 1838–1839* (Harper, N. Y., 1863); Lyell, Chas., *Travels in North America* (London, 1845) and *Second Visit to the United States* (Harper, N. Y., 1849); Mackay, Chas., *Life and Liberty in America* (2 vols., London, 1859); Marryat, Fred., *A Diary in America* (3 vols., London, 1839); Martineau, Harriet, *Society in America* (2 vols., London, 1837) and *Retrospect of Western Travel* (Harper, N. Y., 1838); Olmsted, F. L., *A Journey through the Seaboard Slave States* (Dix and Edwards, N. Y., 1856) and *A Journey in the Back Country* (Mason, N. Y., 1860); Paulding, J. K., *Letters from the South* (Eastburn, N. Y., 1817); Russell, W. H., *My Diary North and South* (Burnham, Boston, 1863); Stuart, J., *Three Years in North America* (2 vols., Edin., 1833); Trollope, Frances M., *Domestic Manners of the Americans* (2 vols., London, 1832); Van Buren, A. de P., *Jottings of a Year's Sojourn in the South* (Review and Herald, Battle Creek, 1859).

III. Autobiography and biography: Considered as literature, several of the most valuable volumes of reminiscence have been noted in the text (see chap. 4). Among

those that have special value for the points involved in
these chapters may be mentioned: Avirett, J. B., *The Old
Plantation* (Neely, N. Y., 1901); Bassett, J. S., ed., *The
Writings of William Byrd* (Doubleday, Page, N. Y., 1901);
Chesnutt, M. B., *A Diary from Dixie* (Appleton, N. Y.,
1908); Clayton, V. V. (Mrs.), *White and Black under the
Old Regime* (Young Churchman, Milwaukee, 1899); Con-
rad, Georgia B., *Reminiscences of a Southern Woman*
(Hampton Inst. Press, 1902); Davis, Reuben, *Recollec-
tions of a Mississippian* (Houghton Mifflin, Boston, 1899);
Devereaux, Margaret, *Plantation Sketches* (Houghton
Mifflin, Boston, 1906); Ford, P. L., ed., *The Writings of
Jefferson* (10 vols., Putnam, N. Y., 1894); Ford, W. C.,
ed., *The Writings of Washington* (14 vols., Putnam, N. Y.,
1889); Gilman, Caroline H., *Recollections of a Southern
Matron* (Harper, N. Y., 1838); Meade, A. H. (Mrs.),
When I was a Little Girl (Lang, Los Angeles, 1916);
Moton, R. R., *Finding a Way Out* (Doubleday, Page, N. Y.,
1920); Pleasants, Lucy Lee, *Old Virginia Ways and Days*
(Banta, Menasha, 1916); Pringle, Elizabeth W. A., *Chron-
icles of Chicora Wood* (Scribner, N. Y., 1922); Polk, Wm.,
Leonidas Polk, Bishop and General (Longmans, Green,
N. Y., 1913); Smedes, Susan D., *A Southern Planter*
(Cushings, Balto., 1887); Sterling, Ada, *A Belle of the
Fifties* (Doubleday, Page, N. Y., 1905); Trent, W. P., *Wil-
liam Gilmore Simms* (Houghton Mifflin, Boston, 1892);
Wallace, D. D., *Henry Laurens* (Putnam, N. Y., 1915);
Washington, B. T., *Up from Slavery* (Doubleday, Page,
N. Y., 1902); Wise, John S., *The End of an Era* (Houghton
Mifflin, Boston, 1899); Wyeth, John A., *With Sabre and
Scalpel* (Harper, N. Y., 1914).

IV. Early slave autobiography: Polemic as they are,
slave narratives offer to the student of plantation life at
least a novel angle of view. Among the more popular of

the early works are: Anon., *Fifty Years in Chains* (Dayton, N. Y., 1858) ; Ball, Chas., *Slavery in the United States* (Taylor, N. Y., 1837) ; Brown, W. W., *Narrative* (Anti-Slavery Office, Boston, 1848) ; Douglass, Fred., *Narrative* (Anti-Slavery Office, Boston, 1845) ; Henson, Joshua, *Life* (Phelps, Boston, 1849, the original of " Uncle Tom ") ; Jacobs, Harriet, *Incident in the Life of a Slave Girl* (ed., Mrs. Child, for author, Boston, 1861) ; Northup, Solomon, *Twelve Years a Slave* (Derby and Miller, Albany, 1853) ; Pickard, Kate, *The Kidnapped and the Ransomed* (Hamilton, Syracuse, 1856) ; Stewart, Austin, *Twenty-Two Years a Slave* (Alling, Rochester, 1857) ; Thompson, John, *Life* (for author, Worcester, 1856).